DATE DUE

NOV 2 7 2003 / NOV 0 5 2005			

DEMCO 38-296

Reconstruction

Reconstruction

CLAUDINE L. FERRELL

Greenwood Guides to Historic Events 1500–1900
Linda S. Frey and Marsha L. Frey, Series Editors

GREENWOOD PRESS
Westport, Connecticut • London

Library of Congress Cataloging-in-Publication Data

Ferrell, Claudine L., 1950–
    Reconstruction / Claudine L. Ferrell.
        p. cm.—(Greenwood guides to historic events 1500–1900, ISSN 1538-442X)
    Includes bibliographical references and index.
    ISBN 0–313–32062–4 (alk. paper)
    1. Reconstruction. I. Title. II. Series.
E668.F39   2003
973.8—dc21   2003042077

British Library Cataloguing in Publication Data is available.

Library of Congress Catalog Card Number: 2003042077
ISBN: 0–313–32062–4
ISSN: 1538–442X

First published in 2003

Greenwood Press, 88 Post Road West, Westport, CT 06881
An imprint of Greenwood Publishing Group, Inc.
www.greenwood.com

Printed in the United States of America

The paper used in this book complies with the
Permanent Paper Standard issued by the National
Information Standards Organization (Z39.48–1984).

10 9 8 7 6 5 4 3 2 1

Copyright Acknowledgments

The author and publisher gratefully acknowledge permission for use of the following
material:

Excerpts from B. A. Botkin, ed., *Lay My Burden Down: A Folk History of Slavery*
(Chicago: University of Chicago Press, 1945).

Excerpts from Philip S. Foner, *The Life and Writings of Frederick Douglass* (New York:
International Publishers, 1950).

Radical Republicans and Reconstruction by Hyman, © Reprinted by permission of
Pearson Education, Inc., Upper Saddle River, NJ.

Excerpts from Richard L. Troutman, ed., *The Heavens Are Weeping: The Diaries of
George Richard Browder* (Grand Rapids, Mich.: Zondervan Publishing, 1987).

Every reasonable effort has been made to trace the owners of copyright materials in
this book, but in some instances this has proven impossible. The author and publisher
will be glad to receive information leading to more complete acknowledgments in
subsequent printings of the book and in the meantime extend their apologies for any
omissions.

CONTENTS

SERIES FOREWORD

American statesman Adlai Stevenson stated, "We can chart our future clearly and wisely only when we know the path which has led to the present." This series, Greenwood Guides to Historic Events, 1500–1900, is designed to illuminate that path by focusing on events from 1500 to 1900 that have shaped the world. The years 1500 to 1900 include what historians call the Early Modern Period (1500 to 1789, the onset of the French Revolution) and part of the modern period (1789 to 1900).

In 1500, an acceleration of key trends marked the beginnings of an interdependent world and the posing of seminal questions that changed the nature and terms of intellectual debate. The series closes with 1900, the inauguration of the twentieth century. This period witnessed profound economic, social, political, cultural, religious, and military changes. An industrial and technological revolution transformed the modes of production, marked the transition from a rural to an urban economy, and ultimately raised the standard of living. Social classes and distinctions shifted. The emergence of the territorial and later the national state altered man's relations with and view of political authority. The shattering of the religious unity of the Roman Catholic world in Europe marked the rise of a new pluralism. Military revolutions changed the nature of warfare. The books in this series emphasize the complexity and diversity of the human tapestry and include political, economic, social, intellectual, military, and cultural topics. Some of the authors focus on events in U.S. history such as the Salem witchcraft trials, the American Revolution, the abolitionist movement, and the Civil War. Others analyze European topics, such as the Reformation and Counter-Reformation and the French Revolution. Still others bridge cultures and continents by examining the voyages of discovery, the Atlantic slave trade, and the Age of Imperialism. Some focus on intellectual questions that have shaped the modern world, such as Darwin's *Origin of Species,* or on turning points such as the Age of Romanticism. Others examine defining economic, religious, or legal events or issues such as the building of the railroads, the Second Great Awakening, and abolitionism. Heroes (e.g., Lewis and Clark), scientists (e.g., Darwin), military leaders (e.g., Napoleon), and poets (e.g., Byron) stride across its pages. Many of these events were seminal in that they marked profound changes or turning points. The Scientific Revolution, for example, changed the way individuals viewed themselves and their world.

The authors, acknowledged experts in their fields, synthesize key events; set developments within the larger historical context; and, most important, present a well-balanced, well-written account that integrates the most recent scholarship in the field.

The topics were chosen by an advisory board composed of historians, high school history teachers, and school librarians to support the curriculum and meet student research needs. The volumes are designed to serve as resources for student research and to provide clearly written interpretations of topics central to the secondary school and lower-level undergraduate history curriculum. Each author outlines a basic chronology to guide the reader through often confusing events and a historical overview to set those events within a narrative framework. Three to five topical chapters underscore critical aspects of the event. In the final chapter the author examines the impact and consequences of the event. Biographical sketches furnish background on the lives and contributions of the players who strut across this stage. Ten to fifteen primary documents ranging from letters to diary entries, song lyrics, proclamations, and posters cast light on the event, provide material for student essays, and stimulate a critical engagement with the sources. Introductions identify the authors of the documents and the main issues. In some cases a glossary of selected terms is provided as a guide to the reader. Each work contains an annotated bibliography of recommended books, articles, CD-ROMs, Internet sites, videos, and films that set the materials within the historical debate.

These works will lead to a more sophisticated understanding of the events and debates that have shaped the modern world and will stimulate a more active engagement with the issues that still affect us. It has been a particularly enriching experience to work closely with such dedicated professionals. We have come to know and value even more highly the authors in this series and our editors at Greenwood, particularly Kevin Ohe. In many cases they have become more than colleagues; they have become friends. To them and to future historians we dedicate this series.

Linda S. Frey
University of Montana

Marsha L. Frey
Kansas State University

PREFACE

There are few periods in American history that have aroused as much debate as have the years immediately after the Civil War—the years commonly referred to simply as "Reconstruction." Reconstruction has inspired strongly worded assertions and counterassertions. Even its time frame has prompted disagreement, although, if one considers the issues at stake, 1862 to 1877 makes enough sense to win general acceptance, if not enthusiasm. The more important substantive issues have pitted historians against each other for almost 150 years, and they have done so with an intensity that has few parallels in the study of American history. The key issues concern individual rights, governmental powers, and racial distinctions.

For most of the years after Reconstruction, the consensus has seen Reconstruction as the playground of vindictive, greedy, petty men who cared more for economic and political gain than they did for the rights of black Americans or the protection of rights in general. Since the 1950s, the consensus has been the reverse: these men, Radical Republicans, cared about economic and political issues, but their commitment to black Americans—what earned them the label "Radical"—was genuine. The significant shift in interpretation came with the civil rights movement and a new thinking about minority rights and the responsibility of the national government for their protection. The shift's explanation—that each generation's thinking about the past is guided by its perceptions and values—suggests that judging Reconstruction by today's standards is natural but that it distorts the period. Most Americans of the twenty-first century have two clear assumptions: all races are equal before the law, and the national government must—or at least *does*—play a significant role in American life. Americans of the mid-nineteenth century did not share these beliefs.

Despite the danger of distortion, however, many questions must be tackled in order to understand the era of Reconstruction: What was Abraham Lincoln's view of the South and his plan for its postwar fate? What impact did his death have on Reconstruction? What motivated Andrew Johnson? How did Southern whites perceive their return to the Union? What motivated the Radical Republicans? Why did they impeach Johnson? What did the Moderate Republicans want to accomplish through Reconstruction? How much did the Reconstruction amendments seek to accomplish? How much *did* they accomplish? How did the former Confederates return to power, and how did they do it so quickly? What was the fate of the freedmen under Reconstruction? What did these Americans want from freedom? Was congressional Reconstruction a good idea badly executed? Or was it a good idea executed as far as the attitudes, values, and goals of the times permitted? Could the Radicals have been more successful? Did they try to do too much or too little? Were their accomplishments—or lack of accomplishments—the result of forces beyond the ability of a handful of men to control? Were there alternatives? And finally, what is the significance of Reconstruction?

ACKNOWLEDGMENTS

Special thanks go to series editors Marsha and Linda Frey for suggesting that I do this book. Since I have always valued their skills as historians, their faith in me was a frequent boost to my work. In addition, I wish to thank the students in my 2001 and 2003 seminars on the era of Reconstruction. Their enthusiasm for the topic and for my approach to it provided needed encouragement. Also at Mary Washington College, Lisa Patton, secretary for the Department of History and American Studies, provided her usual capable, steady, and reassuring help, and Carla Bailey, who handled interlibrary loan requests, did so with her usual speed and efficiency. Several people—including Jack Bales, Thomas Mackey, Cheryl and Duane Clayton, and Vic Fingerhut—provided support and confidence. Finally, escape from the pressure of finding the right words and formulating the clearest explanations came from Hannah and the gang.

CHRONOLOGY OF EVENTS

1861

May 25 | General Benjamin Butler declares slaves to be contraband of war

August 6 | Congress passes First Confiscation Act

1862

April 16 | Congress abolishes slavery in the District of Columbia and in the territories

July 17 | Congress passes Second Confiscation Act

1863

January 1 | The Emancipation Proclamation goes into effect

December 8 | Lincoln issues Proclamation of Amnesty and Reconstruction and announces Ten Percent Plan

1864

July 8 | Wade-Davis Bill is passed and vetoed

1865

March 3 | Congress creates the Freedmen's Bureau

April 15 | Lincoln is assassinated and Johnson assumes presidency

May 29 | Johnson issues Proclamation of Amnesty and Reconstruction

August–October | Southern state constitutional conventions meet

December | Southern states enact first Black Codes

| December 4 | Congress refuses to recognize Southern members elected under Johnson's plan |
| December 18 | Thirteenth Amendment becomes part of the Constitution |

1866

February 19	Johnson vetoes Freedmen's Bureau Bill
February 22	Johnson delivers Washington's Birthday speech
April 9	Congress passes Civil Rights Act of 1866 over Johnson's veto
April 26	Johnson announces official end of Civil War
May 1	Race riot occurs in Memphis
June 13	Congress sends Fourteenth Amendment to the states for ratification
July 14	Congress passes Freedman's Bureau Bill over Johnson's veto
July 24	Tennessee ratifies Fourteenth Amendment and is readmitted
July 30	Race riot occurs in New Orleans
August 28	Johnson's "swing around the circle" begins
December 17	Supreme Court issues ruling in *ex parte Milligan*

1867

January 8	Congress requires black suffrage in Washington, D.C.
March 2	Congress passes Command of the Army Act, First Reconstruction Act, and Tenure of Office Act
April 23	Congress passes Second Reconstruction Act
April 30	Alaska becomes part of the United States
July 19	Congress passes Third Reconstruction Act
September	First state conventions begin meeting under congressional Reconstruction

1868

| February 24 | The House impeaches Johnson |
| March 4–May 16 | Impeachment trial of Johnson |

March 11	Congress passes Fourth Reconstruction Act
June 22	Arkansas is first state readmitted under congressional Reconstruction
June 25	Alabama, Florida, Georgia, Louisiana, North Carolina, and South Carolina are readmitted
July 28	The Fourteenth Amendment is ratified and added to Constitution
August 11	Thaddeus Stevens dies
December 1	Georgia loses readmission

1869

March 4	Grant is inaugurated president
March 18	Public Credit Act becomes law
April 12	Supreme Court issues ruling in *Texas v. White*
September 24	"Black Friday" crash on New York Stock Exchange
October 4	Democrats win control of (redeem) Tennessee
October 5	Democrats win control of (redeem) Virginia

1870

January 26	Virginia is readmitted
February 23	Mississippi is readmitted
February 25	Hiram Revels becomes first African American elected to the U.S. Senate
March 30	Texas is readmitted
	The Fifteenth Amendment is added to Constitution
May 31	Congress passes First Enforcement Act
July 15	Georgia is readmitted for second time
November 3	Democrats gain control of (redeem) North Carolina
December 12	Joseph H. Rainey takes seat as first black Congressman

1871

February 28	Congress passes Second Enforcement Act
April 20	Congress passes Third Enforcement Act
May 24	Treaty of Washington settles *Alabama* claims

October 17	Grant suspends writ of habeas corpus in South Carolina
November 1	Democrats gain control of (redeem) Georgia for second time

1872

May 22	Congress passes general amnesty act for most Confederate soldiers and officials
November 5	Grant defeats Horace Greeley
December 9	Louisiana Governor Henry Clay Warmoth is impeached, removed from office, and succeeded by P.B.S. Pinchback

1873

January 14	Democrats gain control of (redeem) Texas
February	Congress passes Silver Coinage Act ("Crime of '73")
April 13	Massacre in Colfax, Louisiana
April 14	Supreme Court issues ruling in the *Slaughterhouse Cases*
September 18	Failure of Jay Cooke & Company spurs Panic of 1873

1874

September 17	Grant puts down violence in Louisiana with threat of federal intervention
November 10	Democrats gain control of (redeem) Arkansas
November 14	Democrats gain control of (redeem) Alabama
December 7	Race riots in Vicksburg, Mississippi begin Mississippi Plan

1875

January 14	Congress passes Special Resumption Act
March 1	Congress passes Civil Rights Act
November 3	Democrats gain control of (redeem) Mississippi

1876

March 27	Supreme Court issues *United States v. Cruikshank* and *United States v. Reese*

July 7	Race riot occurs in Hamburg, South Carolina
November 7	Presidential election between Hayes and Tilden ends with no winner
November 12	Democrats gain control of (redeem) South Carolina

1877

January 2	Democrats gain control of (redeem) Florida
February 8	Electoral commission awards all disputed votes to Hayes

1883

October 15	Supreme Court issues ruling in the *Civil Rights Cases*

State	Date of Readmission Under Congressional Requirements	Date of Democratic Redemption
Tennessee	July 24, 1866	October 4, 1869
Virginia	January 26, 1870	October 5, 1869
North Carolina	June 25, 1868	November 3, 1870
Georgia	July 15, 1870	November 1, 1871
Texas	March 30, 1870	January 14, 1873
Arkansas	June 22, 1868	November 10, 1874
Alabama	June 25, 1868	November 14, 1874
Mississippi	February 23, 1870	November 3, 1875
South Carolina	June 25, 1868	November 12, 1876
Florida	June 25, 1868	January 2, 1877
Louisiana	June 25, 1868	January 2, 1877

HISTORICAL OVERVIEW

After studying the Civil War, a conflict in which 600,000 Americans died, students usually expect to be bored when they move on to the years immediately following the conflict. It is difficult for them to imagine that the tensions—political, social, economic, and constitutional—that led to South Carolina's secession in 1860, to Abraham Lincoln's use of troops in 1861, and to four years of warfare could be followed by anything that equaled them in intensity and impact. The issues were settled: secession had failed, slavery was over, and the Union had survived. What was left for the nation to do except go back to life as usual, albeit without slavery?

Despite hopeful expectations, the period after the Civil War was a contentious, often bitter one dominated by questions left by the War of the Rebellion:

What Did a Southern Loss *Mean?*

Imprisonment and execution of the failed rebels? An end to the statehood of the former Confederate states? Restrictions on the citizenship of Confederate leaders? Did the Southern states have the "republican form of government" required by Article 4 of the Constitution? If not, how could such a government be restored? Was secession to be looked upon as nothing more than a failed step, legitimate if not constitutional, that could now be forgotten when the South surrendered, the only change being the abolition of slavery?

What Did Freedom *Mean?*

Slavery was dead, but former slaves and their former masters were not. What kind of lives would the freedmen have? With whose help (if any) would they embark on an existence as free men and women? What steps were needed to define and secure this new life? Did freedom mean citizenship, even for people perceived to be inherently inferior by whites? Were black citizens to be the equal of white citizens? If the lowest in Southern society were to be raised by the war, what would become of the highest? Would the South's traditional political, economic, and social elite—who had led their states before and during the war—stay in power? Could they accept social, economic, and political changes in their society?

What Did Wartime Power *Mean* for Peacetime Americans?

The Union had achieved military success, but it had done so with the unprecedented use of the power of the national government, a force that had previously touched the lives of few Americans. How much of the federal government's power would—or should—be exercised after the conflict? How much should the traditional state-based system be disrupted to aid the inferior black? Which branch of the government should handle postwar adjustments? Like all American wars, the Civil War brought up questions of *who* does *what* because, if for no other reason, Congress has the power to declare war—but the president is commander in chief of the military. Add to this problem other complications: the 1861–1865 conflict was a civil war, about which the Constitution says nothing directly. Plus, the war did not end with a treaty listing peace terms. Not only did it end bit by bit, with each Northern victory on Southern battlefields, but the "winners" could not agree among themselves on the peace to impose on the South. As Lincoln explained as the war ended in 1865, "Unlike a case of war between independent nations, there is no authorized organ for us to treat with. . . . We simply must begin with and mold from disorganized and discordant elements. Nor is it a small additional embarrassment that we, the loyal people, differ among ourselves as to the mode, manner, and measure of reconstruction."[1]

Theories

There was no precedent in American history for handling a civil war and its aftermath, for handling claims of secession and counter-claims of rebellion. There were no constitutional provisions that stipulated what should be done and by which branch of government. That left Congress and the president knowing that action was necessary but not knowing what action to take and who should take it. The war years were complicated by this reality; the postwar years were dominated by it. The president's constitutional status as commander in chief during an emergency of unprecedented proportions allowed Abraham Lincoln to exercise substantial power during the war; no such status or immediate threat assisted decision making for his successor Andrew Johnson during Reconstruction. Congress and the president had to reach agreement without the aid of clear-cut constitutional provisions. Their failure to do so helps explain the conflicts, as well as failures, of the succeeding decade. It also provides an explanation for the so-called Second Reconstruction of the 1950s–1970s (the civil rights movement).

Those on the national stage from the war years to the late 1870s could do either nothing or a great deal, depending on how they viewed the Southern states and national power at war's end. If the states had never seceded and were still states, the national government had no power over them after April 15, 1865 (if not even before); if they had seceded, or if they had rebelled and thus ended their status as states, they had to be "fixed." If the latter occurred, did the president's power as commander in chief put him in charge of defining and enforcing terms? Or did Congress's power to control its membership, and to guarantee each state a republican form of government, give it authority over the South's postrebellion fate?

Shortly before his death in April 1865, with the war essentially won against the Southern secessionists, Lincoln maintained that his goal was fixing what was broken, not determining the exact condition of the break. As he explained, "[T]he seceded States, so called, are out of their proper practical relation with the Union." The nation's goal should be "to again get them into that proper practical relation." It was unnecessary to determine whether they were in or out of Union: "Finding themselves safely at home, it would be utterly immaterial whether they had ever been abroad."[2] But as Lincoln knew, their status determined whether the national government—and its Radical members—

had constitutional power and what it might be able to do to secure the results of the war (permanence of the Union and abolition of slavery) and to redefine the South economically, socially, and politically.

Not surprisingly, theories on the impact of secession and war abounded. They wove their way through virtually all aspects of the South's Reconstruction because they determined what could be done—although not necessarily what *would* be done.

Southerners argued before the war that they had left the Union because the nonslave states had repeatedly violated the Constitution. After the war, it suited many of them better to accept the Union's wartime argument that secession was impossible and that they had remained in the Union as states. Under this theory, these states would send representatives to Washington, accept the return of federal agencies and officers, and resume their rightful place in the Union. Neither the president nor Congress had any more power over the South than they did over states that had fought against the Confederacy. Besides the loss of slavery, little would change.

Among those disagreeing were Lincoln's successor and the men with whom he would battle during Reconstruction. With the war's end and Lincoln's death in April 1865, new president Andrew Johnson found himself making Reconstruction policy until Congress convened in December. Like the Southern states, he accepted the idea that they had never left the Union and that the states still existed; Congress had no power over them. But they were not functioning states until he, as president, took steps to make them so, for example, by pardoning their leaders and recognizing loyal governments once they formed. Radical Republicans in Congress went even further and in a different direction. Thaddeus Stevens, the 73-year-old congressman from Pennsylvania, saw the Southern states as conquered provinces. The eleven states had fought the Union; they had discarded the protection of the Constitution. Congress could do with them what it wanted, even ignoring state boundaries. Radical Charles Sumner of Massachusetts, the abolitionist senator who won the label of martyr for his beating in 1856 at the hands of South Carolinian Preston Brooks, presented a similar theory. He argued that secession was impossible and that the states had committed treason—that is, suicide *as states*—when they used force to take this impossible step. Because they had never left the Union, Congress could govern them as states that had reverted to territories.

Ohio Representative Samuel Shellabarger presented a compromise theory of forfeited rights. Like Sumner, Shellabarger concluded that the states, while not losing their boundaries or place in the Union, had changed their relationship to it. In doing so, they had forfeited their rights within it. Because Congress had the responsibility to provide a republican form of government, it alone had the power to reestablish those rights. It could take no action, or it could take years of harsh and exacting steps. It could approve the governments created by the president.[3]

By 1866 the theories and labels had increased to include dead and disorganized states and "disorganized communities, without civil government, and without constitutions or other forms." As the report of the Joint Committee on Reconstruction clarified the last theory, "Having voluntarily deprived themselves of representation in Congress for the criminal purpose of destroying the Union, and having reduced themselves, by the act of levying war, to the condition of public enemies, they have no right to complain of temporary exclusion from Congress. . . ."[4] Whether sharing this particular view or another, most Republicans saw the states in the "grasp of war." Thus, the national government could assert authority in areas traditionally belonging to the states, such as determining the status and rights of blacks.

In *Texas v. White* (1869), the Supreme Court, in its major Reconstruction decision, joined the debate. The rebel state of Texas had sold bonds during the war; the postwar state sought return of the bonds. Supreme Court jurisdiction of the case required clarification of Texas's status: if Texas had seceded from the Union and had not yet been readmitted, it was not a state and could not bring a case to the Supreme Court. Chief Justice Salmon Chase ruled that the Constitution had created "an indestructible Union, composed of indestructible States."[5] As a result, Texas had never left the Union; however, it was not in its normal place as a state and Congress had to take steps to normalize it.

The country was eager for peace, but it was divided by these theories, the political repercussions of civil war. It was also torn by the fate of the freed slave and, to a lesser degree, his former owner. The status and fate of Southern blacks, freed by the war, also required decisions: what would their freedom entail and who would ensure it? The country sought peace, not punishment; but that peace meant deciding who would govern the South and what would happen to the freedmen.

Wartime Origins of Reconstruction

Although it is easy to argue that the Civil War was one event and Reconstruction another, the two were parts of a whole. Reconstruction began during the conflict. In 1861 Abraham Lincoln supported western Virginians, who opposed their state's secession ordinance, as they set up a loyal state government. Lincoln hoped that a base of activist loyalists would encourage others to restore Union control. The plan was to save the Union through restoration of loyal governments, not to remake the domestic institutions of the Southern states. The plan, however, was activated by the president, and even at this early date some Republican members of Congress believed that Reconstruction in whatever form it would take was a congressional responsibility.

In the opening months of his administration, Lincoln responded carefully but with assurance that he had power to act. He called out the militia and announced a blockade of the Confederate coast. The war against the South and the war within the Union government over how to handle the rebellious white Southerners and their black slaves had begun. Congress's and the Supreme Court's approval of Lincoln's response to an emergency did not mean that the former was satisfied to sit back and let Lincoln run the war and, as Union troops took over Confederate territory, administer the Reconstruction of the South. There were too many men who disagreed with his policies and with how he put the policies into motion. These men included many from Lincoln's prewar party, the Republicans: Radicals Thaddeus Stevens of Pennsylvania, George Julian of Indiana, and Henry Wilson and Charles Sumner of Massachusetts, and Moderates Lyman Trumbull of Illinois and William Pitt Fessenden of Maine. They also included Democrat Andrew Johnson of Tennessee, the only member of Congress from a seceded state who did not leave the Union with his state. The Democrats were weakened numerically by the loss of the Southern congressmen and senators and by their widespread opposition to the war, so the country's future was essentially in the hands of Republicans, a mix of Radicals (for their racial views) and Moderates/Conservatives.

As the short war turned into a long one, the initial and single goal of preserving the Union proved to be insufficient, but adding more goals to it was a controversial step during the war and, in terms of its implications, even more so afterward. The issue of slavery's end was a natural, practical outgrowth of the war. As Southern whites went off to war, slaves carried an increasing responsibility for keeping the economy functioning. Their value to the war effort was clear. Even so, the slaves were property of American citizens, and some army commanders returned the slaves who appeared in their camps to their owners. Others, like General Benjamin Butler, who would play a major role in postwar Reconstruction, declared the slaves war "contraband" who would not be returned to their owners and who would not be freed—they would be used as laborers for the Union army. The Confiscation Acts of August 1861 and July 1862 sought to clarify the situation. The first provided for the seizure of all property, including slaves, used for "insurrectionary purposes."[6] The latter provided for the seizure of real and personal property of Confederate officeholders and those aiding the rebellion; slaves of such persons were to be free forever. In addition, in April 1862 Congress ended slavery in the District of Columbia—after having ended slavery in the territories in June 1861—and put enforcement teeth into its laws to end the slave trade. These steps were taken to win the war, but they also reflected broader and more complex goals that would guide—and divide—Americans during the postwar years.

Lincoln's Emancipation Proclamation of 1863 was a war measure: it freed the slaves in Confederate-held areas. This executive order did not end slavery in the United States, as his critics (then and now) were quick to note. Close to a million slaves in the border states and in seceded areas occupied by Union troops were untouched by the presidential order; over three million were touched but still enslaved because they were under rebel authority. Some Northerners criticized the Lincoln administration for changing the war's goals, expecting white men to die for black men, and setting the stage for a black exodus northward. The New York Draft Riots of July 1863 were sparked in large part by the shift in war goals. Some Northerners, however, praised Lincoln's transformation of the war into a war about slavery, freedom, and rights. Regardless, Lincoln's move and Congress's earlier actions hinted at many of the postwar dilemmas that would occupy the nation.

Despite the opposition to abolition as a goal, by January 1865 there was sufficient support—thanks in large part to the Union's growing military successes—for the Thirteenth Amendment prohibiting slavery to receive congressional approval and to be transmitted to the states. Ratification came by the end of the year. But, as the *Cincinnati*

Enquirer lamented, "Slavery is dead, the negro is not, there is the mis-fortune."[7] Would "inferior" black Americans have the same rights as "superior" white citizens? Would states be able to restrict their move-ments, work, and other activities? What did freedom mean? *What did freedom mean to Americans in general?* Ending slavery was only the beginning and only a part of national questions that would complicate the Reconstruction years.

Handling of the postwar problem of the freedmen began during the last weeks of the war with the creation of the Bureau of Refugees, Freedmen, and Abandoned Lands. The Freedmen's Bureau had a multi-plicity of tasks: distributing food and clothing, dividing 800,000 acres of abandoned and confiscated lands for rent and eventual sale, setting up schools and hospitals, and supervising labor contracts involving blacks. Congress rejected Radical Charles Sumner's idea that the Bureau be a permanent one with cabinet rank; instead, Congress settled on a term that would finish one year after the war ended. The short life of the Bureau reflected the discomfort of most Americans with long-term federal guardianship and the desire not to treat the freedmen as a class needing special, permanent protection. To emphasize the government's lack of favoritism for one group, the Bureau also had responsibility for Southern white refugees. This effort to help—but with limitations and strings attached—would characterize many steps taken by the national government after the war.

Lincoln's Plan

Lincoln's formal assumption of authority over Reconstruction came in December 1863 with his Proclamation of Amnesty and Recon-struction. It was, he later explained, "one very proper plan"; others were possible.[8] Part of the country was in rebellion, "many persons" had committed treason, and Congress had authorized him to grant reprieves and pardons to rebels. Thus, in return for an oath of future loyalty (". . . I will henceforth, faithfully support, protect, and defend the Constitution. . . .") and a pledge to accept the "permanent freedom" of slaves, Lincoln offered full pardons and the restoration of all rights (including suffrage but excepting slave property).[9] It was a plan that historian Howard Beale called "kindly, forgiving, moderate."[10] The Pres-ident excluded only high-ranking civil, diplomatic, and military leaders of the Confederacy, plus those who had sworn such an oath before and then violated it to support the Confederacy (including judicial and military officers and former members of Congress).

This step required a second one because statehood, not just individual rights, was at issue. Lincoln explained that, once 10 percent of a state's 1860 voters had taken the oath, they could proceed with the creation of a new state government and a new constitution that accepted the end of slavery. In this way, Lincoln hoped to reestablish loyal governments in the South even as the war was raging; by implication he rejected the argument of Radical Republicans Charles Sumner and Thaddeus Stevens that the rebellious states had reverted to territories and were under congressional authority. His terms were mild and designed to appeal to those who had seceded reluctantly and who could accept the end of slavery but not racial and economic upheaval linked to the Radical goals of black equality under the law and suffrage.

He was seeking a way of undermining Confederate governments by winning over a portion of each state's white voters, but some Republicans in Congress were looking for a change in the very nature of Southern society that would assure blacks' postslavery status and a reworking of the entire Southern order. While few anywhere supported giving African Americans political rights, they did believe that equality before the law was an essential ingredient of freedom regardless of race. Lincoln's plan offered no assurance that such equality was even a possibility. Disagreements over this goal and how to achieve it haunted the nation throughout Reconstruction.

In July 1864 Congress, despite significant opposition, passed an alternative plan. "An Act to Guarantee to Certain States whose Government Have Been Usurped or Overthrown a Republican Form of Government" (the Wade-Davis Bill) was clearly based on Congress's view of its constitutional responsibilities and its belief that Lincoln's plan was too lenient. New state governments would begin forming once 50 percent of a state's white population pledged loyalty and swore an oath of past, present, and future loyalty. Those who took the "iron-clad" oath would then elect a constitutional convention. The new state had to prohibit slavery; those who held high military and civilian office under the Confederacy could not serve in the new state government. Steps would begin once military resistance was over. The president would appoint, with Senate approval, civilian governors to administer the states in the meantime. The bill did not require black suffrage because few Radicals at that time publicly supported equal rights for blacks.

Using a pocket veto, Lincoln argued on July 8, 1864, that he was "unprepared" to lose the new governments established under his plan in Arkansas and Louisiana or to accept Congress's asserted power to abolish slavery. He said, however, that states were free to follow Congress's "very proper plan" instead of his.[11] Lincoln's words did not placate the bill's authors. Senator Benjamin Franklin Wade of Ohio, chairman of the Senate Committee on Territories, was a Radical who wanted the South remade in order to avoid the possibility of slaveholders' regaining their power and of slaves' freedom becoming meaningless; he also opposed the executive branch's assumption of Congress's job of Reconstruction. Together with Congressman Henry Winter Davis of Baltimore, Maryland, who had written the bill, he angrily issued a manifesto which his biographer Hans L. Trefousse calls "one of the most ill-tempered, ill-considered, foolhardy enterprises a politician could undertake in an election year." While Wade may have been affected by his own personal political ambitions and by his wartime disagreements with, dislike for, and distrust of Lincoln, Trefousse links the manifesto to the Senator's determination that ". . . the war would [not] have been fought in vain."[12] Printed in the *New York Tribune,* the statement accused Lincoln of a "rash and fatal act" and of "usurpations"; he was guilty of a "studied outrage on the legislative authority of the people." Lincoln had forgotten "that the authority of Congress is paramount and must be respected" and that ". . . he must confine himself to his Executive duties—to obey and execute, not make the laws. . . ."[13] Issues that divided the country after 1865 and even led to a president's impeachment were evident in Wade and Davis's angry words.

They were also evident in the various "rehearsals for Reconstruction" begun during the war.[14] On the formal, political side were the Lincoln-based governments in Arkansas, Louisiana, Tennessee, and Virginia. For example, a constitutional convention in Louisiana in 1864 abolished slavery in that state, one step among many to undermine planter domination. In addition, the convention reduced the power of planters by changing the base for legislative representation. Still, a totally new order was far from realized: some convention delegates spoke in favor of excluding blacks from the state, and the convention did no more than permit the legislature to enfranchise blacks. For the

Radicals in Congress, Louisiana's Reconstruction vividly demonstrated the flaws of Lincoln's plan.

In other parts of the South, the rehearsals for Reconstruction were less formal but would prove to be equally disappointing to Radicals who saw Reconstruction as the opportunity to remake the South and bring the nation closer to their ideal of equality and liberty. For example, the Union army came into control of coastal areas of Virginia, North Carolina, and South Carolina and of lands along the Mississippi River. Instead of receiving permanent possession of the land and rights as free farmers working to support their families, former slaves were treated more as wage laborers on white-owned plantations.

The problems in these rehearsals suggest the problems facing reform-minded Northerners after the war. Seeking to do more than essentially reestablish the prewar status quo minus slavery, the so-called Radicals in the Republican party had to overcome a variety of hurdles: presidents who saw Reconstruction as an executive duty, a majority of Americans who were firm in their belief that blacks were inferior to whites, the national faith in the sanctity of property and state-based federalism, distracting economic problems that guided Northern voters, and long-standing Southern class divisions and disagreements over slavery, secession, and war.

Thus, the battle of Reconstruction.

Notes

1. Quoted in Howard K. Beale, *The Critical Year: A Study of Andrew Johnson and Reconstruction* (New York: Harcourt, Brace, 1930), 55.

2. Quoted in Michael J. Quill, *Prelude to the Radicals: The North and Reconstruction during 1865* (Washington, D.C.: University Press of America, 1980), 13.

3. Harold M. Hyman and William M. Wiecek, *Equal Justice under Law: Constitutional Development, 1835–1875* (New York: Harper & Row, 1982), 95–96; Howard P. Nash Jr., *Andrew Johnson: Congress and Reconstruction* (Rutherford, N.J.: Fairleigh Dickinson University Press, 1972), 16–17.

4. William E. Gienapp, ed., *The Civil War and Reconstruction: A Documentary Collection* (New York: Norton, 2001), 338.

5. 7 Wallace 700 (1869).

6. David Donald, Jean Harvey Baker, and Michael F. Holt, *The Civil War and Reconstruction* (New York: W. W. Norton, 2001), 281.

7. Quoted in Eric Foner, *Reconstruction: America's Unfinished Revolution, 1863–1877* (New York: Harper & Row, 1988), 31.

8. Harold M. Hyman, ed., *The Radical Republicans and Reconstruction, 1861–1870* (Indianapolis: Bobbs-Merrill, 1967), 137.

9. Walter L. Fleming, ed., *Documentary History of Reconstruction: Political, Military, Social, Religious, Educational and Industrial, 1865 to the Present Time.* 2 vols. (Cleveland: Arthur H. Clark, 1906–1907), 1:109–11.

10. Beale, *The Critical Year,* 54.

11. Hyman, ed., *Radical Republicans,* 136, 137.

12. H. L. Trefousse, *Benjamin Franklin Wade: Radical Republican from Ohio* (New York: Twayne, 1963), 224.

13. Hyman, ed., 147, 144.

14. Willie Lee Rose, *Rehearsal for Reconstruction: The Port Royal Experiment* (Indianapolis: Bobbs-Merrill, 1964).

CHAPTER 1

FORMING BATTLE LINES: THE PRESIDENT, THE SOUTH, AND CONGRESS, 1865–1866

Major Henry Wirz, commander of the Confederate prisoner of war camp in Andersonville, Georgia, was the only man convicted and executed for his wartime acts. He was hanged on November 10, 1865. Officially he was held responsible for eleven deaths at the largest prisoner camp in the war, but publicly he was blamed for the loss of 12,000 Union soldiers who succumbed to disease, lack of food, and exposure. Despite the fears of Southern leaders, no other was even brought to trial. The president of the Confederacy, Jefferson Davis, was confined for two years in a federal prison and then released, despite continued efforts to try him for treason, if not murder; he became president of an insurance company before retiring to an estate in Mississippi. General Robert E. Lee served as president of Washington College in Virginia from late 1865 to his death in 1870; General James Longstreet held a variety of state and federal positions, including minister to Turkey. Vice-President Alexander Stephens of Georgia was in Congress by 1873. Only seven years after the war that took 600,000 American lives and threatened the existence of the Union, most former Confederate leaders could once again hold office, thanks to the Amnesty Act passed by Congress in 1872.

In general, while many Northerners wanted Southern leaders restricted in their political rights if not punished—General George

Armstrong Custer called for the "extermination" of Southern leaders[1]—
most Northern political leaders, journalists, businessmen, ministers,
and military leaders sought a speedy, magnanimous, and lenient peace.
There were many barriers to the realization of this goal. Radical Republicans opposed a peace that did not assure both the war's gains and a
restructuring of the South. Although they had too few votes to make
Reconstruction policy on their own, they were loud and determined.
Their new president, Andrew Johnson, was also determined. As a
result, the first two years after the war were contentious ones that found
little presidential-congressional cooperation in creating peace terms for
the South.

Radicals and Freedom

More important to many Republicans than punishing rebels was
rebuilding the South into "a safe republic" with "free schools, free
churches, free social intercourse" within "a free labor society."[2] A free
labor system, movement toward crop diversification, and abundant natural resources were ready to transform the South into an extension of
the Northern economy and society, but political disruptions had to end
first. Unfortunately for postwar harmony, such Republican interests
were not shared by Democrats, including President Andrew Johnson.

The postwar Democratic party was the minority party in the
national government both numerically and in terms of influence. The
powerful prewar party controlled only a third of the seats in Congress
in 1865. Its Southern members were excluded from national decision
making by their four-year rebellion, and Northern Democrats had few
leaders of experience and influence in Congress. As the war ended, only
one Northern state (New Jersey) had a Democratic governor. The party
sought a speedy readmission of the Southern states and thus a quick
bolstering of its strength in Congress; it also sought Johnson's return to
Democracy.

The majority party, the Republican, was hardly a united force on
any issue, from the status of the Southern states and freedmen to the
tariff and currency. Even each wing of the party—the Moderates/
Conservatives and the Radicals—was internally divided and shifting.
The dominant wing, which included such men as Lyman Trumbull of
Illinois, William Pitt Fessenden of Maine, and John Sherman and James A.

Garfield of Ohio, was opposed to confiscation of planters' lands, black suffrage, lengthy military rule, extending national power over state power, and increased federal expenditures. Moderate Republicans were eager to end Reconstruction expeditiously; they did not share the Radicals' dreams of social reform, although they came to support greater rights and protections for the freedmen. They wanted to accomplish the war's aims of union and abolition and to tackle the troublesome postwar economic problems of the country.

Although some of their positions changed over time, the Radicals accepted the expansion of federal power that had occurred during the war and which, they believed, should continue after it; through that power would come a peace that achieved fundamental changes in the South. The Radicals were committed to black equality and even suffrage, as well as confiscation and redistribution of rebel property. With land taken from whites and in the hands of those who had worked the land for 200 years, the freedmen would have a base from which to rise and fall depending on their abilities, and Southern society would no longer be dominated by the traditional planter class. The South could be rebuilt along egalitarian, free labor lines in a way that provided a fair chance to all.

Although few Radicals, such as Charles Sumner and Thaddeus Stevens, were true racial egalitarians, all stood for some form of equality. Only the most committed Radical argued for social equality; other Republicans did not support political or social equality, viewing suffrage as a state-controlled privilege, not as a right of citizenship, and seeing one's selection of associates as a strictly private, personal issue. Civil rights (rights involving property and treatment by the law), however, were generally seen as an essential aspect of being an American; without them, freedom—and the war to secure it—meant little. On the other hand, a black American might argue that "if I cannot do like a white man I am not free,"[3] but that was not how most white Americans felt, especially if "do[ing] like a white man" included taking the property of Southern whites or voting.

According to the Radicals, then, clarifying the meaning of the end of slavery was critical to ending the war and defining the future for all Americans. Freedom was slavery's opposite, but what was freedom? Was it the same for black Americans as for white ones? If so, what did it mean for white Americans? In other words, the end of slavery presented the Radicals and the rest of the country with a difficult task that is hard for modern Americans to appreciate: defining what it means to be free. As future president James Garfield wondered, "Is [freedom] the bare privilege of not being chained?"[4] If it was more than that, how much more? And what role should the national government take in protecting and aiding the freedmen? By implication, what role should the national government play in protecting and aiding other Americans? Radicals had one answer; few, including the president and most Southerners, agreed with them.

Andrew Johnson

No one knew in April 1865 and no one knows today how Abraham Lincoln planned to handle postwar Reconstruction; no one knows how he would have handled the postwar disputes with Congress or the reluctance of white Southerners to accept anything more than military defeat and slavery's abolition in the most narrow sense. Students of history, however, know how his successor Andrew Johnson dealt with these issues. With Lincoln's assassination in April 1865, Johnson, who was only a few weeks into his vice-presidency, entered the White House. Since Congress was not in session from April to December 1865, Johnson—the Southerner who refused to leave the Union with his state—was virtually free to act on his own. Although many congressmen believed that the legislative not the executive branch was constitutionally responsible for the Reconstruction of the Union, they were willing to give the Tennessean the chance to demonstrate the toughness that permeated his speeches and conversations.

Johnson had climbed from poverty and illiteracy in North Carolina to a successful tailoring business in eastern Tennessee and then to the highest political office in the United States. A Jacksonian Democrat who held a variety of local and state offices in Tennessee before being elected to the U.S. Senate, he strongly opposed secession. He took a tough stand against the slave-owning planters who led the South's secession: "The Constitution declares and defines what is treason. Let us talk about things by their right name! If anything be treason . . . is not levying war upon the United States treason? Is not attempt to take its property treason? . . . It is treason and nothing but treason. . . ."[5] Johnson's loyalty led Lincoln to appoint him military governor of Tennessee in 1862, a position he held until he was elected vice-president on the Republicans' renamed Union party ticket.

Unfortunately for Johnson, his first impression as vice-president was not a good one. On March 4, 1865, weakened by typhoid fever and hoping to steel himself for the inauguration, Johnson drank some whiskey provided by outgoing vice-president Hannibal Hamlin. He then delivered a rambling, mumbling, partially incoherent speech in which he slurred words and made boastful promises suitable for the eastern Tennessee mountains but not for Washington, D.C. Disgraced and embarrassed, Johnson spent the next few weeks out of sight recovering his health. Only on April 14 did he meet with Lincoln for the first time since inauguration day. The image of a drunken Johnson would come back to haunt him, becoming a weapon of his political rivals during Reconstruction and later invoked by critical historians.

On April 15, 1865, the new vice-president—a man who had risen through every level of state and national government—became the new president upon Lincoln's assassination. Despite Johnson's inauspicious introduction to the executive branch, a common view was that he would impose strict requirements on the South. His many years of attacks on the Southern slave-owning elite and his opposition to their "treason," followed by reassuring statements to black Americans that he was prepared to lead them, convinced many that his presidency would be a good one for those who shared Radical views about transforming the South. In fact, Moderate Republican Senator John Sherman of Ohio later recalled that one fear among non-Radicals was that the new president "would err, if at all, in imposing too harsh terms upon these states."[6] They seemed to have reason for worry. In 1861 Johnson had explained,

> Were I the President of the United States, I would do as Thomas Jefferson did in 1806 with Aaron Burr, who was charged with treason; I would have them arrested and tried for treason, and if convicted by the Eternal God they should suffer the penalty of the law at the hands of the executioner. . . . [T]reason must be punished.[7]

Among Radicals, there was a widespread sigh of relief that Lincoln would no longer be an obstacle: "By the Gods, there will be no trouble now in running the government," concluded Senator Benjamin Franklin Wade, because God had provided the nation with "a better man" for Reconstruction. Still, others knew that as military governor of Tennessee Johnson had opposed a "merely retaliatory or vindictive policy" for his state, that he believed the South had never seceded, and that he did not support black suffrage.[8] In fact, he had little interest in black Southerners at all; in 1859 he called arguments about natural rights "clamor and claptrap."[9] The owner of four house slaves and an opponent of abolitionism, he had accepted slavery as a constitutional institution that was entrenched in Southern life, and he shared the poor white's dislike of free blacks and opposition to competition with slave blacks. He saw slavery as an inefficient labor system that also limited opportunities for the white workingman who was subjected to the pressures of the slave-owning elite. His focus was on how slaves had been a key to elite power and how voting freedmen could be used by that elite; rights for the so-called inferior black were of no interest to him.

Like Lincoln, Johnson also believed that Reconstruction was an executive task. Johnson had a broad view of state power and a narrow view of national power. His respect for the rights and powers of states was matched by a strict reading of the Constitution—especially concerning Congress's power—when it came to the reach of the national government. He had opposed secession at the risk of his career and even his life, but he believed that the Southern states, having never left the Union, had rights that the national government could not trample, modify, or ignore.

Johnson's first step came on May 9 when he announced the end of rebel authority in the Confederate states and recognized Lincoln's governments in Virginia, Arkansas, Louisiana, and Tennessee. Then on May 29 he issued two proclamations. His Amnesty Proclamation largely followed Lincoln's policy, granting amnesty to all former rebels who took an oath of future loyalty and accepted emancipation. Six of the exempt categories were similar to Lincoln's, but Johnson's eight others included those who owned taxable property valued at $20,000 or more. This was a logical and necessary exception for a man who blamed many of the South's problems, and certainly the war itself, on the slave-owning elite. Those in the exempt categories had to apply directly to the president. Johnson later explained that he "intended they should sue for pardon, and so realize the enormity of their crime."[10]

The second proclamation focused on North Carolina but was soon followed by others for the rest of the Southern states. Under the direction of presidentially appointed provisional governors, each state had to hold a convention to do three things: abolish slavery, nullify secession, and repudiate the Confederate debt. The conventions were to be elected and manned by those who had taken an oath of present and future loyalty and had been eligible to vote before the war (i.e., white males). After the conventions did their work, the states were to elect new governments. Qualifications for suffrage and office holding were up to the states since setting these qualifications was a traditional state job. While making no explicit statements regarding the freedmen, Johnson did instruct provisional governors to secure statutes protecting the freedman's right to work and to testify in court, and he suggested extending suffrage to blacks if they were literate, owned property, or had served in the Union army. The Southern states did not take his advice, and he did not push.

Although Southerners expected a conciliatory policy, many worried when Johnson spoke of the necessity of punishing traitors.[11] Now they found that they need accept only the most obvious of the war's outcomes. They did not have to provide for black suffrage or equal rights; their leaders were not going to be removed from power. Public reaction in the North, where many people sought a speedy and magnanimous peace, generally accepted Johnson's plan as merciful and dignified. Radical Thaddeus Stevens feared that ". . . before Congress meets [Johnson] will have so be-deviled matters as to render them incurable."[12] Many Northerners were concerned about the failure of Johnson's plan to provide for black rights, but during the summer of 1865 it was unclear where Johnson's plan would lead, so the nation and the Radicals watched.

Johnson's Southern Governments

On December 18, 1865, Johnson reported to the Senate that under his plan "reorganized" Southern states were "'yielding obedience to the laws and Government of the United States' with more willingness and greater promptitude than under the circumstances could reasonably have been anticipated." All but Mississippi had ratified the Thirteenth Amendment, and most had taken or were taking steps "to confer upon freedmen the privileges which are essential to their comfort, protection, and security." In general, Southerners "evince[d] a laudable desire to renew their allegiance" and to make "a prompt and cheerful return to peaceful pursuits." Despite "occasional disorders" in some areas and the continuation of "perplexing questions" regarding the freedmen, "a harmonious restoration" of the Union was occurring.[13]

Many Northerners, and particularly Radicals, saw a very different picture. Despite Johnson's minimalist terms, many in the South dragged their feet. They opposed ratification of the Thirteenth Amendment, two states (Georgia and South Carolina) repealed rather than nullified secession, and many Southerners opposed abandoning their Confederate debts. None took Johnson's suggestion to grant suffrage to property-owning, literate black males. It seemed increasingly obvious that Southern whites were not remorseful for the problems and destruction they had brought the nation and that they could not be trusted with self-government. Many in the North believed that Southerners were "unabashed, unhumiliated, unrepentant, . . . with [their] old swagger, yielding nothing and demanding everything." Where were the "outward signs of inner grace," asked Union Captain Avery Williams. The report of Congress's Joint Committee on Reconstruction, published in June 1866, agreed: "Professing no repentance, glorifying apparently in the crime they had committed, avowing still . . . an adherence to the pernicious doctrine of secession, and declaring that they yielded only to necessity, they insist . . . that they will submit to no conditions whatever . . . to their resumption of power under that Constitution which they still claim the right to repudiate."[14]

Because most Northerners wanted Southern cooperation with whatever Reconstruction policy the national government imposed, numerous travelers visited the South to get a clearer picture of Southern attitudes. These observers, including Senator Carl Schurz and General Ulysses S. Grant, provided conflicting accounts, ranging from eager unionism to determined disloyalty, but many Northern papers reported only problems. The *New York Times* concluded that ". . . the public sentiment is still as bitter and unloyal as in 1861. . . ." The *Boston Evening Transcript* referred to "universal disloyalty."[15] Schurz, a Union general during the war who traveled at Andrew Johnson's request, described freedmen as loyal and in need of the vote for self-protection. Southern whites fell "far short" of "accommodat[ing] themselves to the results of the war in point of spirit."[16] Grant reported a generally more positive picture of the progress of Southern acceptance of the war's outcome. On the negative side, however, he recommended a continued military presence to maintain order and a continued Freedmen's Bureau.

Part of the image of an uncooperative and unremorseful South came from its election of men who could not take the "iron-clad" oath of past, present, and future loyalty that Congress required of its members. These were men who had served in high political and military positions under the Confederacy, including Vice-President Alexander Stephens of Georgia. Choosing these men as governors, state legislators, and members of the Thirty-ninth Congress seemed to indicate a desire to return to the old ways, with nothing changed or learned by the war. The Southerners' choices were probably the result of obtuseness, defiance, and faith in traditional leadership; besides, the South was following the rules laid down by President Johnson. Regardless of Southern reasons, the election of "active secessionists with no love for the Union" revealed, according to the *Newark Daily Advertiser,* that the "reptile spirit of secession is still alive . . . and ready to display its fangs at any moment."[17]

The picture was more complex, however. Only three states—Georgia, Mississippi, and South Carolina—sent no delegates to Congress who could take the iron-clad oath; only 7 of the 77 who were elected to Congress in 1865 had been secessionists, with 44 (including Stephens) having opposed leaving the Union until their states voted to do so. Fifteen had been active Unionists. Among governors elected by the Southern states, none had supported secession, and only three had taken an active role in support of the Confederacy. (On the other hand, 10 men elected to Congress had served as generals in the Confederate Army.) Still, the South's choice of postwar leaders had "embarrass[ed]" its friend in the White House, concluded the *Philadelphia Public Ledger.*[18]

To Northern observers, freedom itself seemed particularly meaningless under the Johnson governments. The freedmen's determination to have economic independence was troublesome to Southern whites who saw in it threats to the social and economic stability of the South. As a result, the states passed a variety of laws in late 1865 and 1866 to limit the rights of the newly freed blacks, the "Black Codes." While legitimizing slave marriages and children, permitting the ownership of property, and allowing blacks to sue and be sued, to contract, and to testify in court in cases involving other blacks—all of which were dramatic steps in the Southern legal systems—the primary goal of the Black Codes was evident in their control of black labor. Seeking to maintain the necessary labor force on plantations (because whites generally believed that the freedmen were too lazy and irresponsible to work on their own) and to prevent whites from competing with each other for laborers, the laws created a category between slavery and freedom through limits on contract rights, definitions of vagrancy, and apprenticeship rules.

Despite the moderation of some of the Codes' provisions, and even though Northern states themselves limited black rights, Northerners were attentive and alarmed. At a minimum, they expected protection of the freedmen's basic (civil) rights and no effort to reenslave the freedmen. But, as one South Carolinian accurately noted, "Our Northern brethren will rightly regard the codes as too much of a white man's law." Senator Lyman Trumbull concluded that, while there was no "precise line" between "where freedom ceases and slavery begins," the Black Codes' restriction on property, travel, and occupations "is certainly . . . in violation of the rights of a freeman. . . ."[19] The *Philadelphia Inquirer* saw in the laws "slavery re-established, regenerated and re-enthralled"; for the *New York Tribune*, they made "emancipation a mockery and freedom a sham." Even the *Jackson* (Mississippi) *Daily Clarion* believed that under its state's laws ". . . slavery would be restored in a far worse form than it was before."[20] The Codes were proof to many in the North that Southern proclamations of loyalty and respect for the outcome of the war were merely words; the "generation of vipers" could not be trusted. It was not illogical for Northerners to believe that, in the words of the *Boston Evening Journal,* the "strong arm of the Federal Government" was needed.[21]

The nation wanted to move past the war, but it needed to do so with signs of Southern loyalty and acceptance of civil equality for the freedmen. Illinois Congressman Burton C. Cook saw the situation simply: "Can we now place the freedmen in the uncontrolled power of their former masters? The Negro codes enacted by the reconstructed Legislatures of Mississippi and South Carolina are our sufficient answer. . . ."[22] Doing so, according to the *New York Evening Post,* would mean that "brave boys who offered their lives upon the Altar of their country" died for nothing.[23]

Congress v. President, 1866

In December 1865, Congress (by a 133–36 vote) created the Joint Committee on Reconstruction, a 15-man committee proposed by Thaddeus Stevens to investigate conditions in the South and determine whether Johnson's Southern governments should be represented in Congress. Congress had decided not to seat the representatives and senators elected by the South. Once these men were seated, Congress's ability to reconstruct the South would be over and the end of the three-fifths compromise would increase the South's power in Congress.

The Moderate-dominated committee of nine representatives and six senators was to determine Southern attitudes and conditions before seating the delegates. Chaired by Moderate Senator William Pitt Fessenden of Maine, the committee spent the early months of 1866 listening to the testimony of witnesses who, despite conflicting reports, convinced many that under the Johnson governments the South could not be trusted to provide justice to freedmen and Southern loyalists. As it did so, Congress took three critical steps to expand the war's accomplishments regarding the freedmen. In response, Johnson took three steps to stop them.

The first two congressional steps came out of the Senate Judiciary Committee, chaired by Moderate Lyman Trumbull. Both were intended to provide the protection for Southern blacks that Johnson's plan did not. To many, therefore, the bills extending the life of the Freedmen's Bureau (a temporary, sectional statute) and clarifying the meaning of the Thirteenth Amendment (a permanent, national measure) were acceptable. Neither would have existed without the war, however, because both were monumental—even revolutionary—strides for a country that held strong racial views and adhered to state-based federalism.

The first bill gave the Bureau jurisdiction in cases involving blacks and allowed it to punish state officials who denied freedmen's civil rights. The bill, which indefinitely extended the life of the Bureau and passed by overwhelming votes of 37–10 in the Senate and 136–33 in the House, emphasized blacks' eventual ability to handle freedom without support from the national government. The Civil Rights Act of 1866 was in large part a response to the South's Black Codes. It sought to provide a clarification of freedom through a fundamental definition of rights for all Americans. It announced a definition of United States citizenship based on birth and naturalization, not race, and listed the rights that defined basic freedom: to sue and be sued, to testify in court, to own and convey property, and to have the "full and equal benefit of all laws and proceedings for the security of person and property, as is enjoyed by white citizens."[24] These were civil rights accepted by most Americans and granted by most Northern states. The bill—passed by votes of 33–12 in the Senate and 111–38 in the House—emphasized civil rights, not political or social ones. As a response to the situation in the South, it added to, rather than replaced, Johnson's plan.

The expectation was that Johnson would sign both measures. Instead, rejecting the opinion of his advisors who urged him not to needlessly antagonize his opponents, he vetoed both. In his February 19 veto of the Freedmen's Bureau Bill, Johnson leveled various charges against Congress. He accused it of acting unconstitutionally by using its military power during peacetime, assuming tasks that belonged to the executive branch, creating a discriminatory welfare system, intruding into the state sphere of education, building a dangerous bureaucracy, and raising unrealistic expectations of federal assistance among blacks. In addition, Johnson argued, how could Congress act when it was unfairly and unconstitutionally excluding the elected representatives of eleven states?

It was a logical, if ill-advised, argument from a president who cared little for blacks, feared for the rights of the states, believed that Congress had no power over Reconstruction, saw Radicals conspiring against him, and knew what would appeal to white Southerners and others whose support he desired. Johnson, however, misjudged Moderate Republicans. As Trumbull explained to the Senate in his response to Johnson's veto:

> The President believes [the bill] unconstitutional; I believe it con-
> stitutional. He believes that it will involve great expense; I believe
> it will save expense. He believes that the freedman will be pro-
> tected without it; I believe he will be tyrannized over, abused, and
> virtually reenslaved without some legislation by the nation for his
> protection. He believes it unwise; I believe it to be politic.[25]

Five weeks after his first veto, Johnson vetoed the Civil Rights Act, a bill that the pro-Johnson *New York Herald* had predicted he would "cheerfully" sign.[26] But Johnson's objections were numerous. Again, the president targeted not just the details of the bill but its underlying theory of black rights protected by national power. He argued that never in American history had either state or national government created what the bill tried to create: "safeguards which go infinitely beyond any that the General Government has ever provided for the white race."[27] He saw in the law favoritism against whites and for blacks. In line with his constitutional thinking, Johnson saw the bill as a threat to federalism and the relationship between individuals and their government(s).

To both Radicals and Moderates the two bills were necessary for the basic protection of Southern blacks, a fact shown by the near passage of the Freedmen's Bureau Bill over Johnson's veto (it failed by two votes, but a modified bill passed in July over another veto) and also by the successful passage of the Civil Rights Act—33–12 in the Senate and 104–33 in the House—on April 9, only the seventh time Congress had overridden a presidential veto and the first time it had done so with a major bill. Historian Dan Carter argues that if the veto had been sustained it "would have marked the end of any federally imposed postwar Reconstruction of the South."[28]

Johnson's third step to stop Congress from modifying his program was quite different from the first two and actually came between the two vetoes. On February 22 Johnson spoke to a crowd outside the White House in honor of Washington's birthday. Only days after his successful first veto, he excitedly attacked Radicals by name, accusing them of comparing themselves to Christ and of being "opposed to the Union."[29] He accused Stevens and Sumner of treason. Was he drunk (again)? Did he simply demonstrate bad judgment fueled by anger and political and philosophical differences? Was he attempting to provoke and isolate the Radicals in his effort to build a party of moderates and conservatives? The Democratic press might have applauded him, but the overall response was negative.

The Fourteenth Amendment

The proposed Fourteenth Amendment was Congress's third step. From January to June 1866 Congress debated possible provisions in a seemingly endless series of proposals and counterproposals. The result was an "imperfect . . . proposition," according to Thaddeus Stevens (who also referred to it privately as a "shilly-shally bungling thing," while fellow Radical George Julian labeled it "a wanton betrayal of justice and humanity").[30] Because it was not a radical measure, however, it drew the much-needed support of the Moderates.

A statement of national principle that made broader and permanent the provisions of the Civil Rights Act of 1866, the first section of the five-section amendment repeated the statute's definition of citizenship and added that "No State" could "abridge the privileges and immunities of citizens," "deprive any person of life, liberty, or property, without due process of law," or "deny . . . any person . . . the equal protection of the laws." In other words, section one clarified the nation's guarantee to every person of equality before the law, however ambiguously it did so. The final section gave Congress "power to enforce" the amendment.[31]

The other sections of the Fourteenth Amendment interest few people today, but they were significant in the 1860s. In fact, sections two and three drew more attention—and controversy—than did section one. Section two deleted the three-fifths clause from Article I of the Constitution and stipulated that a denial of male suffrage for any reason other than participation in the Civil War or "other crime" meant a proportional decrease in the state's representation. Radicals had wanted the amendment to specifically mandate black suffrage; instead they got what Charles Sumner called an "utterly reprehensible and unpardonable" indirect provision that simply threatened.[32] Section three stipulated that no one who had previously taken an oath to the United States and then engaged in rebellion or supported the Confederacy could hold any federal or state, civil, or military office (unless allowed to do so by a two-thirds congressional vote). This restriction did not eliminate the South's traditional planter elite as leaders—they could still be pardoned and they could vote—but it did reduce their powers. Finally, the impact of section four was significant for many states and individuals throughout the South; it voided all debts incurred in support of the Confederate effort and prohibited any compensation for lost slaves. Thousands (including slave owners from the border states and those who had been loyal to the Union) lost millions of dollars as a result.

Despite later claims, the Fourteenth Amendment was not a Radical measure: it was a Republican one. Moderates in the party influenced many of its provisions. Confederates were not disenfranchised, and blacks were not enfranchised. On the other hand, Confederates were disqualified from office holding without a congressional pardon, and if Southerners excluded black voters they faced a loss of representation in the House. (This provision has never been enforced.) As historian William E. Nelson argues,

> What was politically essential was that the North's victory in the Civil War be rendered permanent and the principles for which the war had been fought rendered secure, so that the South, upon read-mission to full participation in the Union, could not undo them. The Fourteenth Amendment must be understood as the Republican party's plan for securing the fruits both of the war and of the three decades of antislavery agitation preceding it.[33]

When Johnson's home state ratified the amendment in July 1866, Congress immediately seated Tennessee's six representatives and two senators. Would it do the same for the other Southern states? Would ratification end Reconstruction? If it did, what would happen to Radical goals, including black suffrage? Section two encouraged but did not require black suffrage, and once Southern states were readmitted Congress could no longer set requirements for the states. Southerners opposed the amendment and, backed by Johnson, refused to act on it. Without their states' votes, the amendment could not be added to the Constitution.

1866 Elections

In the summer and fall of 1866 the nation prepared for and conducted off-year elections that temporarily clarified the position of Northerners on Reconstruction issues and determined the weight of Radical power in the next session of Congress. If candidates supporting Johnson's restoration plan won, Southern states felt assured that their months of limbo would be over and the pressure to ratify the Fourteenth Amendment would end. If they lost, however, the fate of the Southern states would be uncertain. The Republicans had not revealed a substitute plan; they had only pieces, and those pieces were the result of disagreement and compromise, not a shared goal or program. The Radicals in 1866 had enough support to overcome Johnson's veto if they kept their proposals mild, but they needed more if they wished to overturn his program and replace it with a plan that would put into place their vision of equal rights protected by national power.

Two brutal riots hurt the Southern states' hopes. Although Americans familiar with the country's twentieth-century riots think in terms of black rioters, the situation was the reverse—with white rioters and black victims—in the nineteenth century, particularly in the two 1866 riots. Occurring in "restored" states, the riots (or, more accurately, the massacres) in Memphis in May and New Orleans in July suggested the failure of Johnson's lenient efforts and the reality of the freedman's day-to-day status. In all, 80 blacks (and 5 whites) died; in Memphis, hundreds of homes, schools, and churches were destroyed. The three days of violence in Tennessee, which was in Republican hands, grew out of racial tensions involving a growing black population (including black troops garrisoned in Memphis) and city police, many of whom were Irish. Almost four dozen blacks were killed; two whites died. The massacre in New Orleans was the result of political disagreements. Challengers of the Louisiana government and constitution, created under Lincoln's Ten Percent Plan, sought a convention to write a new constitution and enfranchise blacks, a step that would help Republicans outvote their white conservative rivals. Because Secretary of War Edwin Stanton did not inform Johnson of a request for instructions, the Army did not attempt to intervene. When delegates, black and white, and their black supporters attempted to meet, they were stopped by police and a white mob. Next followed "a frightful butchery"[34] that left 34 blacks and 3 white radicals dead. Looking to the fall elections, Horace Greeley of the *New York Tribune* affirmed that not many Northerners would "go to the polls to vote for murder, arson, robbery, torture, cruelty, oppression, systematic swindling and lynch law." Sumner believed that "you may judge [Johnson] by the terrible massacre at New Orleans."[35] Moderate Senators were increasingly ready for national protection of freedmen.

To make matters worse for Johnson's cause, in the weeks after the riots, he did what presidents did not do in the nineteenth century either for themselves or others: he made a campaign tour. During his "swing around the circle" in the Northeast and Midwest, he supported conservative Republicans and Democrats, part of a National Union coalition of supporters of his policies. He avoided mentioning the Fourteenth Amendment, instead emphasizing that the Southern states were loyal and that state issues (such as suffrage) should be left to the states. Unfortunately, making the same mistake as he did during his Washington's Birthday speech, Johnson responded to hecklers at some stops, calling his Radical opponents traitors and betrayers equal to Judas.

Johnson's candidates did not do well that fall. Republicans won control of every Northern state government and three border state governments (Missouri, Tennessee, and West Virginia), as well as an overwhelming majority in the House. As one pleased observer of the 1866 elections noted, "The House of Representatives can [now] send a dozen members off to a picnic and yet leave a majority large enough to pass a radical measure over the President's veto."[36] It is too easy to say that the reason was Johnson's policies, the Southern riots, or the president's campaigning. It is also too easy, as well as inaccurate, to credit the Republicans' success to a unified vision of Reconstruction. Such a vision did not exist, but many Northerners supported the general principles in section one of the Fourteenth Amendment (especially if they meant that the Southern blacks would have no reason to migrate to their states from the South). Significantly, the Republicans' campaign had emphasized sections two, three, and four, which allowed candidates to attract votes for anti-South positions rather than potentially lose them for problack stands. So, although Johnson had tried to avoid making the Fourteenth Amendment an election issue, it was.

Despite the election results, Johnson did not end his opposition to the Fourteenth Amendment, and he continued to encourage the Southern states not to ratify. They hardly needed his encouragement. Florida's governor explained the Southern white's view: "We will be taxed without representation, we will quietly endure the government of the bayonet . . . but we will not bring as a peace offering the conclusive evidence of our own self-created degradation."[37] White Unionists and freedmen saw the situation differently, as both stood to benefit from the amendment's reduction of the power of the traditional Southern political elite. In fact, white loyalists in states of the Deep South, where their numbers were few but black numbers were large, were coming to believe that only with black votes could they assure their own power. In Congress, Moderates who believed that protection of blacks required the amendment were frustrated by the delay and increasingly interested in new requirements for the Southern governments created under Johnson's plan.

Congress Takes Over

Despite historian Howard Beale's claim that "after November 1866, [Radicals] were supreme," and even with the South's "self-inflicted wound[s]" of 1865–1866, nothing was going to be easy for Johnson's Radical opponents. The long-standing argument has been that the Radicals quickly and easily seized control of Reconstruction and imposed their vision of government, economics, and race on the South. Historian William A. Dunning wrote in 1907, " . . . there was left to the moderates only the function of a drag on the reckless and revolutionary policy to which the radicals gave an irresistible impulse."[38] But the Radicals faced obstacles in all three branches of the national government. In Congress they needed Moderate support, and even the Radicals were divided among themselves about the direction to take in early 1867 when members of the new Fortieth Congress would be seated. (The second session of the old Thirty-ninth Congress met from December to March; the newly elected Congress was not to convene until December 1867, but a bill passed in January 1867 provided that future Congresses would convene immediately after their predecessors had ended. Thus, the Republicans could proceed with a revised Reconstruction in March 1867.) The questions facing the Radicals—and the Moderate congressmen whose votes they needed—involved how to insure Southern white loyalty, how to protect the rights of the black Southerner, and what test the Southern states needed to pass in order to end their nonstate status. For the Moderate Republicans the goal was to end the process quickly and to move on to other national concerns; for the Radicals, the goal was broader, the stakes higher. For the Radicals, what was done in 1867 and in the following years would not only determine the fate of black Southerners and rebel whites but also affect the nation's promise of liberty and freedom for all Americans, white and black, Northern and Southern.

The Radicals also still needed Johnson's cooperation, if not support, because, as chief executive with patronage and appointive powers, he would play a role in any Reconstruction program. And they had to be ready for the Supreme Court's playing a spoiler's role. In December 1866 the Court issued a ruling that threatened to undermine Radical goals. In *ex parte Milligan* the Court unanimously overturned a conviction by a wartime military court in Indiana; because the state's civilian courts were operating at the time of the trial, there was no reason to use a military tribunal. Although dealing with a wartime situation and not postwar Reconstruction, the decision raised doubts about how Freedmen's Bureau courts in the South, where civilian courts were operating, would fare with the Justices. One Southerner saw hope if the Court and the president stood against the Radicals: "What can they do without the army and in opposition to the united purpose of the South?"[39] The possibility of a Court opposed in general to Reconstruction efforts in the Southern states was also increased by two rulings in January 1867 against state-required loyalty oaths (*Cummings v. Missouri* and *ex parte Garland*).

Thus, the nation ended its second year of peace primed for further tension and division. Congress was divided, the South was determined and resistant, the president felt embattled, and the Radical Republicans were seeking a fresh start. It was an ideal situation for conflict and for a renewal of Reconstruction.

Notes

1. Michael J. Quill, *Prelude to the Radicals: The North and Reconstruction during 1865* (Washington, D.C.: University Press of America, 1980), 65.

2. Thaddeus Stevens and Carl Schurz, quoted in Eric Foner, *Reconstruction: America's Unfinished Revolution, 1863–1877* (New York: Harper & Row, 1988), 235, 236.

3. Henry M. Turner, quoted in ibid., 78.

4. Quoted in Foner, *Reconstruction*, 66.

5. Quoted in Lately Thomas [Robert Steele], *The First President Johnson: The Three Lives of the Seventeenth President of the United States of America* (New York: William Morrow, 1968), 163.

6. Quoted in Foner, *Reconstruction*, 177.

7. Quoted in Chester G. Hearn, *The Impeachment of Andrew Johnson* (Jefferson, N.C.: McFarland, 2000), 51.

8. Both quoted in Foner, *Reconstruction*, 177.

9. Quoted in David Warren Bowen, *Andrew Johnson and the Negro* (Knoxville: University of Tennessee Press, 1989), 134.

10. Quoted in Howard K. Beale, *The Critical Year: A Study of Andrew Johnson and Reconstruction* (New York: Harcourt, Brace, 1930), 31.

11. Michael Perman, *Reunion without Compromise: The South and Reconstruction: 1865–1868* (London: Cambridge University Press, 1973), 35–40.

12. Quoted in Beale, *The Critical Year*, 63.

13. Walter L. Fleming, ed., *Documentary History of Reconstruction: Political, Military, Social, Religious, Educational and Industrial, 1865 to the Present Time*, 2 vols. (Cleveland: Arthur H. Clark, 1906), 1:187–88.

14. Quoted in James P. Shenton, ed., *The Reconstruction: A Documentary History of the South after the War: 1865–1877* (New York: G. P. Putnam's Sons, 1963), 103; in Dan Carter, *When the War Was Over: The Failure of Self-Reconstruction in the South, 1865–1867* (Baton Rouge: Louisiana State University Press, 1985), 86; and in Patrick W. Riddleberger, *1866: The Critical Year Revisited* (Carbondale: Southern Illinois University Press, 1979), 51.

15. Quoted in Quill, *Prelude to the Radicals,* 127.

16. Harvey Wish, ed., *Reconstruction in the South, 1865–1877: First-Hand Accounts of the American Southland after the Civil War, by Northerners and Southerners* (New York: Farrar, Straus and Giroux, 1965), 46.

17. Both quoted in Carter, *When the War Was Over,* 228.

18. Quoted in Quill, *Prelude to the Radicals,* 135.

19. Quoted in Riddleberger, *1866,* 87–88.

20. Quoted in Quill, *Prelude to the Radicals,* 130; Theodore Brantner Wilson, *The Black Codes of the South,* Southern Historical Publications, no. 6 (University: University of Alabama Press, 1965), 70; and Carter, *When the War Was Over,* 226.

21. Quoted in Carter, *When the War Was Over,* 226, 228; and in Quill, *Prelude to the Radicals,* 129.

22. Quoted in Wilson, *The Black Codes,* 117.

23. Quoted in William E. Nelson, *The Fourteenth Amendment: From Political Principle to Judicial Doctrine* (Cambridge: Harvard University Press, 1988), 43.

24. Fleming, ed., *Documentary History,* 1:197–98.

25. Quoted in Riddleberger, *1866,* 83.

26. Quoted in Mark M. Krug, *Lyman Trumbull: Conservative Radical* (New York: A. S. Barnes, 1965), 241.

27. Quoted in Hearn, *The Impeachment of Andrew Johnson,* 86.

28. Carter, *When the War Was Over,* 236.

29. Quoted in Hearn, *The Impeachment of Andrew Johnson,* 99.

30. David Donald, Jean Harvey Baker, and Michael F. Holt, *The Civil War and Reconstruction* (New York: W. W. Norton, 2001), 544; Victor B. Howard, *Religion and the Radical Republican Movement, 1860–1870* (Lexington: University Press of Kentucky, 1990), 126.

31. Fleming, ed., *Documentary History,* 1:197–202.

32. Donald, Baker, and Holt, *The Civil War and Reconstruction,* 546.

33. Nelson, *The Fourteenth Amendment,* 61.

34. Thomas, *The First President Johnson,* 474.

35. Quoted in Howard, *Religion and the Radical Republican Movement,* 130–31; and in George C. Rable, *But There Was No Peace: The Role of Violence in the Politics of Reconstruction* (Athens: University of Georgia Press, 1984), 59.

36. Theodore Tilton, quoted in Howard, *Religion and the Radical Republican Movement,* 143.

37. Quoted in John Hope Franklin, *Reconstruction: After the Civil War* (Chicago: University of Chicago Press, 1961), 67.

38. Beale, *The Critical Year,* 9; Rable, *But There Was No Peace,* 60; William A. Dunning, *Reconstruction, Political and Economic, 1865–1877* (1907; reprint, New York: HarperTorchbook, 1982), 88.

39. Quoted in Perman, *Reunion Without Compromise,* 249.

CHAPTER 2

TAKING AIM AT THE SOUTH AND A PRESIDENT: CONGRESSIONAL RECONSTRUCTION, 1867–1869

The Fortieth Congress passed four Reconstruction bills in 1867 and 1868, all based on its war powers and all but the last over presidential vetoes. Congressman James A. Garfield, a Moderate, was among many Republicans of all hues who believed that the time for congressional action had come:

> I have been in favor of waiting to give [the southern states] time to deliberate and act. They have deliberated. They have acted. The last one of the sinful ten has, . . . with contempt and scorn, flung back in our teeth the magnanimous offer of a generous nation. It is now our turn to act. They would not cooperate with us in building what they destroyed. We must remove the rubbish and build from the bottom.[1]

This view had momentous implications for the South and the nation, for black American and white. With Moderates and Radicals working together, or at least compromising together, the Republicans used the victories in the 1866 election to ensure that Reconstruction of the South was more than just Johnson's "restoration" of the antebellum South minus slavery. The president's determination to thwart their efforts, and the Republicans' counterefforts, led the country to its first-ever presidential impeachment and to the possible disruption of national checks and balances.

The First Reconstruction Act

The Reconstruction Act of March 2, 1867 voided the governments set up under Johnson's plan and started over, announcing that "no legal State governments or adequate protection for life or property" existed in the South. (Technically, Johnson's governments continued to operate until they were replaced by new governments.) The act divided the 10 states that had not ratified the Fourteenth Amendment (i.e., all of the Confederate states except Johnson's Tennessee) into 5 military districts: Virginia; North and South Carolina; Georgia, Alabama, and Florida; Mississippi and Arkansas; and Louisiana and Texas. Each district was to be commanded by a general appointed by the president. The First Reconstruction Act stipulated that blacks were to vote for state consti-tutional conventions; whites barred from office-holding under the Fourteenth Amendment could not vote. The new constitutions had to guarantee black suffrage and the disenfranchisement of those who par-ticipated in the rebellion. Once a majority of eligible voters approved the constitution and elected new state and federal officers, and once the new legislature under that constitution ratified the Fourteenth Amend-ment, the ". . . State shall be declared entitled to representation in Con-gress. . . ."[2]

These requirements, not surprisingly, prompted a presidential veto on March 23. According to Andrew Johnson, Congress had taken power that belonged to the states, had made black suffrage the single test of a state's having a "republican form of government," and had necessitated a standing army and heavier taxes. Their intention was both to create new governments and to support black governments that could not maintain themselves. If black suffrage was the test, Johnson pointedly suggested that ". . . the work of reconstruction may as well begin in Ohio as in Virginia, in Pennsylvania as in North Carolina."[3]

In effect, what Congress did was return to the beginning, laying out new requirements for returning the Southern states to their old sta-tus as states. It was doing what black abolitionist Frederick Douglass had earlier argued that it should do: "begin with a clean slate, and make clean work of it," treating Johnson's "pretended governments . . . as shams and impositions."[4] This new start two years after the Civil War explains much of the bitterness tied to Reconstruction, bitterness that has led to Radical leaders' being called partisan, petty, vindictive, and spiteful racial demagogues for overturning two years of labor under the president's plan and requiring Southerners to accept Northern, national, military, black, and Republican interference. In 1865 white Southerners had known that the war was lost, the Confederacy was over, and abolition was a fact; they expected terms from the victors, they got the terms, and they followed them. Yet in 1867, Congress said that they had to start over.

Because congressional Reconstruction was to be implemented by the military, Congress also passed the Tenure of Office Act on March 2 to protect the Army's ability to do its job without presidential obstacles. This measure limited the president's ability to remove and replace appointed federal officials without Senate approval. If an officer's appointment required Senate approval, so too did his removal by the president. Only when the Senate was not in session could the president remove an appointee, but when it was back in session he had to present his reasons to the Senate.

As it turned out, this law, which today seems technical and unimportant on first reading, proved to be the spark that set off the final battle between Johnson and the Republicans. The controversy revolved around the section dealing with the removal of cabinet officers. A compromise resulted in the following requirement: such officers would retain their positions "for and during the term of the President by whom they may have been appointed, and for one month thereafter, subject to the advice and consent of the Senate."[5] The key figure at issue was Edwin M. Stanton, the secretary of war appointed by Lincoln during his first term and the cabinet's strongest supporter of congressional Republican views. If Johnson could replace him with a man who shared his views, then the president would be better able to undermine Congress's Reconstruction efforts. But did the Tenure of Office Act apply to Stanton? The president who appointed him had died almost two years earlier. Johnson's response was to veto the bill, saying that the president's removal power was "settled . . . by construction, settled by precedent, settled by the practice of the Government, and settled by statute."[6] Congress overrode, 138–40 in the House and 35–11 in the Senate.

Another important March measure aimed at restraining Johnson was the Army Appropriations Act. This act, an annual piece of legislation, included an important new element in 1867 as Congress sought to ensure that the General of the Army, Ulysses S. Grant, and not Johnson supervised its *military* Reconstruction plan. A rider to the bill required that the general's headquarters be in Washington, D.C., and that he not be removed or assigned elsewhere except by his request or except if the Senate agreed beforehand. In addition, it required that all orders to the army from the president or secretary of war go through the general. Johnson's disagreement with the measure did not lead to a veto because the rest of the appropriations bill was necessary to the functioning of the military.

Was the congressional Reconstruction plan that these two measures sought to protect "Radical"? Did it deserve the charges leveled against it by Southern whites and by many historians even through the twentieth century? Was it, as Kentuckian George Browder called it, "extreme, unjust, illiberal, & radical"?[7] The South was to be under temporary, not prolonged or permanent, military rule; wartime leaders were reduced in but not eliminated from power; and black suffrage was required of the South only. The Johnson governments were not immediately dissolved but stayed in power for months; Radical goals of land reform and black education were ignored. Radicals required Moderate support to pass any plan (recall the Moderate role in the framing and passage of the Freedmen's Bureau Bill, the Civil Rights Act of 1866, and the Fourteenth Amendment). As a result, any congressional plan was going to be "milder" than what the most committed Radical desired. The 1867 act was a compromise that failed to achieve the broad and long-range goals sought by men like Stevens, Sumner, and Wade.

Congressional Reconstruction Continues

Republicans quickly discovered that the First Reconstruction Act, written and enacted amidst deep party disagreements, had "loopholes" everywhere. For example, while the statute required the registration of voters, it did not specify who would be responsible. The result was that Johnson's governors did little to speed a process that would lead to their removal from power. The Second Reconstruction Act, passed on March 23, 1867, clarified the responsibility of the military commanders for registering voters, calling constitutional conventions, and scheduling elections.

The Third Reconstruction Act came in the summer of 1867 after months of problems over military commanders' lax use of their powers to remove civilians disqualified by the Fourteenth Amendment and after Johnson's removal of General Philip Sheridan as commander of the Texas-Louisiana district. The Civil War hero, unlike his peers, was willing to remove civilian officials, going so far as to replace the governor of Louisiana. The new statute sought to push military commanders to remove any official who was "disloyal to the government of the United States" or who "hinder[ed], delay[ed], prevent[ed] or obstruct[ed] the due and proper administration" of Reconstruction. Responding to opinions from Attorney General Henry Stanberry, the third act also included a provision that no Southern Reconstruction official was "bound . . . by any opinion of any civil officer of the United States." It clarified that all provisions of the various Reconstruction Acts were to "be construed liberally, to the end that all the intents thereof may be fully and perfectly carried out."[8] In other words, congressional goals upon which the acts were based were not to be undermined.

The fourth and final Reconstruction Act was prompted by a situation in Alabama. Since the act of March 2, 1867, required that a majority of all registered voters—not just a majority of those voting—approve the new constitutions, opponents stayed away from the polls. Even an overwhelming vote in favor of a new constitution would be insufficient if fewer than 50 percent of registered voters went to the polls. Alabamans decided to resist congressional Reconstruction by not taking part in the vote on the new constitution. In February 1868, only 70,000 of 167,000 eligible voted. Congress declared that a majority of those voting was all that was necessary, no matter how few. Not cooperating was no longer a strategic option. In this measure, as in the preceding three, Moderates and Radicals achieved their divergent goals: to move Reconstruction more speedily to a conclusion and to eliminate the influence of Johnson's governments, respectively.

The Road to Impeachment

Congress's concerns that Johnson would undermine Reconstruction by controlling the military seemed justified when the president decided in the summer of 1867 to heed conservative advisers' urgings to remove Stanton as secretary of war. Having made the decision to keep Lincoln's cabinet in April 1865, Johnson had found himself with an "inside agent" in the person of the second most powerful man in the executive branch. Stanton slowly but steadily had come to oppose Johnson's Reconstruction policies and to serve as the eyes, ears, and (careful) voice of the Radicals.

When the Senate, adjourned for the preceding months, refused to accept Johnson's reasons for firing Stanton and his interim appointment of Grant (required by the Tenure of Office Act), it ordered the secretary's reinstatement on January 13, 1868. On February 21 the president continued his efforts to eliminate Stanton and to control the Army with another interim appointment (Lorenzo Thomas); he would later argue, and some historians still believe, that he removed Stanton only to create a legal challenge to the Tenure of Office Act. Such an appointment when the Senate was in session violated the act.

Support in Congress for Johnson's removal as a barrier to Reconstruction had been growing for several months. Radicals had discussed it for over a year, but Moderates had refused to cooperate, even using their numbers to waylay Radical efforts in the summer of 1867 and to vote down resolutions of impeachment in late 1867. Radicals, such as James Ashley, had long argued that Johnson was hindering Congress's ability to do its job. Although Moderates believed that Reconstruction needed to function without undue interference, they did not agree that removal of the president was necessary, at least not until the spring of 1868. Instead, they sought nonimpeachment alternatives in the form of refinements of the Reconstruction Acts and other limitations on the president's ability to undermine congressional efforts; for example, the Army Appropriations Act limited his control over the general of the army. Moderate James W. Grimes of Iowa concluded: "We have very successfully and thoroughly tied his hands, and, if we had not, we had better submit to two years of misrule . . . than subject the country, its institutions, and its credit, to the shock of an impeachment. . . . [E]verybody is now apparently coming to [this] conclusion."[9] With the North's reaction to—and virtual rejection of—the Radical agenda (especially black suffrage) in the 1867 elections, the Moderates were concerned about the impact on Northern voters if the Republican party as a whole was perceived as Radical, which it would be if the Moderates supported such major Radical initiatives as impeachment. As Horace Greeley wrote, "We shall have burdens enough to carry in the next campaign without making Johnson a martyr and carry him also."[10]

Yet the Moderates joined the Radicals in early 1868 to impeach a president still popular with many voters, particularly Democrats. The Radicals were able to secure sufficient House votes for impeachment in late February 1868 only because they had Moderate support that had not existed only three months earlier. At that earlier time 66 House Moderates (along with 42 Democrats) stopped an impeachment resolution that had 57 supporters. The votes existed in 1868 because Johnson had managed to turn the Moderates' many reasons not to support impeachment into reasons to back it. Because he did "provoking things," Moderates responded with "a necessary defensive move."[11] Having already removed Sheridan, Johnson replaced four other military commanders. All this was in addition to his removal of Secretary of War Stanton and appointment of Thomas while the Senate was in session. With appointees who had no sympathies for Republican Reconstruction efforts, the fate of Reconstruction was at stake, as was Congress's authority. Johnson had done enough to shift Moderate thinking from concerns about their party's becoming too radical to fears of losing everything that congressional Reconstructionists sought. He was able to do so despite their concerns about Johnson's successor if he was convicted: Senator Ben Wade of Ohio, who was speaker pro tem, was a Radical whose views on everything from black rights to high tariffs and women's suffrage made him suspect. As Conservative Republican Austin Blair told his fellow legislators,

> I have been among those who have hesitated long before resorting to this measure. I had thought it better . . . that we should bear much and suffer very much rather than resort to this extreme measure . . . but at last I am convinced, as I believe all at least upon this side are, that there is to be no end of this [defiant presidential] course of action.[12]

Republicans were so ready to act against Johnson that, while the House did not decide on the charges (articles of impeachment) until March 2 and 3, it voted 126–47 to impeach on February 24. A seven-man committee that included four Radicals and two Moderates then presented the House with 11 charges. The first eight involved Stanton's removal and Johnson's alleged violation of the Tenure of Office Act. The ninth involved an alleged violation of the Army Appropriations Act. The tenth, encouraged by Thaddeus Stevens and written by Ben Butler, accused Johnson of bringing Congress "into disgrace, ridicule, hatred, contempt, and reproach" and of "excit[ing] the odium and resentment of all the good people of the United States against Congress and the laws by it duly and constitutionally enacted." It noted "certain intemperate, inflammatory, and scandalous harangues," as well as "loud threats and bitter menaces . . . against Congress." Johnson's actions and words were, according to the article, "peculiarly indecent and unbecoming in the Chief Magistrate" and brought the office "into contempt, ridicule, and disgrace." The eleventh or "omnibus" article pulled together the charges involving Stanton and accused Johnson of denying the authority and legality of Congress through references to its representing "only part of the States."[13]

In essence, the *legal* charges were 1) violating the Tenure of Office Act, 2) removing Stanton and appointing a replacement when the Senate was in session, and 3) seeking to interfere with the enforcement of congressional laws related to Reconstruction. The *political* charges were encapsulated in the eleventh article. The team of seven sent to the Senate to "prosecute" Johnson on these charges was made up of Moderates and Radicals, including Butler and Stevens.

If the impeachment and subsequent Senate trial seem partisan to today's students, that is because they were. Impeachment in the nineteenth century was generally seen as a political tool; the "high crimes and misdemeanors" required by the Constitution did not have to be actions that were indictable in regular courts. If Congress's control of Reconstruction was shaky, preventing Johnson from weakening its plan was essential; thus, removing him before he could undermine Reconstruction was not a vindictive act but a logical (and constitutional) political one. Plus, if the Republicans were "partisan" in their support for removal, Democrats were equally so in their opposition to it and steadfast support for Johnson.

Because the Republicans had the necessary numbers in the Senate to convict Johnson—a two-thirds vote was required—the question becomes how Johnson avoided removal in such a partisan situation. Historians over the years have come up with a variety of answers, many of them centering on the high moral stand taken by the handful of

Republicans who voted "nay" despite significant Radical arm-twisting. Practically, for some Senators, the prospect of Wade as Johnson's successor was probably sufficient to acquit. For others the two months between the beginning of the trial (March 30) and the final votes (May 16 and May 26) generated uncertainty about whether Johnson had removed Stanton in an honest attempt to test the constitutionality of the Tenure of Office Act or whether he had simply broken the law—or whether the law covered Stanton at all. Anyone who worried that conviction would disrupt or even destroy the executive/legislative balance also had enough time to contemplate what a vote to convict might mean. Chief Justice Salmon P. Chase, whose manner of presiding over the trial emphasized the legal rather than political nature of the proceedings, also likely played a role in influencing those who developed doubts about Johnson's guilt.

Whatever their reasons, the seven Moderates who voted not to convict—including such well-respected figures as William Pitt Fessenden and Lyman Trumbull—ignored the emotional appeals of the Radical House prosecutors and gave Johnson a one-vote escape, 35–19, on the three articles considered. In other words, because of Moderate support there were sufficient votes to impeach Johnson, and because of Moderate opposition, there were insufficient votes to convict him.

While Johnson's acquittal may have protected future presidents from similar political efforts at removal and thus secured the constitutional balance within the national government, the effort to remove the president also had an immediate impact. Realizing that his actions influenced the Moderates, Johnson controlled his provocative behavior during the trial and even afterwards. The result was that the reconstruction of the Southern states proceeded along the lines established by Congress and with a speed that satisfied Moderates; Congress seated the representatives and senators from Arkansas (on June 20) and from Alabama, Florida, Georgia, Louisiana, North Carolina, and South Carolina (on June 25), overriding two presidential vetoes to do so. After Georgia's legislature expelled its black members in September 1868, Congress refused to seat its Congressmen, investigated racial violence and "political murders" in the state,[14] and imposed new requirements on the state, including ratification of the Fifteenth Amendment. Georgia's second readmission came in the summer of 1870. Just a few weeks earlier, after late or redirected starts, Mississippi, Texas, and Virginia were readmitted. With their constitutions approved and their representatives and senators seated, the states were now largely inaccessible to Congress. Nowhere was land taken from former rebels and given to former slaves; nowhere did the reach of the national government into local affairs—for example, education and property—continue. As a result, key Radical goals went unachieved; the Radical vision remained just that.

The first year of congressional Reconstruction was thus a period of compromise, presidential vetoes, and congressional overrides, of Moderates provoked to challenge the president, and of frustrated but hopeful Radicals. It was a year of limits: on what the Radicals wanted, on how far the Moderates would bend, and on the role Andrew Johnson would play in Congress's Southern plan.

One major accomplishment during the year was black suffrage, which the First Reconstruction Act imposed on the South. The commitment of some of the Radicals to black suffrage was shared by few others, although many black Americans, including Frederick Douglass, saw voting as an essential ingredient of citizenship, of freedom. The argument that the right to vote would eliminate the need for the national government to play guardian or to play a long-term role in protecting the freedmen did appeal to many Moderates. In fact, allowing blacks to vote would reduce the need to disenfranchise whites, thus reducing that element of national intervention. Plus, if millions of Southern blacks voted, and if they voted Republican, the party had a chance of maintaining its national prominence—and control over national policy and protection of rights—even with the return of the Democratic South to the Union. Most importantly for the Radicals, these black voters could help secure protection for black rights and could secure the loyalty of the Southern states, that is, congressional Reconstruction goals.

There were other problems with the idea of expanding the suffrage. Doubts were widespread about blacks' ability and preparation to exercise the franchise. What was the likelihood that the freedmen's former masters would not try to take advantage of blacks and control their votes? Of what value would be the *right* to vote if the freedmen did not have the *ability* to vote for candidates who spoke for their interests? Being a wage laborer or a sharecropper did not provide the type of economic independence that would protect suffrage. If black Southerners lost power, Radical goals would be threatened if not destroyed.

Regardless of the concerns, the significance of suffrage for men who were enslaved just months before should not be overlooked by students today who find the nineteenth-century American's ideas of racial differences to be illogical and offensive. Whites of that time shared a racism that grew out of immediate, not historical, evidence; yet, in 1867 some were willing to share political power, something they would not do even with white women for another half century. Would they share it with African Americans in the rest of the nation? The answer to that question, and to the fate of most of the Republican governments in the South, came during the presidency of Johnson's successor, Ulysses S. Grant.

Notes

1. Quoted in Howard P. Nash Jr., *Andrew Johnson: Congress and Reconstruction* (Rutherford, N.J.: Fairleigh Dickinson University Press, 1972), 121.

2. H. L. Trefousse, *Reconstruction: America's First Effort at Racial Democracy,* updated ed., Anvil Series (Malabar, Fla.: Krieger, 1999), 111, 113.

3. Harvey Wish, ed., *Reconstruction in the South, 1865–1877: First-Hand Accounts of the American Southland after the Civil War, by Northerners and Southerners* (New York: Farrar, Straus and Giroux, 1965), 101.

4. Glenn M. Linden, ed., *Voices from the Reconstruction Years, 1865–1877* (Fort Worth, Tex.: Harcourt Brace, 1999), 142.

5. Walter L. Fleming, ed., *Documentary History of Reconstruction: Political, Military, Social, Religious, Educational and Industrial, 1865 to the Present Time,* 2 vols. (Cleveland: Arthur H. Clark, 1906–1907), 1:404.

6. Quoted in James E. Sefton, *Andrew Johnson and the Uses of Constitutional Power,* ed. Oscar Handlin (Boston: Little, Brown, 1980), 149.

7. Linden, ed., *Voices from the Reconstruction Years,* 118.

8. Trefousse, *Reconstruction,* 119, 121.

9. Quoted in Michael Les Benedict, *The Impeachment and Trial of Andrew Johnson* (New York: W. W. Norton, 1973), 25.

10. Quoted in Victor B. Howard, *Religion and the Radical Republican Movement, 1860–1870* (Lexington: University Press of Kentucky, 1990), 161.

11. Quoted in David Donald, *The Civil War and Reconstruction* (New York: W. W. Norton, 2001), 568; Sefton, *Andrew Johnson,* 150.

12. Quoted in Benedict, *Impeachment and Trial,* 104.

13. Trefousse, *Reconstruction,* 129, 130, 133, 134.

14. James E. Sefton, *The United States Army and Reconstruction, 1865–1877* (Baton Rouge: Louisiana State University Press, 1967), 200.

CHAPTER 3

FADING DREAMS: CONGRESSIONAL RECONSTRUCTION ENDS, 1869–1877

Ulysses S. Grant was nominated by the Republican party with both Radical and Moderate support, the former because he had supported congressional Reconstruction and the latter because of his nonextreme views on Reconstruction and the economy. He won the 1868 presidential election with ease, taking over 80 percent of the electoral votes in his race with Democrat Horatio Seymour of New York. Clearly the Democrats' success in the 1867 congressional and state elections had not been the beginning of an undetoured comeback for the party, although election results had suggested that Northerner voters were not supportive of the Radical package of land confiscation, black suffrage, and broad use of federal power. Historian Martin Mantell concludes that the 1868 election showed "soft spots" in the Republicans' Northern branch and much "fluid[ity] and [rapid] political change" in the Southern branch,[1] but the spots and changes continued erratically through the final years of Reconstruction. Concerns about corruption and the economy loosened the Republican grip on Congress and added to the country's growing interest in abandoning the uneasy work of remaking the South. By the 1870s all the Southern states had been readmitted. Many had also been "redeemed," with Democrats replacing the Republican governments. This step—not the readmission of the state—is usually used by historians to mark the end of Reconstruction in a Southern state.

By early 1870, when the last three Southern states were readmitted, many Republicans recognized that Reconstruction of the South might be a short-term accomplishment at best. Southern white Democrats might have reluctantly accepted the reality of congressional Reconstruction, such as new governments that included black suffrage and office-holding restrictions on the traditional elite, but now they were gaining control of those governments. With national power removed—except for the occasional intervention of federal troops to restore order and support Republican administrations—the politics of each state began to be more internally directed. As a result, loyalist whites (Unionists), cooperative whites (scalawags), Northerners relocated in the South (carpetbaggers), and blacks found their numbers, and certainly their votes, thinned by intimidation, violence, and power plays. Whites who found their states "ruled" by blacks, Northerners, and Republicans in the late 1860s used a variety of tools to win elections and thus save their states from these outsiders.

While the Democratic victories were in part the result of violence and fraud, there was little that the national government could do either constitutionally or practically. The constitutional reach had been limited and controversial even in 1865–1868; the practical reach, restricted by public views of blacks and national power, as well as budget and manpower limits, no longer even had much support from those who had once sought to protect the Civil War's accomplishments. National laws passed to enforce the new amendments permitted intervention, but tactically they were an unclear and inconsistent national strategy, even at a time when Republicans controlled both the executive and legislative branches. The use of those laws was up to the enforcers, and the enforcers were increasingly interested in economic rather than Reconstruction issues, as were their constituents. Radicals such as Charles Sumner were still dedicated to their task, but their numbers were thinning. Death (including Stevens' in 1868 and Sumner's in 1874), retirements, frustrations with the South, and the influence of competing issues were all turning the nation's eyes away from the South.

The Grant Years

It was up to the presidency of a war hero to ensure that the accomplishments of Reconstruction—limited as they might have been in the eyes of Radicals—were not lost. Ulysses S. Grant did not have the same commitment to black rights or to the Republican Southern state governments as did Charles Sumner, and he did not have a cohesive Southern policy when he took office or at any time during his eight years in Washington. Yet, his first term demonstrated a determination to follow through on the basic plan set out by Congress.

Grant's Southern policy has been called inconsistent, nonexistent, and lackadaisical. The *New Orleans Daily Picayune* referred to his actions in the South as an "incomprehensible muddle and mystery, a parable that cannot be understood, a riddle that defies all guesswork."[2] His support for congressional Reconstruction existed, whereas Johnson's had not; however, he varied from action to passivity, with responses to situations in the South often guided by political considerations. Influences on Grant included a Northern population increasingly interested in sectional harmony and general economic issues, as well as his own desire to be reelected in 1872 and to help his party win state and national elections. He was a conciliator in Virginia, an intervener in South Carolina, an observer in North Carolina, and a periodic force in Louisiana. His support for Republican governments in the South was real but inconsistent and hard to predict, especially by his second term when growing Northern frustration with Southern political troubles meant that intervention would likely cost the Republicans Northern votes. The result was, in the words of abolitionist James Redpath who investigated Mississippi's 1875 election, "dastardly surrender" by the Grant administration.[3] But if it was surrender, it was by the president, the Congress, and most white Americans.

Fifteenth Amendment

The Fifteenth Amendment was not surrender; it was compromise. In 1868 only the former Confederate states were required to have black suffrage. Most Northern and Western states still limited voting to white males. The proposed Fifteenth Amendment, which passed Congress on February 26, 1869, made black suffrage nationwide: "The right of citizens of the United States to vote shall not be denied or abridged by the United States or by any state on account of race, color, or previous condition of servitude." It was in some ways the last major stand on principles for the Radicals, who had sought black suffrage as a way of assuring equality of citizenship and equal protection of the laws. Whatever the opposition of most Americans to black suffrage, the elections of 1868 had given Republicans control of the executive branch for four years and of both houses of Congress for at least two years, as well as of the states whose votes were needed for ratification.

Motives for extending suffrage by amendment were complex, involving both political gain and egalitarian commitment. For Moderates, the Fifteenth Amendment was in some ways a defeat because they disliked overriding state control of suffrage requirements. Suffrage was seen as a privilege selectively given (e.g., to men, not to women). It was not a natural corollary to citizenship. On the other hand, because Radicals had sought explicit provision for black office-holding; because the amendment prohibited the denial of suffrage "on account of race, color, or previous condition of servitude" but did not state a guaranteed right to vote; and because discrimination could proceed on racially neutral grounds (e.g., through literacy and property requirements), the amendment was another compromise that undercut Radical goals. Those who wanted more from the amendment found themselves supporting it as better than no amendment at all. Still, even as section one of the amendment left loopholes for the creative disenfranchiser who wished to deny blacks the vote on the basis of some apparently nonracial basis, section two empowered Congress to act if the amendment was violated.

For many Northerners, black suffrage was the final step of Reconstruction: ". . . the work of the Republican party . . . ends with the adoption of the Fifteenth Amendment," concluded the *New York Times*.[4] (The amendment was added to the list of Reconstruction requirements facing the still-unadmitted Mississippi, Texas, and Virginia.) With suffrage guaranteed by the Constitution, Southern freedmen no longer needed a protective federal presence. Others saw it as only a step: Henry Wilson of Massachusetts argued that "we have had to gather every triumph of human rights step by step, a little at a time; but by the blessings of God the final fruition will come some time, and we will work for that end." Another supporter saw it as "a fort built to secure the advance" of progress.[5] The amendment, however, meant no more than the national commitment to enforce it and the South's determination to accede to it. Despite the best hopes of Radicals, Southern white Democrats controlled their states' economies, were steadily regaining political control of their states, were using terrorist organizations to intimidate and control, and still rejected black claims of even civic equality. African Americans may have had the weight of a constitutional amendment behind their vote, but those exercising their suffrage in the South risked their lives; and those who threatened lives and suffrage in the South faced inconsistent punishment regardless of section two.

The Enforcement Acts

Congress—with presidential support—did not completely or abruptly abandon its Southern efforts. It could and did act under the authority of the Thirteenth, Fourteenth, and Fifteenth Amendments. It was obvious to Radicals that the rights of blacks were insecure, if not nonexistent, in many areas of the South, and it was logical to them that the rights defined by the national constitution and by federal law should be protected by national power. Thus, Congress enacted the Enforcement Acts of 1870 and 1871 to cover not only organized violence but also racial discrimination in elections.

The Enforcement Act of May 30, 1870, was prompted by the continuing harassment of black voters in Southern states. It reenacted the Civil Rights Act of 1866 and stipulated that election officials had to insure that there was no "distinction of race, color, or previous condition of servitude" in qualifying to vote. It prohibited "any person" from using "force, bribery, threats, intimidation, or other unlawful means" (including firing them from a job, evicting them from a house, and refusing to renew labor contracts) to limit potential voters from qualifying to vote or from voting. "If two or more persons shall band or conspire together, or go in disguise upon the public highway, or upon the premises of another" in order to violate the Enforcement Act or "to prevent or hinder [a person's] free exercise and enjoyment of any right or privilege granted or secured to him by the Constitution or laws," they faced fines up to $5,000 and imprisonment up to 10 years. Enforcement was in the hands of the new Department of Justice, and federal district courts had jurisdiction over alleged violators.[6] In July 1870, Congress added coverage of congressional elections in cities with populations of 20,000 and larger. Sixty-three of the 68 cities with such populations were outside the South, suggesting lawmakers' political interests in Democratic-dominated Northern cities, but the political and humanitarian motives often blended: protection of Republican voters in the

South and North would help secure the party's power and thus help secure the protection it believed that voters—black and white—needed.[7] (A rider to the Civil Appropriations Act of June 10, 1872 expanded election supervision to rural areas.)

While the Enforcement Act of February 28, 1871, enlarged the powers of election officials and provided a process for the appointment of supervisors for registration and voting for Congress, the third act, commonly known as the Ku Klux Klan Act of April 20, 1871, specifically targeted terrorist groups in the South. Broader in what it sought to protect than the 1870 law, the KKK Act prohibited a variety of activities, including acting "under color of any law, statute, ordinance, regulation, custom, or usage" to deny "rights, privileges, or immunities secured by the Constitution." It also prohibited conspiracies to overthrow or oppose the United States, to prevent the enforcement of its laws, and to prevent anyone from voting, holding office, testifying, or being impartial jurors. Importantly, it prohibited

> . . . go[ing] in disguise upon the public highway or upon the premises of another for the purpose . . . of depriving any person or any class of persons of the equal protection of the laws, or of equal privileges or immunities under the laws, or for the purpose of preventing or hindering the constituted authorities of any State from giving or securing to all persons within such State the equal protection of the laws, or . . . conspir[ing] together for the purpose of in any manner impeding, hindering, obstructing, or defeating the due course of justice in any State or Territory, with the intent to deny to any citizen of the United States the due and equal protection of the laws. . . .

Victims of such actions could sue in federal court for injuries and loss of rights. If violations "so obstruct[ed] or hinder[ed] the execution of the laws" as to deny "any portion or class of people" their constitutional rights, and if they could not be handled by the state authorities, the state was in violation of the Fourteenth Amendment and the president could use federal military forces. If a state could not control the activities or was "in complicity with" the violators, the situation was "a rebellion against the government of the United States"; the president could suspend the writ of habeas corpus.[8]

Enforcement of the new laws was a difficult task for the few remaining federal troops in the South. Counting those in Texas assigned to handle Native Americans, there were fewer than 6,000. In addition, the Justice Department operated with little money and victims were reluctant to testify. While there were thousands of indictments, particularly in Mississippi, North Carolina, and South Carolina, there were relatively few convictions, and South Carolina was the only state where Grant used the powers given him by the KKK Act to suspend the writ of habeas corpus. However, suspended sentences with the threat of more severe penalties for further offenses, the flight of thousands to avoid prosecution, and the conviction of key figures helped accomplish the laws' short-term goal of protecting the lives and rights of black Southerners. Still, as historian Eric Foner points out, ". . . the need for outside intervention was a humiliating confession of weakness for the Reconstruction [Republican] regimes."[9] If a Republican government could not protect its citizens, its claims of legitimacy were weak, increasing the reluctance of Northerners to intervene and adding to the determination of Southern Democrats to head to the polls and resort to further violence and intimidation.

Federal response to the violent successors to the Klan did not come often, for a variety of reasons that historians still debate. Many of the dedicated Radicals in Congress had died or lost political power; many Northern members of the Republican party were more interested in economic issues, especially because of the depression that began in 1873. In addition, Northerners, skeptical of strong federal power, were increasingly uninterested in Southern issues, especially those involving black rights and dishonest and unstable government, or "monstrosities," as President Grant called the state governments in 1874);[10] they responded less and less when Republicans "waved the bloody shirt" (reminded listeners of the South's wartime disloyalty). Federal troops sent to the aid of a Republican state government were a sign of that government's weakness and inability to govern. Why should the nation's resources be used to prop it up? To the *New York Herald*, the Republican governments in the South were "dead weight." A Northern Republican confirmed in 1875: "The truth is our people are tired out with this worn out cry of 'Southern outrages'!!! Hard times & heavy taxes make them wish the 'nigger,' 'everlasting nigger,' were in _____ or Africa." Grant's widely quoted explanation for not sending troops cited Northern public opinion: "The whole public are tired out with these annual autumnal outbreaks in the South, and the great majority are ready to condemn any interference on the part of the Government."[11] Yet a year later, in a reflection of the difficulty with which Republicans abandoned the South entirely, he pledged that "neither Kuklux [sic] Klans, White Leagues, nor any other association using arms and violence to execute their unlawful purposes can be permitted in that way to govern any part of this country."[12] And he authorized the War Department in 1875 to use troops to counter the most significant outbreaks of intimidation and violence.

Use of federal troops or prosecutions in states that were unlikely to see Republican wins was unappealing to many Republican party leaders. Grant's administration had little interest in federal enforcement "except when an election was pending," Radical Senator Carl Schurz concluded. Thus, even when Mississippi Governor Adelbert Ames requested federal troops in 1875, Grant did not send them as he had earlier in the year to Louisiana. Instead, he listened to Northern voters: "Grant decided to save Ohio and sacrifice the Negroes of Mississippi," concludes historian Kenneth Stampp. Ames seemed to agree, noting that "I was sacrificed last fall that . . . [a Republican] might be made Gov[ernor] of Ohio."[13]

The Last Years of Congressional Reconstruction

In the early 1870s Congress tackled economic problems exacerbated by depression, and Grant battled numerous scandals and the revolt of the Liberal Republicans against his 1872 reelection bid. The impact on Reconstruction of the South was significant.

During the war the nation solved some of its financial problems by issuing $433 million in United States notes, or what were commonly called "greenbacks." Many Americans believed that only a gold and silver currency was wise economically and that only coins were proper constitutionally. These ideas and the inflation of the postwar years led to repeated demands to contract the currency by calling in greenbacks and resuming payment in gold. The battle over currency policy, as well as tariff levels, split the electorate and the Republican party. It forced the latter repeatedly to make Reconstruction issues secondary to economic ones.

In addition, while Southern Democrats leveled charges of corruption against Southern Republicans, especially the Northern so-called carpetbaggers, the Grant administration itself was feeling the brunt of various scandals and allegations. Even though Grant himself was personally honest, his support of friends and appointees accused of corruption and illegalities helped fragment the Republican party and build opposition to his election to a second term. That opposition, the Liberal Republicans, was not only outraged by the corruption but disagreed with Grant's Southern interventions, and they wanted amnesty for Confederate leaders. They also wanted currency reform (the gold standard), free trade, and limited government. Their fusion with the Democrats had little success in stopping Grant's reelection in 1872 but did push the Republicans to respond to some of the reformers' issues. Congress reduced the tariff and turned away from silver; it also provided amnesty for most former Confederates. Republicans also sought to undercut the Liberals' Southern plank by considering a version of a civil rights bill proposed by Charles Sumner.

The threat from the Liberal Republicans may have fizzled, but the Democratic challenge only grew until, two years later in 1874, Democrats won control of the House, the first time that the Republicans had suffered a significant national defeat. Then, when the newly elected state legislatures met, they selected fewer Republicans, thus cutting the party's majority in the Senate by half. Democrats also took 19 gubernatorial races and lost only 6. Undoubtedly the Democratic victories were due to a wide range of concerns, including economic depression, corruption, and Grant's interest in a third term. But they also reflected Northern views on Reconstruction, particularly aid to blacks and the use of federal troops to prop up weak Republican governments. An explanation for Democratic successes that was unique to the South was the use of violence by successors to the Klan.

With Democratic control of the next Congress, the Republicans met in December 1874 in a lame-duck session and sought to make changes in economic policy, to strengthen voting protections, to add new states (Colorado and New Mexico) in order to gain more Senate votes, and to protect the remaining three Republican governments in the South (Florida, Louisiana, and South Carolina). They also sought passage of Charles Sumner's controversial civil rights proposal. Earlier Congressional actions had targeted civil and political rights; this bill focused on what most people defined as social relations between the races, from eating, sleeping, and traveling to education and burial (although schools and cemeteries were excluded from the final bill). For some the bill was a tribute to the recently deceased Massachusetts senator. For other Republicans it was likely a last effort to return to the party's egalitarian vision, as well as a response to pressure from black voters. For many in the North and South it was simply going too far. As the *New York Tribune* summarized white concerns: "Do you wish to be buried in a nigger grave-yard? Do you wish your daughter to marry a nigger? Are you going to send your boy to a nigger school?"[14] A Kentucky newspaper clarified Southern white concerns:

> The graveyards you have selected, beautified, and adorned . . . must be desecrated . . . [with] choice places given to the negro, even if it should require the exhuming of friends long buried. You must divide your pew in church, even if your wife and child are forced to sit on the floor, and no complaint must be made should Sambo besmear the carpet you have placed there with juice of tobacco. Your children at school must sit on the back seat and in the cold, whilst the negro's children sit near the stove and on the front seats, and enjoy in every instance the money you toil for, whilst Sambo is sleeping and stealing.[15]

Still, the measure passed. Targeting individual, private discrimination, the statute sought to enforce the Fourteenth Amendment's requirement of equal protection. It prohibited racial discrimination by "inns, public conveyances on land or water, theaters, and other places of public amusement." The law also prohibited disqualification from jury service because of "race, color, or previous condition of servitude."[16] Criticism came from Republicans and Democrats, from Northerners and Southerners, and from blacks and whites. Few saw hope of enforcement or of practical changes resulting from the law. They were right.

The Force Act

Even though Northern interest in the Southern black and the Southern Republican party was ebbing, black and white Republicans in the South sought further protections for black suffrage. White Republicans, whose numbers were never large, saw their fate, and that of the national party, at risk if black voters were not free to cast ballots for them. Even with the Enforcement Acts already on the books, Grant pushed for further protections in late 1874 with the 1876 elections looming in the near future. The extensive violence associated with the 1874 elections was evidence that additional aid was necessary. A proposal, backed by Radicals and passed by the lame-duck House, proposed protection against election frauds and such suffrage barriers as the poll tax; it allowed the president to suspend the writ of habeas corpus, authorized federal marshals to make arrests, and prohibited carrying arms on election day. However, the "Force bill" died in the Senate.

Reconstruction and the Supreme Court

Unfortunately for the long-term accomplishments of the Radicals, the Enforcement Acts and the Civil Rights Act ran into a Supreme Court which, like most postwar Americans, was guided by a devotion to state-based federalism and a general lack of interest in and even opposition to racial equality.

In the *Slaughterhouse* cases of 1873, the Court in a 5–4 decision held that the Thirteenth and Fourteenth Amendments existed to protect black rights; they could not be used by white Louisiana butchers to stop their state from limiting the butchering of livestock to one area near New Orleans and to the facilities of one corporation. The amendments had enlarged the rights of black Americans, not all Americans. While the Civil War increased the power of the national government, it had not eliminated states' powers, including their power over "the rights of person and of property,"[17] and most citizenship rights were tied to states, not the nation. Traditional federalism, therefore, was not much changed by the new amendments, a conclusion that would bode ill for later efforts to use federal power under the articles to ensure the limited accomplishments of Reconstruction.

In 1876, *United States v. Reese* restricted the usefulness of the Fifteenth Amendment, voiding sections of the 1870 Enforcement Act and holding that the amendment did not confer voting rights—it merely prohibited voting restrictions based on race. States could limit voting for reasons other than race. In the *Reese* case, the restriction was the poll tax.[18] The same year, *United States v. Cruikshank,* which involved the successful prosecution of one of the white participants in the Colfax massacre of April 1873 (in which over a hundred blacks died), further limited the Fourteenth and Fifteenth Amendments. The Supreme Court held that they did not "add any thing to the rights which one citizen has under the Constitution against another."[19] In targeting the actions of individuals, rather than of states, the Enforcement Acts had reached outside the amendments. Under the acts, the national government had improperly indicted dozens of whites, supporters of a rival Democratic government, for their attack on blacks loyal to Louisiana's court-backed Republican government. Only nine had been tried, and only three of those nine were convicted, but the Court held that the amendments had given the national government no such reach into the action of private individuals.

Then in 1883 came the Court's ruling on the Civil Rights Act of 1875. By the 1880s the nation had moved past Reconstruction of the South, but the Supreme Court's decision was important in confirming just how far. In the *Civil Rights Cases,* the Justices limited Congress's power under the Thirteenth Amendment, holding that the article "has only to do with slavery and its incidents." Refusing someone service at an inn or restaurant was not such an incident. The Court rejected the argument that ". . . the act of a mere individual . . . refusing the accommodation . . . [could] be justly regarded as imposing any badge of slavery or servitude . . ."; "it would be running the slavery argument into the ground, to make it apply to every act of discrimination which a person may see fit to make as to the guests he will entertain." Disturbingly for those concerned about black rights under the Constitution, the Court's eight-man majority concluded, "When a man has emerged from slavery, and by the aid of beneficent legislation has shaken off the inseparable concomitants of that state, there must be some stage in the progress of his elevation when he takes the rank of a mere citizen, and ceases to be the special favorite of the laws." In lone dissent, John Marshall Harlan could not "resist the conclusion that the substance and spirit of the recent amendments to the Constitution have been sacrificed by a subtle and ingenious verbal criticism." He argued that the "badges and incidents" of slavery were covered by the Thirteenth Amendment and that railroads, inns, and other public accommodations were "agents or instrumentalities of the State" and thus covered by the Fourteenth Amendment.[20] These were arguments that would have to wait over a half-century for support; as a result, the goals of Reconstruction embodied in its amendments were delayed until the so-called Second Reconstruction of the 1950s–1970s.

The 1876 Election and the Compromise of 1877

At the start of 1876, three Southern states—Florida, Louisiana, and South Carolina—still had Republican governments; the other eight had been restored to Democratic rule. A year later, every Southern state was in Democratic hands. As a result, historians usually use the event that helped precipitate that change, the election of 1876, to mark the end of Reconstruction. As 1876 opened, most Americans were hoping that the nation had "finished the work of readjusting our national life to the new [post-slavery] order of things" (*New York Evening Post*); yet, ". . . a large section of the country . . . [was still] disturbed by violence and paralyzed by misgovernment . . ." (*Springfield Republican*).[21] Were black lives still at risk in the South? Was it time for the national government to give up its support for Southern governments and allow local rule to decide the fate of those lives? The 1876 election provided answers, but not because it pitted two conflicting views of Reconstruction against each other.

The Republicans did not offer Grant the chance of a third term; instead, it nominated the honest and able governor of Ohio, Rutherford B. Hayes. He was the perfect compromise candidate because he had few enemies and a limited, reform-based record. As a member of the House immediately after the war, he had supported congressional Reconstruction but had also supported state control over suffrage requirements, as well as educational requirements for both whites and blacks. As governor, he helped obtain Ohio's ratification of the Fifteenth Amendment, which he believed marked the end of Reconstruction. By 1875 he avoided Reconstruction issues, focusing on a Southern policy that emphasized economic development, a demand for "thorough, radical, and complete" civil service reform, and specie payments. The Republicans' platform, while affirming a general commitment to Reconstruction, suggested a retreat from it. Especially telling was the party's shrugging off of Frederick Douglass's pointed questions at its 1876 national convention: "[W]hat is your emancipation?—what is your enfranchisement? What does it amount to, if the black man, after having been made free by the letter of your law, is unable to exercise that freedom; and, having been freed from the slaveholders' lash, he is to be subject to the slaveholder's shot-gun?"[22] The Democrats nominated their own reform candidate, Governor Samuel J. Tilden of New York, and offered their own conciliatory platform.

As many foresaw after the 1874 elections, 1876 was another violent election year in the South, highlighted by the massacre in Hamburg, South Carolina. After an incident between a black militia unit and local whites, hundreds of whites surrounded the armory where the unit had fled for safety. When gunfire killed one of the whites, they responded with cannon fire. Upon the surrender of the militia, the whites released its leaders, only to shoot six of them in the back as they tried to run away. The violence steered the election toward what the South could do and what the nation was willing to accept. As Hayes privately explained the Northern dilemma, "The true issue in the minds of the masses is simply, Shall the Rebels have the Government?"[23]

Although Tilden won the popular vote and seemed the new president—minus *one* electoral vote—as election day ended, the three Southern states still in Republican hands had not reported, and neither had the Pacific Coast states. The Pacific Coast votes—except for one disputed vote in Oregon—soon went to Hayes; therefore, the decisions of the returning boards of Florida, Louisiana, and South Carolina were critical to the selection of the next president. At issue were four, eight, and seven votes, respectively, as well as the one vote in Oregon. Democrats claimed fraud in the boards' considerations of disputed votes, and Republicans cited violence and intimidation against Republican voters. A constitutional crisis was at hand: the Senate (Republican) and House (Democratic) were unable to agree on a way to count the contested votes. Kentucky minister George Browder was not alone in January, with a president still not chosen, when he hoped "that the Presidential question will be settled without war."[24]

That same month, however, the two houses agreed on an electoral commission made up of five members each from the Senate, House, and Supreme Court. The Democrats and Republicans would be equally represented, with the fifth justice impartial. As the electoral votes were counted, disputed votes would go to the commission; both houses, however, could overrule its decision.

On February 1 the count began. Alphabetically, all went smoothly until Florida's disputed votes came up for counting. Democrats argued for challenging the decision of the state board; Republicans argued against doing so. The commission accepted the Republican position in an 8–7 vote, thus assuring the state's votes went to Hayes; Tilden failed to get the single vote he needed. The same occurred for Louisiana and South Carolina. Hayes won all of the disputed votes. The angry Democrats in the House tried to delay the official count. There was little, if anything, for them to gain from this step, and their Southern members—assured that Hayes would not support the threatened Republican state governments, would back a Southern-based transcontinental railroad, and would appoint a Southerner to his cabinet—ended their support of a filibuster, as did some Northern party members who saw the pointlessness of the exercise. The stalled vote count ended on March 2. Hayes was sworn in privately on March 3 and publicly two days later.

Hayes and Reconstruction

Did Hayes' election end Reconstruction? Did the "Compromise of 1877" that allegedly put him into office spell the demise of federal efforts in the South? It would be a simplification to say yes, because the Republican party had largely already abandoned both its Reconstruction focus and its platform, and Hayes had indicated throughout the campaign a clear lack of interest in monitoring of Southern states and federal protection of African Americans in the South. Hayes supported Southern "home rule." He explained that he wished to force whites to deal with blacks as they did with all voters, putting aside race as a divisive point. Future president James Garfield concluded, "The policy of the President has turned out to be a give-away from the beginning. He . . . discontinued prosecutions, [and] offered conciliation everywhere in the South. . . ."[25] President Hayes refused to provide troops to back up the unpopular Republican governments in Louisiana and South Carolina. As one Northern observer explained, "You can't expect us in the North to allow our party to be torn to shreds in an attempt to uphold and defend the sort of government you have in South Carolina."[26]

If Reconstruction depended on Republican control of the Southern states, then Reconstruction was over at the start of Hayes' presidency. Democrats had won control of Florida, Louisiana, and South Carolina—the three Southern states still, technically, in Republican hands by the 1876 election. Unsure of federal response to overt violations of the Reconstruction amendments and supporting statutes, the

Democratic Redeemers were cautious initially, although some states quickly began dismantling the various services and reforms put in place by the Republican constitutions and governments. Not until the next decades would they begin their assault on the constitutional accomplishments of Reconstruction. The North's attention was on its own problems—from urbanization and immigration to "robber barons" and strikers—and it was more than willing to turn over the "Negro problem" to Southern whites. The result of the Radical vision of a remade South with legal protections for the freedmen was a blurred outline. It would take another group of Americans in another century to fill in the outline and give it life.

Notes

1. Martin E. Mantell, *Johnson, Grant, and the Politics of Reconstruction* (New York: Columbia University Press, 1973), 147.

2. Quoted in William Gillette, *Retreat from Reconstruction, 1869–1879* (Baton Rouge: Louisiana State University Press, 1979), 166.

3. Quoted in ibid., 169.

4. Quoted in David Donald, Jean Harvey Baker, and Michael F. Holt, *The Civil War and Reconstruction* (New York: W. W. Norton, 2001), 612.

5. Quoted in Victor B. Howard, *Religion and the Radical Republican Movement, 1860–1870*, 207, 208.

6. H. L. Trefousse, *Reconstruction: America's First Effort at Racial Democracy*, updated ed., Anvil Series (Malabar, Fla.: Krieger, 1999), 154–56.

7. Gillette, *Retreat from Reconstruction*, 48–49.

8. Trefousse, *Reconstruction*, 171–72.

9. Eric Foner, *Reconstruction: America's Unfinished Revolution, 1863–1877* (New York: Harper & Row, 1988), 459.

10. Both quoted in Gillette, *Retreat from Reconstruction*, 182.

11. Quoted in Donald, *Civil War and Reconstruction*, 624, 626.

12. Quoted in ibid., 625–26.

13. Kenneth M. Stampp, *The Era of Reconstruction, 1865–1877* (New York: Knopf, 1965; New York: Vintage Books, 1967), 210; quoted in Donald, *Civil War and Reconstruction*, 615.

14. Quoted in Gillette, *Retreat from Reconstruction*, 223.

15. Quoted in ibid., 217.

16. Trefousse, *Reconstruction*, 176.

17. 16 Wallace 36 (1873).

18. 92 U.S. 214 (1876).

19. 92 U.S. 542 (1876).

20. 109 U.S. 3 (1883).

21. Quoted in Gillette, *Retreat from Reconstruction*, 301.

22. Glenn M. Linden, ed., *Voices from the Reconstruction Years, 1865–1877* (Forth Worth, Tex.: Harcourt Brace, 1999), 278.

23. Quoted in Brooks D. Simpson, *The Reconstruction Presidents* (Lawrence: University of Kansas Press, 1998), 202.

24. Linden, ed., *Voices from the Reconstruction Years*, 220.

25. Quoted in Simpson, *The Reconstruction Presidents*, 216, 226.

26. Ibid., 207.

CHAPTER 4

Fighting Old and New Enemies: The South, 1865–1877

As the South's election of former rebels in 1865, its passing of Black Codes in 1865–1866, and the massacre in Hamburg in 1876 indicated, there was much going on south of Washington. It was not just what Andrew Johnson saw as acceptable under the Constitution or what the Radicals wanted for the country that determined the future of white and black Southerners. It was also what those white and black Southerners did that decided their fate and that of future generations.

With the end of the Civil War came more than military defeat and the end of slavery. The South was a region of physical and human destruction, with 20 percent of its adult white male population (260,000) dead in the war, the largest number of them small farmers. Thousands more were wounded, with many unable to work. Many widows and wives had to take on the burden of trying to farm lands on which soldiers had recently fought. To pull themselves out of debt, their focus shifted from self-sufficiency to planting cotton, a plan undermined in large part by the falling prices for that crop. Immediately after the war, hungry and desperate men, alone and in groups, survived by "impressing" livestock, blankets, and food from Confederate storehouses and from private citizens; the South was a region of "widespread outlawery."[1] One former Confederate general, Braxton Bragg, lived for a time in a slave cabin after he returned to find his Alabama home uninhabitable. Thousands of former slave-owners soon found themselves leaving the South for Europe or the North or even Brazil; many white Southerners of all social and economic ranks managed the many postwar adjustments, including the reality that "we are whipped," by honoring the region's valiant Lost Cause.[2]

In response, federal troops provided some semblance of order and protection, as well as distributed relief, but most of the troops were in Texas dealing with Native Americans and protecting the border with Mexico. "Vast stretches of the rural South were practically free of the Federal presence."[3] In addition, "a penny-pinching Congress" soon reduced the size of the Army as it struggled to handle the high cost of administering Reconstruction in the South.[4] According to historian James E. Sefton, approximately 186,000 troops were scattered throughout the 11 Southern states in the months immediately after the war; over 45,000 were in Texas. Six months later, with rapid demobilization taking place, the total number was down to less than 90,000, with 25,000 in Texas; by April 1866, the total was 38,700. Shortly after the Republican-dominated Congress took over Reconstruction in 1867, only 20,000 troops remained in the South, a quarter of them serving in Texas. When the Grant administration battled the Ku Klux Klan and other terrorist groups in the early 1870s, fewer than 8,000 soldiers were stationed in the former Confederate states. Arkansas and Virginia had only one garrison each; South Carolina had eight garrisons, the most of any Southern state (outside of Texas with 15). In 1876 the total authorized force of the Army for the nation was 27,442.

However few their number and impact, the white and black "blue-coated dogs of despotism," who sought to maintain order, were too much for Southern whites, who saw them as brutish and illegitimate occupiers sent by a national government for whom they had little, if any, respect.[5] As historian George C. Rable points out, Southerners "had to change national allegiance three times in less than five years," and the allegiance required of them after April 1865 did not come easily when they saw behind it bayonets, especially those wielded by black troops.[6] The removal of most black troops from the South by mid-1867 eased some tensions.

The end of the war brought not only troops, farmlands, and homes destroyed by battling armies but also the carrying out of Lincoln's Emancipation Proclamation in the Southern states, as well as the implementation of the Thirteenth Amendment. As joyous as freedom was for the freed men, women, and children of the South, a world without slavery was "a world turned upside down" for white Southerners who traditionally distrusted change. According to Joseph Buckner Killebrew, a Tennessee planter, "All the traditions and habits of both races had been suddenly overthrown, and neither knew just what to do, or how to accommodate themselves to the new situation."[7] The result, explains historian Edward L. Ayers, was that "the South in 1865 was a society without a center, a sense of control, a sense of direction. All certainties had been destroyed." White Southerners saw the fate of a non-slave South "in apocalyptic terms," because they believed in a world in which the status of one race automatically raised or lowered the status of others. In 1871 the *Augusta* (Georgia) *Chronicle and Sentinel* called attempts to "raise the negro to the station and dignity of the Southern white race . . . as silly and futile as the attempt of Xerxes to bind the ocean with an iron chain."[8] Views and treatment of the freedmen varied widely, but for some whites the new reality was clear: "our own interests, although it result in [the freedmen's] total ruin and annihilation, must alone dictate the course for us to pursue."[9] As a poem in the *Raleigh North Carolinian* explained in early 1868:

> Shall low-born scum and quondam slaves
> Give laws to those who own the soil?
> No! by our grand-sires' bloody graves! . . .
> The WHITES shall rule the land or die.[10]

Worsening the tense and unsettled situation, in the first months following the end of the war, rumors spread throughout the South of planned black uprisings. Although there was no substantive evidence of conspiracies and plans for a vengeful race war, the stories spread easily. They reflected the reality that white Southerners expected, particularly with the provocative presence of Northern white teachers and officials and black Union troops (who, reported the *Natchez Daily Courier*, came with "bright muskets and gleaming bayonets").[11] An insurrection was a logical step for the inferior freedmen, so evacuation of white women and children and appeals to federal officials for protection were realistic, not hysterical, precautions. The expected race war did not materialize, although white attacks on alleged black conspirators were common.

Southern fears were not surprising considering general racial beliefs of the mid-1800s and the fact that even in the North blacks were excluded, segregated, and discriminated against in jobs, housing, schools, voting, and public accommodations. Despite such notable exceptions as Charles Sumner and Thaddeus Stevens, throughout the country the general perception of blacks was that they were mentally, physically, and emotionally inferior to whites. If blacks did not demand their rights, they were seen as submissive, dependent, and inferior; if they asserted themselves, they were seen as threats to their white superiors. Such views made it hard for the national administration to frame and implement a Southern policy, and they played a major role in white Southerners' responses to both abolition and Reconstruction.

Freedom

Freedom meant many things to the former slaves. While it meant some purposeless wanderings to test their new status—slaves needed passes, free men did not—it also led to calculated travel to search for long lost friends or relatives, to return home, or to find better employment. Although most former slaves stayed in the South, some moved from rural to urban areas, doubling the number of African Americans in the South's ten largest cities by 1870. The overcrowded cities soon meant segregation, low-paying menial jobs, disease, and inadequate housing. As a Richmond, Virginia, tobacco factory worker lamented, "They say we will starve through laziness[;] that is not so. But it is true we will starve at our present wages."[12] In addition, some blacks went West and became soldiers, miners, businessmen, and cowboys, including the famous Deadeye Dick (Nat Love).

Freedom meant legalized marriages and two-parent families. It meant taking new surnames and being addressed as Mr. or Mrs., not by first names or as "boy." Freedom meant owning firearms, drinking alcohol, wearing colorful clothes, controlling religious services, holding political rallies, and not taking orders from whites. Most freedmen were cautious in their demonstrations of freedom, sometimes doing no more than not tipping their hats to whites or not stepping off sidewalks to allow whites to pass. For whites, even these were dangerous signs of blacks' forgetting "their place" and needing controls.

With rising state taxes, declining land values, falling cotton prices, scarce credit, natural disasters such as floods and insects, and uncertain and shifting political realities, landowners found the prospect of laborers who would not labor frightening and frustrating. Worried whites were "restless, despondent, almost despairing," particularly because the changing work behavior of blacks helped explain declining agricultural production after 1865. A Tennesseean concluded that the freedmen were "a trifling set of lazy devils," while another Southerner determined that the freedmen did "only two-fifths of what they did under the old system." Some blamed Union troops for "poison[ing] the mind of our negroes" and looked to foreign immigrants, mainly Asians, to replace the allegedly inefficient and lazy freedmen. The effort was generally a failure, but it reflected white determination to rebuild "a rural economy that was in a tailspin."[13]

Some freedmen's unwillingness to work was a problem, especially immediately after the war, but a more widespread and long-lasting problem was their opposition to working for wages that were paid only monthly or after the crop was harvested. In their eyes, such wage labor was no better than slavery, especially if freedmen worked in gangs for the same bosses they worked for under slavery, lived in the same quarters they occupied as slaves, and worked the same crops they farmed for their masters before emancipation. Wage labor was also unappealing to many white farmers. The shortage of capital made a wage labor system difficult, but it was an unappealing system for another reason: "What can be done with an irresponsible laborer who throws down his spade and walks off?" asked George Trenholm, a former member of Jeff Davis's cabinet.[14] Planters needed dependable (controllable) laborers if they hoped to recover from the war's devastation.

Most freedmen wanted little to do with any type of wage labor and preferred to farm subsistence food crops rather than the "slave crop" (cotton). They wanted to own land. Land ownership, all Americans believed, meant independence and political and social status; it meant freedom. As one freedman explained in 1865, "What's de use of being free if you don't own land enough to be buried in? Might hyst as well stay slave all yo' days."[15] Former slaves, however, seldom had the necessary purchase money and seldom lived in a community whose whites were willing to advance credit or sell them property.

At the war's end, it had seemed both logical and fair to many freedmen that they should receive at least some of the land on which they had labored without recompense for so many years. Despite rumors of land confiscation and distribution to the freedmen, and support from the Radicals, the national government never took that step.

What it did was sporadic, and it was soon cancelled out by concepts of private property and presidential orders. The 1865 act creating the Freedmen's Bureau gave the federal agency control over lands seized under the 1862 Confiscation Act and the 1863 Captured and Abandoned Property Act. It could rent, and eventually sell, 40-acre tracts to freedmen and white refugees. In January 1865, General William Tecumseh Sherman issued Special Field Order No. 15, which provided freed families with 40 acres of land in the Sea Islands and below Charleston. This step, however, was only a temporary way of caring for the many blacks who had joined Sherman's army in his march to the sea. Any hope raised by these steps soon ended; President Johnson restored lands to their original white owners once they were pardoned, and the Radicals could not raise enough support in Congress.

The country's reverence for property overrode any perception that the freedmen required land in order to establish full freedom. However much leaders of the Southern rebellion deserved punishment, confiscation of property punished not only ex-Confederates, but also their heirs. It was an unacceptable step, even worse than disenfranchisement or elimination of office holding. Constitutional historian Harold M. Hyman explains the situation simply: "Mid-nineteenth-century Americans believed that property, especially land, was simply too sacred to trifle with, even to punish rebels."[16] As W.E.B. Du Bois adds in *Black Reconstruction:* "To give land to free citizens smacked of 'paternalism'; it came directly in opposition to the American assumption that any American could be rich if he wanted to, or at least well-to-do; and it stubbornly ignored the exceptional position of a freed slave."[17]

For some historians, this failure is the failure of Reconstruction. As Joe Gray Taylor has argued, " [M]ost politicians should have known that without some form of economic foundation, black political power [and self-protection] was, at best, uncertain. . . . On the contrary, . . . [freedmen] were allowed to become the equivalent of serfs or peons." On the other hand, Southern historian John Boles has explained that " . . . the wrenching economic conditions . . . were so severe that land ownership would probably not have made a substantial difference in the long run unless blacks had opted for a peasantlike existence outside the market-crop market."[18]

All of this is not to say that no land came under black ownership. Through the Southern Homestead Act of 1866, 45 million acres of public land were made available in five Southern states (Alabama, Arkansas, Florida, Louisiana, and Mississippi). Until 1867 all land was reserved for the freedmen. However, of the 4,000 freedmen who responded to the act, few had the means to move or to buy supplies, seeds, animals, and equipment. Still, some individuals and groups found ways to buy land and farms. The "exceptional and lucky Negroes," according to Du Bois, took advantage of cheap land, with Virginia blacks acquiring almost 100,000 acres.[19] In Kentucky, Missouri, and Tennessee, the number of black landowners rose from 775 to 6,538 by the end of the 1860s. By 1870, one-twelfth of Mississippi black families owned land; by that same year, 408 blacks in Wilmington, North Carolina, owned real property.[20]

For many of the remaining millions (and for thousands of whites) there was a next-best alternative, one that was also acceptable to the planter who needed workers for his fields but seldom had the necessary money to pay wages: a tenancy system that included sharecropping and that soon employed thousands of former slaves and their families. It reduced the landowners' need to supervise reluctant workers, and it gave landless farmers more control over their lives and more privacy than under wage labor. The system allowed blacks (and whites) who needed only land and a house (share tenants) to receive them from the landowner in exchange for a percentage of the crop produced (e.g., a third of the corn and a quarter of the cotton). Those who also needed work animals and farming tools (sharecroppers) received them in exchange for turning over a larger percentage of their crops at the end of the harvest. In addition, country stores and landowners-turned-merchants provided clothing and food on credit, with credit rates averaging nearly 60 percent.

In the 1860s, sharecropping offered hope for both landowner and landless. However, this system became increasingly exploitative. Receiving only half of the crop he produced, the sharecropper often had nothing left after he paid his debt to the merchant. As a result, he began another year in debt. State laws would permit creditors to require that borrowers legally bind the crop to the creditor. This crop was often cotton, which the creditor required because it often drew high prices. Cotton exhausted the soil, leading to reduced harvests and pressuring sharecroppers to cut back on their production of food crops. The result for the cropper was an even greater dependence on others and thus an even greater need to borrow. Regardless of this future scenario, in the 1860s sharecropping offered hope for both landowner and landless.

Black Codes and the Freedmen's Bureau

In 1865 and 1866, concern for controlling blacks and for maintaining a labor system led to the Black Codes, whose restrictions were similar to those of the antebellum slave codes. For white Southerners, these lists of black rights and restrictions were a logical approach to emancipation. They acknowledged the end of slavery but also the black's innate inferiority, the need for labor, and the white-dominated social and economic order. Few Southern whites doubted the logic of governing blacks under different legal codes than whites since, according to the *Macon Daily Telegraph*, "there [was] such a radical difference in the mental and moral constitution of the white and the black race. . . ." To be guided by "absurd theoretical notions of legal equality would be to abandon common sense and self-respect. . . . ," concluded the *Atlanta Daily Intelligencer.*[21]

Mississippi was the first state to complete its Black Codes. Its severe restrictions drew attention in the North in late 1865, although Theodore Brantner Wilson has argued that many of its limitations on black workers were "in line" with regulations imposed by the Freedmen's Bureau.[22] Freedmen who "misspend what they earn, or do not provide for the support of themselves or their families" and those who "habitually misspend their time . . . [in] houses of ill-fame, gaming-houses, or tippling ships" were vagrants and subject to $100 fines and 10 days imprisonment. Those "with no lawful employment or business" faced a $50 fine and 10 days in jail. A freedman or freedwoman who "quit the service of his or her employer before the expiration of his or her term of service without good cause" was to be returned to the employer. No black could own firearms or knives without a license. In addition, freedmen who made "insulting gestures" or "committ[ed] any other misdemeanor" faced fines up to $10 and jail for up to 30 days.[23]

The laws of other states dealt with the same general areas of control. South Carolina's laws limited freedmen to being farmers and servants (unless they paid a special tax), and Louisiana's put employers in charge of settling disputes with black employees; freedmen in Florida who broke labor contracts faced whipping and the sale of their labor for up to a year. Some states prohibited activities, such as hunting and fishing, that permitted freedmen to survive outside of white controls. Laws throughout the South permitted state judges to order the "apprenticing" of children who were orphans or whose parents could not support them, giving first choice to former owners; in many cases, parents were not informed of the legal step. As one black veteran wrote in frustration, "If you call this Freedom, what do you call Slavery?"[24]

Congress responded to these limitations on black freedom with the Civil Rights Act of 1866 and the Fourteenth Amendment and through continuation of the Bureau of Refugees, Freedmen, and Abandoned Lands. The Bureau represented an effort to protect the accomplishments of the war and to provide relief and rehabilitation across the South; to the South, it represented Northern, military, Republican, and national interference.

Created in early 1865, the Freedmen's Bureau was a temporary agency under the War Department and under the leadership of Oliver Otis Howard, a young professional soldier from Maine who was also an evangelical Christian humanitarian. The Bureau's agents were caught between protecting the former slaves' new freedom and responsibility for helping the South recover economically. For some, all the sympathy was with the planters. The *New Orleans Tribune* reported in October 1867 that the agents were merely "the planter's guards": agents did not help freedmen but instead worked "to furnish the planters with cheap hands."[25] Sharing many of the racial views of Southern whites, officers of the Freedmen's Bureau worried that blacks would not work without coercion and supervision and would not follow the terms of labor contracts, a serious concern in the first months after the war when black wage labor seemed as if it would be the replacement for slave labor. For others, however, whites were targets for correction because of the "abuse and mistreatment" of freedmen.[26]

Southern whites found themselves dealing with Bureau courts, whose goal was "to set the law in motion" when state courts would not. The courts' acceptance of the testimony of blacks led community leaders to conclude that the white man's word was being weighed against a "passel of ignorant field hands." Such a new reality—one that did not exist in numerous Northern states—was "literally turning the slave into the master and the master, slave," complained a North Carolina white who faced the "absolute disgrace" of being treated with "no more dignity or respect than is shown the negro."[27]

Throughout the South in the late 1860s, the Bureau's work was massive and ranged widely. As one agent, John W. De Forest, explained his job in late 1868:

> [Freedmen's complaints] might refer to an alleged attempt at assassination or to the discrepancy of a bushel of pea vines in the division of a crop. They might be against brother freedmen, as well as against former slave owners and "Rebs." More than once have I been umpire in the case of a disputed jackknife or petticoat. . . . Everybody, guilty or innocent, ran with his or her griefs to the Bureau officer; and sometimes the Bureau officer, half distracted, longed to subject them all to some huge punishment. Of the complaints against whites the majority were because of the retention of wages or of alleged unfairness in the division of the crops.[28]

Complicating the Bureau's job in the first years after the war were the state officials, laws, and practices of Johnson's quickly restored governments. Local officials often released whites accused of crimes against blacks or ignored freedmen's complaints in general, arguing that black attitudes justified violent white responses. A Tennessee white reported that freedmen were working well but "they have had to be shot sometimes." A Bureau agent in Alabama complained in November 1865: "Upon the most frivolous pretexts and charges, [freedmen] are arrested and after a mere mockery of a trial are incarcerated in some loathsome prison, there to drag out days of miserable wretchedness."[29]

Congressional Reconstruction changed little. A Mississippi magistrate turned away a black plaintiff who claimed he had been shot by his white employer, asking, "Do you suppose I am going to insult a white man for you niggers? [G]o away." General Philip Sheridan concluded "that the trial of a white man for the murder of a freedman in Texas would be a farce." Then, once the states completed congressional requirements and were readmitted, ". . . agents were completely powerless"; they were no more than "friend and . . . advisor" when it came to ensuring that the freedmen were protected by the law.[30]

The Bureau's task was, in the words of General William Tecumseh Sherman, "Hercules' task." The general warned the determined and dedicated Howard that ". . . it is not in your power to fulfill one tenth part of the expectation of those who formed the Bureau. . . . It is simply impractical."[31]

Education

Of particular concern to many freedmen was obtaining an education. They flocked to schools, whether established by the freedmen themselves, the Bureau, or various freedmen's aid societies, secular and religious. If education was an essential ingredient of the Republicans' definition of good citizenship, for the former slave, education was an essential ingredient of a free life, even if the "teacher" was a barely literate former slave. School subjects included the "three R's" (reading, writing, and arithmetic), industrial skills, and the responsibilities of freedom ("Be Industrious," "Respect One Another," "Be Temperate"),[32] although some educators urged a standard academic program, arguing that anything less was preparing the freedmen for lives of inferiority. By 1870, 150,000 students attended Freedmen's Bureau schools alone. By 1870, well over 3,000 male and female (black and white) teachers representing 50 organizations staffed black schools; by 1869, the majority of teachers were black (varying from 35 percent in some states to as high as 75 percent in North Carolina and Louisiana). These teachers were a source of hope for the freedmen, as well as a source of concern for whites because their activities often went well beyond the classroom. As a female teacher from New York explained, "I preach & teach & civilize & reconstruct generally."[33] While some white teachers saw blacks as inferiors, those who treated blacks as social equals antagonized whites. Schools were burned and teachers assaulted. An education would make freedmen poorer workers and more "uppity."

By the 1870s, almost a dozen colleges and universities, as well as over 50 normal (teacher-training) schools, were preparing blacks for teaching but also for professional and leadership careers; these included Howard University in Washington, D.C., Hampton Institute in Virginia, and Fisk University in Tennessee.

Ku Klux Klan

The Ku Klux Klan and other secret societies, such as the Knights of the White Camellia, the '76 Association, and the White Brotherhood, used violence in the late 1860s and early 1870s to right an upside-down world in which blacks went to school, voted, and held office. Like the other groups, the Klan, founded in Tennessee in 1866 as a social club by young Confederate veterans, was a natural development in the South's long history of group violence. Night-riding and disguises of hoods and gowns for both men and horses became common occurrences in many areas of the South.

The goal of the Klan was to unite whites against the threat of black (and Republican) disruption of society and politics, a threat clearly escalated in 1867 by congressional Reconstruction's creation of black voters. It sought to restore home rule by undermining Republican governments and demonstrating to white and black Republicans that their governments were incapable of protecting them. The groups were responding to the threat of social anarchy as they saw it: the South, which valued localism, found itself with unequal citizens imposed on them from the outside. As Reconstruction historian Michael Perman argues, "The objective was not simply to destroy the Republican governments by attacking and dispersing their supporters, but to enable the Democrats to regain power by winning elections. Ironically, the intention was to use violent and illegal means to win power legitimately, through the electoral process."[34]

Although the Klan and other similar groups often mutated into violent criminal organizations, they were led—or, at least, supported—by the "best men" of the state, including merchants and Democratic politicians, and used a variety of techniques to accomplish their ends, including ostracism, bribery, and pranks played on allegedly gullible and superstitious blacks, as well as arson, beatings, and murder. Centralized control did not exist; leaders often did not know what local groups were doing. Targets were usually average black and white Republicans, including officers and teachers of the Freedmen's Bureau. Targets also included political candidates and office holders; the Klan killed an Arkansas congressman and three members of the Georgia legislature. In addition, their victims included black workers who tried to leave employers and white women who associated with black men.

Local officials were usually unable or unwilling to act against terrorist organizations. State officials were often hesitant to use militias against whites, especially since the militias had black members and were thus violently opposed by most Southern whites. Nevertheless, state action took place in Texas, Arkansas, and North Carolina. North Carolina's carpetbagger governor William W. Holden was impeached and removed from office in part because of his efforts in the so-called

Kirk-Holden War of 1870 against the Klan. This militia campaign in Alamance and Caswell counties ended with a hundred arrests but no convictions. Violence continued, and both the governor and his general, Colonel George W. Kirk, fled the state. In March 1871 Holden was impeached for exceeding his authority in raising the militia and ordering arrests. He was convicted and removed from office, the first state governor to suffer that fate.

By the late 1860s and into 1870, many in the North and in Congress were losing interest in Southern problems and in the Negro; however, the extent of the violence convinced Congress to act. The result was the Enforcement Acts of 1870 and 1871, which authorized the president to use military force against violations of civil and political rights. The April 1871 statute, also known as the Ku Klux Klan Act, made it a federal crime to "go in disguise . . . for the purpose . . . of depriving any person or any class of persons of the equal protection of the laws. . . ."[35] Under the acts' authority, President Grant suspended the writ of habeas corpus in parts of South Carolina in 1871. There were, however, few convictions, because of lack of funds (federal attorneys often spent their own money on cases), Klansmen who evaded capture, intimidation of officials, heavy case loads, an inadequate number of federal troops, and a wavering commitment by federal marshals, attorneys, and judges. The *Nation* called the failure to support the laws with adequate personnel and funding "a wretched mockery," and the *Springfield Republican* called the anti-KKK effort "an entire and lamentable failure."[36] Nevertheless, the federal troops, investigations, and trials were sufficient essentially to break the Klan in the early 1870s.

That did not, however, mean the end of violence and intimidation. Irregular militia units drilled and marched in black-populated areas, broke up Republican meetings, and prevented freedmen from registering to vote. They assaulted and murdered Republicans. They used economic pressure: vote Republican and lose your job. Because their goal was to demonstrate the ineffectiveness of Republican administrations, they carried out their intimidation openly and publicly. The strategy was known as the Mississippi Plan, and groups were known as White Leagues, Red Shirts, and rifle clubs. In some states, the violence resulted in the deaths of numerous freedmen; most notably, over 100 blacks died in attacks in Colfax, Louisiana, in spring 1873.

Black Republicans

Despite intimidation and violence against them, freedmen voted and were elected to office. Reconstruction was not, however, a period of "black rule," as many early Reconstruction historians alleged. South Carolina's lower house had a brief period during which African Americans had a majority, but that was a unique occurrence. Although blacks made up anywhere from 30 to 60 percent of state populations, they never held offices in numbers that came close to these percentages. Southern African Americans were, however, politically active, if not radical. Blacks joined the Union League, a Republican political organization that also helped build black schools and churches, assisted the sick, and gave advice on contracts. Some served in the conventions that met from late 1867 to spring 1868 to draw up new constitutions for their states. They made up about a quarter of the delegates; Southern whites accounted for over half.[37] About 1,500 African Americans were elected to office. While more than 600 were elected to state legislatures, most held local positions such as sheriff and justice of the peace. Black Republicans, realizing that appealing to white voters required running white candidates, were willing to support such candidates, at least in the early years of Republican Reconstruction. Few blacks were radical enough to resist this strategy or vindictive enough to support disenfranchisement of former Confederates.

A handful of Southern blacks won national and statewide office. Sixteen were elected to the United States House of Representatives—the first being Joseph H. Rainey of South Carolina. Hiram Revels and Blanche K. Bruce, both from Mississippi, were elected to the Senate. Revels filled the seat vacated in 1861 by Jefferson Davis. A slightly larger number held high statewide office. Five served as lieutenant governors; others served as state treasurers, secretaries of state, and state superintendents of education. Only in South Carolina did an African American serve on a state supreme court, and the only black serving as state governor was Pinckney B.S. Pinchback, Louisiana's lieutenant governor who briefly replaced the impeached Henry Clay Warmoth in 1872.

Pinchback was one of the many Southern black office holders who had been born free or who had gained their freedom before the war; many of these men were well-educated, wealthy, and natural leaders.

Others were Northern-born or Southern African Americans who had gone to the North for their education. James Lynch, who served as secretary of state in Mississippi, was an Army cook during the war and decided to work in the South afterward for the Methodist Episcopal Church. He explained that "I have convictions of duty to my race as deep as my own soul. . . . They impel me to go [to] a Southern state, and unite my destiny with that of my people." James G. Blaine watched his black colleagues in Congress and concluded that "they were as a rule studious, earnest, ambitious men, whose public conduct . . . would be honorable to any race."[38]

Scalawags and Carpetbaggers

The Republican party in the South also included "prewar opponents of secession, consistent Unionists and wartime peace advocates, reform-minded yeoman [*sic*] and artisans, upper-class moderates and realists, regional representatives seeking some shift in state policy and power, and whites especially receptive" to principles of racial equality and free labor.[39] These "scalawags" were indeed a diverse group of Southern "traitors." Many scalawags were non-slave-owning farmers from the hill country who had opposed secession, as well as slavery, before and during the war. Their goal was to prevent the old planter elite from returning to power, and cooperation with Republicans was the only way of doing that. The choice, according to a North Carolina newspaper, was "salvation at the hand of the Negro or destruction at the hand of the rebel."[40] It was not a pleasant choice for most scalawags, but as a result of making it many found themselves sitting on juries, voting, and holding office for the first time.

Other scalawags, who had been secessionists and had fought for the Confederacy, had returned to find themselves facing foreclosures. They hoped that Republican governments would enact legislation that protected debtors. Still other scalawags were among the South's richest and most successful business leaders; many had been Whigs and continued their prewar and wartime hostility to the Democrats. Their goal was to move past slavery and the war and to focus on economic development that would allow the South to compete with the rest of the country. To them, the Republican party offered the best hope of achieving this outcome.

Working with Republicans and freedmen was not easy. The result was often social ostracism, threats, and physical attack. Support for the Republicans subjected whites to violence and to the label "nigger lover." Such a label was difficult to bear for Southern white Republicans, who opposed black political equality and a truly biracial party and supported rights for blacks only for pragmatic reasons. William Henry Lusk, a Mississippi scalawag who broke with the Republicans, explained that "I cannot afford to have [my daughters] suffer the humiliating consequences of the social ostracism to which they may be subjected if I remain in the Republican party."[41]

Southern Republicans also included the carpetbaggers. Called "radical carpet-bag vultures—the leeches who are sucking the life-blood out of the south" by the *Arkansas Gazette*,[42] carpetbaggers were actually migrants from the North who came South for a wide variety of reasons. True to the stereotype, some moved South to gain personally from economic and political deals. Others, however, were teachers and officials of the Freedmen's Bureau or competent and honest businessmen and professionals who saw in the South opportunities for success that did not exist in the North. The latter invested considerable sums in businesses and farms. Many Union soldiers who had fought in the South returned there after the war, intrigued with its beauty, its cheap land, and its potential for growth. Northern publications, including the *New York Commercial and Financial Chronicle,* urged men to take advantage of Southern opportunities: the South was a "true El Dorado of the times."[43] In addition, many Southerners, at least initially, urged Yankees to bring their ideas and money South. Soon, however, being from the North automatically won Southern distrust. So too did alliance with blacks and scalawags. Carpetbaggers were charged with controlling the South, an illogical charge since they made up only about two percent of the potential voters. Still, Northerners did play a significant role as office holders. They were governors of six states, and dozens represented Southern states in Congress. Their positions made their political influence significant and encouraged charges of exploitation and corruption, not all of them undeserved.

Republican Accomplishments, Railroads, and Defeat

Accomplishments of the Republican governments created under Reconstruction were many, but the Republicans often took the South in directions that Southern whites had long been resisting. In spite of the relative moderation of these governments and of the new constitutions upon which they were based, white Southerners found their efforts on behalf of black civil and political rights and general reforms to be threatening and radical. Such efforts required resistance and repeal. For example, the new state constitutions generally ended property and race requirements for both voting and office holding; five states passed public accommodations laws that prohibited discrimination on the basis of race. Legislatures provided protection for debtors and reformed tax systems to shift more of the burden to property owners; imprisonment for debt was also ended in some Southern states. The Republican governments also began the states' first public schools and built hospitals, penitentiaries, and asylums for orphans and the insane, all of which were generally segregated but nevertheless open to both races. (Only Louisiana's and South Carolina's constitutions permitted mixed schools and only Louisiana attempted such a system.) The Republicans funded the construction of railroads and provided jurors with daily pay; they modernized divorce laws and expanded the rights of married women. (Whatever the problems in the constitutions, the new ones passed by Democrats after they "redeemed" their states often worked few major changes into the new documents. Those of Mississippi in 1890 and Virginia in 1902, for example, were similar to their Reconstruction predecessors.)

Much corruption by and many allegations against these governments were the result of the widespread appeal of the railroad. Railroad representatives were everywhere, in Virginia and Kentucky as well as New York and Illinois. States wanted railroads, and the railroads wanted state subsidies, as well as tax exemptions, land grants, and bond endorsements. Recovery of the Southern economy to a large degree hinged on building the region's transportation system, and railroads were seen as central to this system. As a result, state activities were extensive and varied.

With over 25,000 miles of track built in the South and the West in 1865–1873, opportunities for profit and profiteering—for dishonest and self-serving shenanigans—were numerous. Some lines were never built; some railroad stock was worthless; many railroads had insufficient capital to operate profitably; and many states were left with higher taxes. Contributing to these problems was the South's capital shortage and its inability to provide sufficient traffic to support the lines. Thus, problems were the result both of honesty and dishonesty, of competence and incompetence.

By late 1873 both Northern and European investors had grown leery of investing in Southern railroads (as well as those in other parts of the country). Within weeks of the economic Panic of 1873, which was precipitated by the collapse of the banking firm of Jay Cooke, 16 Southern railroads were in default; many more would follow, with those poorly built and operated among the first to go. By 1883 all major Southern lines that had failed were being run by non-Southerners and integrated into wider rail networks. It was an unpleasant reality for many Southerners. As Robert L. Dabney of Virginia commented in 1882, "Each of these roads points virtually to New York."[44] As a result, in the 1870s many Southerners viewed railroad companies as outsiders who required regulations. They simply joined the list of Northern agents who threatened Southern home rule.

With the railroads failing, Republican governments in the South faced a growing taxpayers' revolt that took the form of Taxpayers' Conventions. Southerners, unused to high taxes supporting public services before the war, were now stepping up their demands for tax cuts. The rates set by Republican governments were higher than Southerners had ever paid, and their states were too economically weak to afford them, as well as county, school, and poll taxes. In addition, Democrats argued, the wrong people were levying the taxes. Restrictions on office holding left those who owned little or no property in control of the legislatures. (Plus, Southern whites bristled at allotting tax dollars for educating poor and inferior blacks.) Such arguments were true, but so too were the Republicans' counterarguments that the tax rates were still relatively low and that state governments needed the money to operate efficiently and to provide essential services, such as schools. Nevertheless, one by one Reconstruction governments studied ways to limit their debts, including resisting new railroad legislation. The states had moved from "railroad mania" to fiscal responsibility.

But it was too late for the Republicans. While the Reconstruction legislatures demonstrated little vindictiveness in terms of suffrage restrictions against former Confederates—thus, ironically, simplifying the latter's task of regaining political control—these governments were targets of a variety of complaints, some legitimate, many not. The Republicans had not convinced white Democratic Southerners—or even some of their own white Southern members—to accept black voting and office holding (or even equality under the law), and they had not brought prosperity to the South.

"Redemption"

Democratic (or Conservative) opposition quickly succeeded in some Southern states, although Republicans held most of the states for at least four years. In 1869 and 1870 Democrats (and some disenchanted Republicans) were able to win control of the state governments in Tennessee, Virginia, and North Carolina. Georgia followed in 1871, Texas and Alabama in 1874, and Arkansas in 1874. Virginia's Democrats never lost control of the state, the only one that the Republicans failed to win. The redemption of the remaining three states—Florida, Louisiana, and Mississippi—took a bit longer, but all were again in Democratic hands by 1877. Thus, 1877 has traditionally been used as the year that marks the end of Reconstruction: if Reconstruction meant the Republican restructuring of the rebel states, then the year when the last state was subject to restructuring can serve as a convenient conclusion to the effort. With Republicans in control (and backed to one degree or another by Northern and congressional interest), a state generally protected African Americans and the goals of Republican Reconstruction; with Democrats in control, that protection ended, at varying speeds and degrees.

There were a variety of factors favoring a Democratic victory beyond a general determination to redeem the states from outsiders; they included racism, misdirected economic policies, class antagonisms, and violent intimidation. The Republican governments often made policy and administrative decisions that failed to provide their states with equitable and fair taxes, promised services, or economic recovery. Economic recovery based on railroads turned out to be "a political time bomb that eventually exploded in [Republican] faces."[45] Another explosion was the corruption in the Grant administration and the Liberal Republicans' revolt in 1872. When Republicans joined the Liberal Republicans—who urged an end to Reconstruction—and thus turned over party roles to blacks, the Southern party became even more offensive to Southern whites. In some states, as the party's problems grew, it sought to keep black voters by emphasizing racial issues and reforms. The strategy worked to a degree, but it also meant that the Democrats could, in logical response, present themselves as the party for white supremacy. By the early 1870s Democrats were raising racial issues to attract white voters to the polls. Blacks thus saw little reason to leave the problack Republicans and whites saw little reason to leave the prowhite Democrats.

The widespread, organized violence also had an impact. It led to deaths and intimidation of voters, keeping blacks and other Republicans from the polls and eliminating opposition leaders. The violence may have spurred the enforcement efforts, but the decreasing influence of Radicals in the North and the North's general refocusing of interests away from Reconstruction issues and toward economic ones were effective counters. Increasingly, Northern Republicans were suggesting and even arguing that the freedmen had the basic tools and would have to care for themselves in the future, that is, without federal government aid. Increasingly, Reconstruction was not seen as a national policy in response to Southern rebellion but as interference in local matters in the Southern states. The Southern branch of the Republican party, along with the black Southerner, was cast adrift.

The ingredients that were necessary to accomplish a remade South—land reform plus more time, troops, money, and bureaucracy—were unacceptable to most Americans in the 1860s–1870s. They certainly were unacceptable to white Southerners and were also beyond the power of black Southerners to influence, much less control. The result was a period of both triumph and failure, regardless of one's perspective.

Notes

1. Dan Carter, *When the War Was Over: The Failure of Self-Reconstruction in the South, 1865–1867* (Baton Rouge: Louisiana State University Press, 1985), 20.

2. Eric Foner and Olivia Mahoney, *America's Reconstruction: People and Politics after the Civil War* (New York: HarperPerennial, 1995), 50.

3. James P. Shenton, ed., *The Reconstruction: A Documentary History of the South after the War: 1865–1877* (New York: G. P. Putnam's Sons, 1963), 72.

4. James E. Sefton, *The United States Army and Reconstruction, 1865–1877* (Baton Rouge: Louisiana State University Press, 1967), 208.

5. Quoted in George C. Rable, *But There Was No Peace: The Role of Violence in the Politics of Reconstruction* (Athens: University of Georgia Press, 1984), 11.

6. Ibid., 197, n. 43.

7. Carter, *When the War Was Over,* 1; quoted in James L. Roark, *Masters without Slaves: Southern Planters in the Civil War and Reconstruction* (New York: W. W. Norton, 1977), 141.

8. Quoted in Edward L. Ayers, *Vengeance and Justice: Crime and Punishment in the Nineteenth-Century American South* (New York: Oxford University Press, 1984),150; and in William Gillette, *Retreat from Reconstruction, 1869–1879* (Baton Rouge: Louisiana State University Press, 1979), 192.

9. Quoted in Roark, *Masters without Slaves,* 145.

10. Quoted in David Donald, Jean Harvey Baker, and Michael F. Holt, *The Civil War and Reconstruction* (New York: W. W. Norton, 2001), 594.

11. Quoted in Carter, *When the War Was Over,* 198.

12. Quoted in Noralee Frankel, "Breaking the Chains: 1860–1880," in *To Make Our World Anew: A History of African Americans,* ed. Robin D. G. Kelley and Earl Lewis (Oxford: Oxford University Press, 2000), 263.

13. Quoted in Roark, *Masters without Slaves,* 153, 161; ibid., 170.

14. Quoted in Carter, *When the War Was Over,* 205.

15. Quoted in John B. Boles, *Black Southerners, 1619–1869* (Lexington: University Press of Kentucky, 1983), 202.

16. Harold M. Hyman, ed., *The Radical Republicans and Reconstruction, 1861–1870* (Indianapolis: Bobbs-Merrill, 1967), 200.

17. W. E. B. DuBois, *Black Reconstruction in America, 1860–1880* (1935; reprint, New York: Atheneum, 1992), 601–2.

18. Quoted in Joe Gray Taylor, "Louisiana: An Impossible Task," in Otto H. Olsen, ed., *Reconstruction and Redemption in the South* (Baton Rouge: Louisiana State University Press, 1980), 222; Boles, *Black Southerners,* 203.

19. DuBois, *Black Reconstruction in America,* 603.

20. Loren Schweninger, "Black Economic Reconstruction in the South," in Eric Anderson and Alfred A. Moss Jr., eds., *The Facts of Reconstruction: Essays in Honor of John Hope Franklin* (Baton Rouge: Louisiana State University Press, 1991), 180–81.

21. Quoted in Carter, *When the War Was Over,* 216–17.

22. Theodore Brantner Wilson, *The Black Codes of the South,* Southern Historical Publications, no. 6. (University: University of Alabama Press, 1965), 67.

23. Walter L. Fleming, ed., *Documentary History of Reconstruction: Political, Military, Social, Religious, Educational and Industrial, 1865 to the Present Time,* 2 vols. (Cleveland: Arthur H. Clark, 1906), 1:284, 288, 290.

24. Quoted in Eric Foner, *Reconstruction: America's Unfinished Revolution, 1863–1877* (New York: Harper & Row, 1988), 215.

25. Quoted in William E. Gienapp, *The Civil War and Reconstruction: A Documentary Collection* (New York: Norton, 2001), 384.

26. Quoted in Carter, *When the War Was Over,* 214.

27. Donald G. Nieman, *To Set the Law in Motion: The Freedmen's Bureau and the Legal Rights of Blacks, 1865–1868* (Millwood, N.Y.: KTO Press, 1979); quoted in Carter, *When the War Was Over,* 221, 222.

28. Gienapp, ed., *The Civil War and Reconstruction,* 383.

29. Quoted in Rable, *But There Was No Peace,* 29–30, and in Nieman, *To Set the Law in Motion,* 26.

30. Quoted in Nieman, *To Set the Law in Motion,* 201, and in Rable, *But There Was No Peace,* 21; also Nieman, *To Set the Law in Motion,* 208.

31. Quoted in Patrick W. Riddleberger, *1866: The Critical Year Revisited* (Carbondale: Southern Illinois University Press, 1979), 59.

32. Robert C. Morris, "Education Reconstruction," in Anderson and Moss, eds., *The Facts of Reconstruction,* 159.

33. Quoted in ibid., 147.

34. Michael Perman, "Counter Reconstruction: The Role of Violence in Southern Redemption," in Anderson and Moss, eds., *The Facts of Reconstruction,* 132.

35. H. L. Trefousse, *Reconstruction: America's First Effort at Racial Democracy,* updated ed., Anvil Series (Malabar, Fla.: Krieger, 1999), 172.

36. Quoted in Gillette, *Retreat from Reconstruction,* 31, 37.

37. Martin E. Mantell, *Johnson, Grant, and the Politics of Reconstruction* (New York: Columbia University Press, 1973), 73.

38. Quoted in Frankel, "Breaking the Chains," 251; and in John Hope Franklin and Alfred A. Moss Jr., *From Slavery to Freedom: A History of African Americans,* 7th ed. (New York: McGraw-Hill, 1994), 244.

39. Olsen, *Reconstruction and Redemption,* 9.

40. Quoted in Foner and Mahoney, *America's Reconstruction,* 104.

41. Quoted in Kenneth M. Stampp, *The Era of Reconstruction, 1865–1877* (New York: Knopf, 1965; New York: Vintage Books, 1967), 199.

42. Quoted in Rable, *But There Was No Peace,* 93.

43. Quoted in J. Michael Quill, *Prelude to the Radicals: The North and Reconstruction during 1865* (Washington, D.C.: University Press of America, 1980), 115.

44. James W. Ely Jr., *The Guardian of Every Other Right: A Constitutional History of Property Rights* (New York: Oxford University Press, 1998), 69.

45. Quoted in Donald, Baker, and Holt, *The Civil War and Reconstruction,* 592.

A campaign banner supporting Abraham Lincoln for president and Andrew Johnson for vice president, 1864. Library of Congress.

Victims and enemy through Northern eyes: Andersonville Prison and President Jefferson Davis. Library of Congress.

Radical members of the first South Carolina legislature after the war. Library of Congress.

A Radical's view of Andrew Johnson's veto of the Civil Rights Act and Freedmen's Bureau Bill in 1866. Library of Congress.

1872 cartoon mocking the opposition of the Liberal Republicans, including Horace Greeley and Charles Sumner, to the acquisition of Santo Domingo. Library of Congress.

1868 drawing by Thomas Nast for *Harper's Weekly* that emphasizes Democrats' violent efforts against African Americans. Library of Congress.

THE FREEDMEN'S BUREAU.—Drawn by A. R. Waud.—[See Page 467.]

The Freedmen's Bureau intercedes in the South, as pictured by *Harper's Weekly* in 1868. Library of Congress.

CHAPTER 5

THERE WAS MORE TO RECONSTRUCTION THAN RECONSTRUCTION: NON-SOUTHERN ISSUES

Many of the non-Reconstruction events and issues of the 1860s and 1870s seem unimportant when compared to those linked to presidential impeachment and civil rights. Yet without them, any analysis of the period after the Civil War is one dimensional. Americans' interest in and battles over the tariff and currency, corruption and civil service reform, and even foreign expansion did not stop in the 1850s and pick up again only in the late nineteenth century. Americans during Reconstruction argued and fought tenaciously over these issues, which often took attention away from the battle over Reconstruction, as well as dividing the always splintered Republicans. Many voters cared more about the war's economic legacy than its ideological repercussions, a fact that pragmatic political leaders had to face.

The Tariff

The tariff (a tax on imports levied by Congress) was a divisive issue from the earliest days of the new republic. In the first years of independence, some Americans wanted an opportunity to develop new industries without foreign competition; states imposed tariffs to provide such protection for their infant manufacturing sectors. Under the new Constitution during the 1790s, protective tariffs imposed by Congress were part of the Financial Plan of Secretary of the Treasury Alexander Hamilton. Hamilton's tax, which succeeded in stimulating manufacturing, was the beginning of the national debate over the tariff. The Constitution authorizes the national government to levy tariffs, but the question was *how*—and even *if*—tariffs should be used. Should tariffs be used only to raise revenue? Or should the national government use them, as Hamilton did, to guide the economy, essentially favoring certain groups and aspects of the economy over others? High tariffs provided stimulation for whatever industry—manufacturing or agricultural—whose foreign-made products were blocked from American markets; low tariffs provided revenue rather than protection.

After rising in the 1820s and 1830s—thus prompting South Carolina in the early 1830s to announce its "nullification" of national tariffs that it believed harmed the state's economy—tariff rates declined in the 1840s and 1850s. Interest in the tariff dropped as Americans were caught up in the swirl of slavery and Western expansion. The Panic of 1857 and the Civil War changed the downward drift. Those hurt by the depression, such as the iron industry, demanded greater protection. The war itself brought expenses, and government spending increased 1,000 percent. During the Civil War, without the opposition of Southern congressmen, Congress raised the tariff to higher and higher levels until the average duty in 1865 was 47 percent above that in 1857. The goal of the wartime tariff was both to protect certain American industries from foreign competition and to raise badly needed money for the federal treasury. As Abraham Lincoln explained, Republicans believed that raising tariffs would "secure to the workingman liberal wages, to agriculture remunerative prices, to mechanics and manufacturers an adequate reward for their skills, labor and enterprise and to the nation commercial prosperity and independence."[1]

The end of the war brought years of heated discussions about the tariff. The internal taxes passed during the war to raise revenue were fairly easily eliminated. Not so the tariff. While the postwar Republicans, including Thaddeus Stevens, were the party of the protective tariff for the very reasons Lincoln enunciated, some, including Westerners, wanted reduced tariffs; other Republicans wanted free trade (i.e., no tariffs); and others, such as Charles Sumner, had no strong view on the tariff. This division helps undermine arguments that the Republicans, especially the Radicals, were engaged in an economic conspiracy to benefit Northern business interests rather than in a crusade to protect Southern black interests. Farmers and importers, who argued that tariffs hurt them, found the tariff of more immediacy and personal importance than questions related to Southern blacks and the Fourteenth Amendment. The tariff affected prices and jobs. Southern issues were distractions that could easily ruin the nation's economy.

By 1870 many Americans wanted reductions. For example, Westerners were upset by high prices on manufactured goods and low prices for agricultural products induced by tariff levels. The demand for lower rates was particularly strong, because the national government took in considerably more money than it spent; in both 1870–71 and 1871–72 the government had a surplus of $100 million. The result of complaints and surpluses was the Tariff Act of 1872. It provided for a 10 percent reduction in duties on all cotton, wool, iron, steel, metals, paper, glass, and leather, with significant reductions for salt and coal; tea, coffee, hides, and paper stock were to be admitted duty free. Protection continued but revenue tariffs declined. The Panic of 1873, however, brought repeal of the 10 percent reduction. President Ulysses S. Grant and his secretary of the treasury even urged the return of duties on coffee and tea to raise revenue.

Currency

The currency debate also involved questions of national power, constitutionality, party direction, and uneven benefits. In its simplest form, the debate was between advocates of specie, or gold and silver coins (hard money), and paper money, mainly greenbacks (soft money).

Since 1785 the United States had issued gold and silver currency in the form of dollars. In 1791 Congress created a Bank of the United States and authorized it to issue notes receivable in payments to the national government; notes had to be redeemable in gold or silver coin. In the Coinage Act of 1792, Congress confirmed its use of both gold and silver, with the gold value of the dollar determined on a 15:1 silver-to-gold ratio. This plan meant that the U.S. monetary system would be affected every time the market price for the two metals changed. For example, with the discovery of gold in California in 1848 came a rapid increase in the amount of gold in circulation (from $4 million in 1846 to $37 million in 1856). Gold's value thus declined and silver's increased; silver coins became hard to find, with the result that the nation operated on an essentially gold-based currency.

During the Civil War, the government decided to issue "United States notes" to supplement the three types of money already in circulation: specie, state bank notes, and demand notes (that were payable on demand in gold but were not legal tender for private debts). The new United States notes were commonly referred to as "greenbacks." Created by the Legal Tender Act of February 25, 1862, they were black, white, and green; the one dollar note pictured hard-money Secretary of the Treasury Salmon P. Chase. (The rule prohibiting living people from being portrayed on paper money came in 1866.) The non-interest-bearing greenbacks were lawful money and legal tender in payment of all debts contracted before and after their issuance. While intended to be temporary and redeemable after the war, the $433 million issued became permanent currency. Objections to the issuance of the notes and to their permanence dominated the debate over currency during Reconstruction, with few public leaders taking a neutral stand.

Elbridge G. Spaulding, president of a bank in Buffalo, New York and a member of the House Ways and Means Committee that proposed the Legal Tender Act, called greenbacks "a war measure—a measure of *necessity,* and not of choice."[2] Chase, who said that he opposed any currency except gold and silver, agreed that the war had made greenbacks "indispensably necessary."[3] So too did Thaddeus Stevens. Although Chief Justice Roger Taney wrote an undelivered opinion that greenbacks were unconstitutional because the national government had no constitutional power to issue paper (just coins), Abraham Lincoln referred to the government's need for the notes to pay troops. He called the greenbacks "unavoidable," but he also emphasized that "a return to specie payments . . . as the earliest period compatible with due regard to all interests concerned, should ever be kept in view."[4] Still, after the war there was little agreement on how and when to take this action—and, for some, even if doing so was the correct step.

Predictions that greenbacks would depreciate and help increase inflation were accurate. The cost of living almost doubled from 1860 to 1865; in 1865 it took $157 in greenbacks to buy $100 in gold. In fact, the term "inflation" as it is used today gained usage in the 1860s to explain the impact of the greenbacks on the economy. With almost a half-billion dollars in greenbacks in circulation, the country had difficult decisions to make after 1865. Views on ending the use of green-backs varied. Although the sides of the currency debate varied significantly over the next ten years, in general Eastern bankers approved of a tight currency, restricting money in circulation by returning to gold and ending greenbacks; Westerners, who faced a problem of too little currency in their region, supported inflation, which often meant keeping greenbacks. "Give us greenbacks we say and build cities, plant corn, open coal mines, control railways, launch ships, grow cotton, establish factories, open gold and silver mines, erect rolling mills," urged George Francis Train, a speculator. As banker Jay Cooke added, "These men who are urging on premature resumption [of gold] know nothing of the great & growing west which would grow twice as fast if it was not cramped for the means necessary to build. . . ."[5] But most of those who claimed to understand economic issues in the mid-1800s believed that gold and silver were not only unchallengeable economically but also divine choices. Charles Sumner allegedly explained in 1868 that "to my mind [idols and paper money] are equally forbidden by the Ten Commandments. If one commandment enjoins upon us not to worship any graven images, does not another say expressly, 'Thou shalt not steal?'"[6]

Both Republicans and the Democrats harbored divergent views on currency within their ranks. Within the Republican party were soft-money men, men who supported contraction and the speedy return to gold, and men who wanted both gold and greenbacks—some out of principle, some out of political expediency. The radical wing of the party was split. Some focused on redeeming the greenbacks as a return to specie or because doing so would be keeping faith with the war's sacrifices. Republicans, including Stevens, Benjamin Wade, Benjamin Butler, and John Sherman, generally had close ties to such industries as textile manufacturing, real estate, banking, and railroads and worried about the impact of currency contraction on manufacturing. The Democrats, who went from being essentially a hard-money party to a soft-money one (especially in the West), nevertheless also included supporters of gold-redeemable bank currency and old-line gold-silver advocates.

President Andrew Johnson, who had little interest in finance or money policy, left Secretary of the Treasury Hugh McCulloch, a successful Indiana banker, in charge of determining the fate of greenbacks. McCulloch believed that greenbacks "were war measures, and, . . . ought not to remain in force one day longer than shall be necessary to enable the people to prepare for a *return* to the *constitutional* currency," gold.[7] In early 1866, with government costs down and taxes bringing in sufficient income, Congress approved his proposal—the Contraction Act—to reduce the greenbacks in circulation.

By October the amount in circulation was down to $399 million. Within months the economy had begun to slow. Prices on many products dropped. Was the reduction in greenbacks the cause? The *Chicago Republican* thought so, arguing that ". . . if this policy of contraction is pursued, it cannot fail to interfere very materially with business prospects for the next year. . . . This work of burning 'greenbacks' must be stopped."[8] Democrats wanted to make an election issue of the Republicans' financial policy, and Republicans recognized the need to deal with currency as well as the South in their Northern campaigns. J. C. Devin, an Ohio Republican, lamented that "the currency question is now attracting more attention than the [proposed Fourteenth] Amendment of the Constitution." Republican Burke A. Hinsdale concluded: "[T]he Fall elections [in Ohio] as a whole have settled two things: 1. The negro will be less prominent for some time to come; 2. Financial questions will be more prominent." The owner of the Republican *Chicago Tribune,* Joseph Medill, summarized the situation: "The very fact that the reconstruction question is drawing rapidly to a conclusion will hasten the disintegration of our party, unless our leaders reflect public sentiment on financial questions as accurately as they have heretofore done on questions of freedom and personal rights."[9]

Complicating the decision about greenbacks were questions related to government bonds. Purchased by millions of Americans during the war with depreciated currency, payment of their principal or interest in gold or undepreciated currency would mean significant profits for bondholders. Affecting the most holders were 5–20 bonds, tax-exempt securities paying 6 percent interest in gold. Chase and others argued that gold was necessary to pay both interest and principal; Stevens and Butler were two of the few Republicans who said that paper currency was legal for redemption of both. The Pendleton Plan or "Ohio Idea" of George H. Pendleton, who had opposed the greenback bill in 1862, called for the 5–20 bonds to be paid for in greenbacks. While the plan helped make Pendleton a candidate for the Democratic presidential nomination in 1868, it split the Democrats, most of whose

Eastern members opposed the plan, and it was opposed by the Republicans, Stevens and Butler being exceptions.

Even though Congress ended further withdrawal on February 4, 1868, leaving $356 million in circulation, contraction—or not—joined Reconstruction as a major issue in the 1868 presidential elections. Both parties emphasized key issues, Reconstruction or the economy, depending on the interests of voters. The presidential victor that year, Ulysses S. Grant (who declared that payment of the national debt and a return to gold was a matter of the nation's honor), signed the Public Credit Act in early 1869. In apparent contradiction to the repeal of contraction a year earlier, it announced that the "faith of the United States is solemnly pledged to the payment in coin or its equivalent" of national debts.[10] Most Republicans, the founding fathers of greenbacks, voted for the measure, as did most Democrats, although the latter's vote was split regionally with all but one Western congressman opposing the measure. Financial conservatives among the Republicans had taken over the direction of the party's financial policy, even as such progreenback Republicans as Butler fought on. (Stevens died in August 1868.)

The Supreme Court's decisions on greenbacks reflected the Republicans' and the country's postwar divisions on the government's paper money. A seven-man Supreme Court took on the question of the greenbacks' constitutionality in 1870, specifically looking at their use as legal tender for debts contracted *before* their creation. Chief Justice Salmon P. Chase (the hard-money Secretary of the Treasury who had supported greenbacks in 1862) and three other members of the Court surprised the nation by ruling in *Hepburn v. Griswold* that the notes violated the Constitution. A little over a year later, with two appointments by Grant having raised the number of justices to nine, the Court reversed itself in a 5–4 decision. The *Legal Tender Cases* held greenbacks constitutional for prior contracts as well as those made after their creation. The justices explained that any other ruling would lead to "great business derangement, widespread distress, and the rankest injustice." The wartime need to protect "the government and the Constitution from destruction" supported the Act.[11] The decision, however, did not end the national debate.

When the economy plummeted with the Panic of 1873, Republicans—in power since 1860—received the bulk of the blame (and in 1874 lost control of Congress). To stimulate the economy, the Treasury

Department reissued $26 million in greenbacks, for a total of $382 million. The Republicans also passed an Inflation Bill, pushed by Southerners and Westerners, that called for an increase in the amount of greenbacks. Grant, however, surprised the nation by vetoing the bill. Heeding the complaints of Easterners and even Western businessmen who bristled at the thought of the national government's adjusting the money supply in response to changes in the economy, Grant argued that the Republicans had promised to return to gold at the earliest possible time. He called the bill "a departure from the principles of finance, national interest, the nation's obligations to creditors, Congressional promises, party pledges . . . , and of personal views and promises made by me."[12] The business community and the press applauded the veto as the equivalent of Grant's battlefield victories.

While the public's interest in currency issues was receding, the congressional debate over redemption and greenbacks was not over, particularly within the Republican party. Seeking to unite the party and avoid currency questions in the 1876 elections, Republicans pushed through the Resumption Act, which Grant signed in January 1875. The measure, as its name implies, provided for resuming the redemption of greenbacks in coin (gold, due to the Coinage Act of 1873 or "Crime of '73," which controversially ended the government's coining of silver, as well as adding "In God We Trust" to all currency). Beginning in 1879, when the government had rebuilt its gold reserve, holders of greenbacks could turn them in for specie; the law, however, provided no mechanism for specie payment. The law, which was pushed by Moderate Republicans but pleased no one completely, did not end greenbacks, and an 1878 measure stopped the withdrawal of greenbacks with $346 million in circulation. Still, opposition to limits on greenbacks and to currency contraction in general led to the formation of the National Greenback party, a group supporting repeal of the Resumption Act and the issuance of more soft money. It drew one million votes in the 1878 elections.

Corruption

Because of anti-Republican publicists and the perspective of early-twentieth-century historians, Reconstruction is often associated with corruption. Allegations center on the Grant administration (due in large part to the Credit Mobilier and Whiskey Ring scandals) and to Northern carpetbaggers who allegedly despoiled the South politically and economically. The association with the Republicans, particularly those in the South, is not untrue; it is just *part* of the story. One need only think of the Democratic Tweed Ring of New York City, which defrauded the city of New York of millions of dollars, to obtain a more accurate picture of a period justifiably known for its ethical shortcomings, influence peddling, and bribery, graft, and corruption. One can think of the selling of divorces by Pennsylvania legislators or Kansas's reputation as "the Rotten Commonwealth." As historian Rembert Patrick has explained, "The majority of Americans remained honest, but their indifference [especially to local illegalities] enabled the few to milk the public. Dishonesty was characteristic of the times; it was not limited to one race, one party, or one section."[13] So-called scandals were often the result of no more than individual incompetence or negligence, if not greed or dishonesty. Much of what was called scandalous was in the "lackluster credentials rather than the larceny," argues historian Mark Summers.[14] Bribes and kickbacks were a businessman's accepted way of working the system.

But because a case could be easily made against the Republicans— Louisiana Governor Henry Clay Warmoth, a carpetbagger, noted that corruption was "all the fashion" in his state[15]—it helped undermine the Republicans' efforts for the freedmen. White Southerners were already worried about vast changes in their lives, and because corruption and dishonesty, as well as general betrayals of public faith—in government and in business—did exist, it was easy to believe the reports. Newspaper stories and rumors both carried weight. As a result, public faith in the Republican party waned; they were not the purifying reformers. And the issue mattered. It was an instrument used by Southern Democrats against their Northern and black opponents; it was an argument for those who believed in limited government; and it was a simplistic way of explaining why dreams turned into nightmares.

A Democratic satire expressed the case that many made against the Republicans in general and President Grant in particular:

> Rotten custom house inspectors,
> Public thieves and Ring directors,
> White House military hacks,
> Leeches on the people's backs.

Grant us, therefore, ease and booty,
Sinecure devoid of duty;
Anything you have to give.
Anything to let us live;
We must steal, for work we can't,
Save us and feed us, U.S. Grant.[16]

Among the corrupt practices linked to the Grant administration, none are more famous than Credit Mobilier and the Whiskey Ring. Officials of the Credit Mobilier, a construction company whose members were corporate directors of the Union Pacific Railroad, hired their own dummy company to build the railroad. The former charged excessive amounts and paid for them (i.e., paid themselves) with United States bonds that had been appropriated to aid with the construction; they then subcontracted the actual work. Among those involved was Massachusetts Representative Oakes Ames. To avoid a congressional inquiry into their activities, Ames bribed congressmen (all Republicans) by selling them reduced-cost company stock. Most of this activity occurred before Grant became president, but it became public knowledge in 1872, thus inspiring critics of his administration. Congress investigated. Ames and James Brooks of New York (also a director of the Union Pacific) were censured by the House; outgoing Vice-President Schuyler Colfax, Vice-President elect Henry Wilson, and Representative (and future president) James Garfield were all tainted.

The Whiskey Ring involved Grant's personal secretary and friend, Orville Babcock. The aide who stood behind Grant at Lee's surrender at Appomattox, Babcock allegedly accepted bribes in return for helping delay federal prosecution of men who had attempted to defraud the government. The scandal also involved a Grant appointee and friend, John McDonald of St. Louis, who was collector of internal revenue for seven states. Discovered by Grant's Secretary of the Treasury Benjamin Helm Bristow in 1874, the illegalities dated back at least to 1870. Bristow learned that whiskey distillers and distributors had long bribed federal tax agents to ignore illegalities, such as mismeasuring the amount of whiskey in bottles and issuing more stamps than taxes collected. Millions of dollars in taxes were evaded.

Grant was not involved in the bribes or fraud. When he learned of the corruption in mid-1875, he initially cooperated with investigators and supported prosecutions, asserting that ". . . no guilty man [should] escape if it can be avoided."[17] Over three hundred arrests followed. Babcock, who vouched for McDonald's honesty and innocence, was indicted by a federal grand jury, but Grant was willing to testify at Babcock's trial because he had come to view the circumstantial case against his secretary as baseless. McDonald was convicted, fined $5,000, and sentenced to three-and-a-half years in prison; Babcock was acquitted with the help of the president's deposition.

Grant was an honest man. His respected Secretary of State Hamilton Fish believed that ". . . it would [not] have been possible for Grant to have told a lie, even if he had composed it and written it down," and Ebenezer Rockwood Hoar, Grant's attorney general, "would as soon think Saint Paul had got some of the thirty pieces of silver" as think the president corrupt.[18] But Grant's refusal to acknowledge the dishonesty in others caused much concern. He was a president who repeatedly demonstrated bad judgment in picking the men he listened to and in overseeing their actions. For example, his own brother-in-law was duped into trying to trick Grant to help Jay Gould and Jim Fisk corner the gold market. The result of that effort was Black Friday (September 24, 1869), when gold prices collapsed and upended the economy for months. The wife of William W. Belknap, his secretary of war, received payoffs for helping men gain licenses from her husband to trade with the Indians; Belknap, who received the payments ($20,000) after his wife's death, resigned but was still impeached by the House and tried by the Senate. With many questioning whether the Senate had jurisdiction over a man who no longer held office, he was acquitted, 37–25. Grant's administration also faced criticism for Secretary of the Navy George M. Robeson's extravagance and contract improprieties, for Secretary of the Interior Columbus Delano's concealment of a featherbedding scheme, and for Attorney General George Williams's personal use of government monies and extravagant lifestyle at the government's expense.

Plus, the Republicans did little to help Grant's or their cause when in early 1873 they raised the salaries for the president (from $25,000 to $50,000), vice-president, cabinet officers, members of the Supreme Court, and members of Congress (from $5,000 to $7,500), the last retroactive for two years even for those retiring or defeated in the recent election. Despite arguments that their higher salaries were justified, those congressmen who voted for the "salary grab" and "back-pay steal" found themselves under intense criticism. Within months Congress eliminated its pay raise.

Civil Service Reform

In July 1881 Charles Guiteau, who had unsuccessfully sought a government job, shot and killed President James Garfield. In many ways the problems that led to the assassination began 50 years earlier, when president Andrew Jackson argued for rotation in office: the work of government was simple, and too long in office led a man to corruption. Americans as democrats should be willing and able to serve in government and then return to life as private citizens. But with the increasing importance of party loyalty, administrations discovered that contributors who supported office seekers expected something in return for their help; they also were certain that those who opposed them would work against their policies if left in office. As the national government expanded—adding, for example, departments of agriculture and justice in 1862 and 1870, respectively—the possibilities for both good and harm grew. According to Mark Summers, "[T]he broadened authority of government permitted the lucky partisan a fresh, and entirely legal, source for pickings." By these years appointments of the unethical and unqualified reflected on both parties and government—bringing "six months of scramble and forty-two of muddle"[19]—and prompted reformers who were offended by inefficient, maladministered, profiteering, and sometimes corrupt government.

Demands for civil service reform during the 1860s and 1870s had much justification. And it was not just because unqualified men received government jobs in exchange for campaign contributions. Government work offered numerous opportunities for profit: inspectors and tariff collectors were bribed and products disappeared in transit. The job of supervisor of internal revenue for upper New York State was known to be worth a half-million dollars a year. In addition, in the days before the secret ballot, officeholders could easily require federal workers (even those hired only for the period preceding and including election day) to vote for a certain party or candidate. Government workers were assessed campaign "contributions" in many other ways, including direct monetary donations and indirect contributions in the form of tickets to partisan get-togethers. Seldom were pay-or-be-fired threats necessary; the workers knew the system.

What type of reform would fix these problems? Selection of better men would not fix poor procedures, weak bookkeeping requirements, insufficient personnel, and poor pay. And reform could not be allowed to undermine party power; officeholders in favor of reform wanted a method that did not disrupt or weaken their influence. Some sought reform merely as a way of removing others and assuming office themselves. A pragmatic President Grant saw little hope for total reform: it was "human nature to seek power and use it to help friends."[20]

On the national level, the threat posed by the Liberal Republicans prompted Grant—whom some reformers had seen in 1868–1869 as the candidate for honesty and reform, because he was "no more afraid of [politicians] than he was of rebels"[21]—to push reform in order to undermine the Liberals' demands for clean government. In his 1870 State of the Union address, the president called for civil service reform. In response, Congress gave Grant the power to establish a commission to write guidelines for government hiring and firing. The commission's recommendations included competitive exams, promotions based on experience, a board of examiners chosen by the commissioners, and the ending of political appointments. Grant agreed in late 1871 to follow the recommendations on the hiring and firing of federal workers; however, old practices continued for positions not covered by the commission. The rules, which the *New York Graphic* referred to as "the merest baby of a reform,"[22] had little impact, because Congress was reluctant to fund the commission even as it spoke in favor of the commission's work on a theoretical level. By early 1875 Grant was ordering executive offices to abandon the rules because Congress was no longer funding civil service reform.

In 1876 Republican presidential candidate Rutherford B. Hayes urged "thorough, radical, and complete" civil service reform,[23] but reform came only with the disappointed Guiteau's murder of a president. The 1883 Pendleton Civil Service Act, which followed up on the rules established by Grant's commission, created a bipartisan commission to administer competitive exams that would be used for making appointments to federal jobs. Over 13,000 federal workers were covered in 1884; the number reached 95,000 by 1900.

Liberal Republicans

The Liberal Republican party was a nationwide response to the mix of Reconstruction, economic problems, and corruption issues. The party began in three border states—Missouri, Tennessee, and West Virginia—where Republicans demanded the end of federal Reconstruction in the South and to the state laws that denied suffrage to former Confederates. They also opposed the corruption associated with Republican rule in their states. Getting nowhere with their arguments within their own party, these Republicans made common cause with at least some Democrats in the late 1860s and 1870.

The various views of the Liberal Republicans, who shared no common set of principles or goals, except opposition to Grant, make an impressive and intriguing list. They wanted an end to corruption, cutbacks in expenditures, currency reform (a dollar should be worth a dollar), tax reductions (including an end to the federal income tax created during the war), and civil service reform. All of these steps would help restore honesty and integrity to government. To accomplish this goal and to achieve a sound financial policy, they also sought free trade and the gold standard. They wanted limited government on both the national and the state level; every opportunity for subsidy and support (including land grants to railroads) was an opportunity for graft and corruption and an opportunity to benefit one group at the expense of another. Supply and demand should guide the economy. Amnesty for former Confederate leaders and an end to Reconstruction were also on the Liberal Republican agenda; both would allow the South's best men to guide their states and keep intellectually and morally inferior blacks from endangering the South. Similarly, the Liberal Republicans sought to remove the barriers (including city machines and patronage) that limited men such as them from being in their proper places of power and influence. As the *Nation* explained in July 1867, "Let us be content with securing equal justice in the South, and then combine to attack corruptions nearer home." "Other duties" must be attended to. Five years later the *Nation* echoed its earlier appeal: "Reconstruction and slavery we have done with; for administrative and revenue reform we are eager."[24] There were enough laws—too many—for the freedmen; now, they had to do for themselves. Not surprisingly, Democrats eager to remove unpopular Republican governments from the South found a receptive audience in the Liberals when the Democrats focused on blacks' weaknesses as political persons and on corruption and class legislation in the states.

These positions brought the Liberal Republicans to national prominence in 1872, having added to their membership Moderate Republicans, including Lyman Trumbull, and even some Radicals—including ex-congressmen James Ashley and George Julian and, in time, Charles Sumner. Also among them were Supreme Court Justices Salmon P. Chase and David Davis, former Secretary of the Navy Gideon Welles, poet and editor William Cullen Bryant, former minister to Great Britain Charles Francis Adams, and Edwin Godkin of the *Nation*. Most had been pushed out of influence (with Julian gerrymandered out of his congressional seat in 1870) and were seeking a way back.

At the Liberal Republicans' 1872 national convention in Cincinnati, the party had a wealth of capable, experienced men from whom to choose a presidential candidate to challenge Grant, the man most identified with the ills facing the nation. The party, however, passed on such men as Justice Davis and Senator Trumbull to select *New York Tribune* editor Horace Greeley, a choice that Indiana congressman Michael C. Kerr called "a most stupendous and illogical blunder."[25] Despite his eccentric looks, behavior, and causes (including women's rights, labor organizations, and vegetarianism), Greeley was popular; still, he was a disastrous choice because he represented few Liberal positions. He cared little for civil service reform, he favored protective tariffs, he opposed specie, and he supported a variety of reforms that required the use of government power. He had made a career of denouncing Democrats whom the Liberal Republicans needed as allies if they had any hope of replacing Grant.

Greeley garnered just 62 electoral votes to Grant's 286. He won three states in the former Confederacy—Georgia, Tennessee, and Texas—and just three in the rest of the South—Kentucky, Maryland, and Missouri. He won no states in the North or West. (Technically, he won no votes, since by the time the electoral votes were counted he was dead and electors had to make other selections.) Grant took 56 percent of the popular vote, the highest percentage between Andrew Jackson in 1828 and Theodore Roosevelt in 1904. The Liberal Republicans may have failed, but their efforts helped spell the end of Reconstruction. Some issues, such as black rights and security under law, still drew support, but the Liberals helped fragment the Republicans, drawing some Radicals to their fold and helping some Democrats-turned-Republicans return to their first loyalty; Trumbull and Julian were both supporting Democrats by the 1876 elections.

The Liberal Republicans reflected a Northern electorate that increasingly saw economic and political issues as more in need of attention than the racial and Southern issues that had more or less dominated the preceding half-decade. Republicans in the North were increasingly reluctant to defend or support governments in the South and willing to focus on non-Reconstruction issues. In addition, during the campaign the Republicans had sought to counter Greeley by eliminating some of the reformers' issues. Congress reduced the tariff and provided amnesty for most former Confederates. Republicans also sought to undercut the Liberals' Southern plank by passing a version of Sumner's civil rights proposal, which died in the House. In the meantime, Democrats toned down the racial angles of their platform in an attempt to appeal to white and black voters. Their new emphasis on economic and reform issues made their "fusion" with the Liberal Republicans logical.

The Democrats' (temporary and incomplete) move away from racial issues put them in a position to take advantage of other issues—corruption, suspicious financial deals, taxes, and the developing depression—while the failure of the Liberal Republicans and the failure to win black Southern voters away from the Republicans convinced Democrats that "fusion" was not the answer. Appeals to whites' racial concerns would end the voter apathy that hurt so many Democratic candidates throughout the South in 1872, especially because Republican governments in the South increasingly emphasized their commitment to black interests in order to assure their hold on the African American vote.

Santo Domingo (and Alaska)

Although Americans and their political leaders had a wealth of domestic issues to dominate their time and thinking, they also had interests outside the nation's borders. Americans' expansionist interests in the 1860s and 1870s focused both northward and southward. To many in the early 1870s Santo Domingo (the Dominican Republican) was a controversial and riveting issue. Its acquisition was a goal of the Grant administration; preventing that annexation inspired heated debate and attacks that helped fuel the Liberal Republicans' break with Grant, as well as Grant's disenchantment with the Radicals in general and Charles Sumner in particular. The purchase of Alaska caused little damage to the country's domestic political relationships, but it too engaged the nation in debate.

In 1867 the United States purchased the 370 million acres of Russian America for $7,200,000. Russia's sale of Alaska was prompted by its recent defeat in the Crimean War, focus on Asian lands to the south, need for capital, concern that American settlers would soon be arriving, difficulty defending the distant location, and preference for American rather than British expansion. The United States' purchase was spurred by a desire for naval stations and by broad strategic concerns, always an interest of Secretary of State William Seward, who also purchased Midway Island in 1867 as a way station in the Pacific. In the years preceding the Alaska purchase, Californians and the Washington legislature had expressed interest in the area's furs, fishing, and harbors.

Despite differences in their party, many Republicans supported the treaty, including both Representative Thaddeus Stevens and Charles Sumner, who was chair of the Senate Foreign Relations Committee. However, when the treaty was signed on March 30, 1867, and sent to the Senate for its approval, Congress had just passed the First Reconstruction Act and the Tenure of Office Act over Andrew Johnson's vetoes. Some Senators were reluctant to accept any measure that came from Johnson's administration; some were unhappy about not being informed of the negotiations. In addition, while the acquisition aroused the support of Pacific Coast interests, the Senate Foreign Relations Committee was dominated by men from the Atlantic side of the country. And while many newspapers supported the treaty, Horace Greeley's *New York Tribune,* at least initially, attacked it for diverting the nation's attention from important domestic issues. Many observers predicted swift Senate rejection.

Ratification, however, came easily, 37–2, spurred by Sumner's lengthy speech in defense of the treaty. Reasons for supporting the purchase included not wanting to antagonize a country that had been friendly during the Civil War, taking a step that would eventually remove Great Britain from North America, and simply taking advantage of a good deal for the United States (two cents an acre). Sumner listed Alaska's resources (including fish, gold, and fur seals), as well as its closeness to Asian markets; he also noted the importance of extending the American republican system. Still, House appropriation of the purchase money prompted a variety of complaints about the acquisition of a land of polar bears, icebergs, and volcanoes. Benjamin Butler concluded that only an "insane" man would want Alaska.[26] Nevertheless, on July 27, 1868, the House appropriated the necessary funds.

Johnson's successor in the White House, Ulysses S. Grant, had less success in his efforts at expanding the nation into the Caribbean, even though Americans had long coveted parts of Mexico, Cuba, and Central America. For some the Danish West Indies (Virgin Islands) and the Dominican Republic were also suitable targets for Americanization. Grant himself believed that the Caribbean and a future isthmian canal would play critical roles in the country's security and prosperity; however, he was concerned that support for Cubans rebelling against Spanish rule would hurt American claims against the British for the latter's aid to the Confederacy during the Civil War. In addition, interest in the Caribbean was not unanimous. In early 1867 the House announced that it would not provide the money "unless there is greater present necessity . . . than now exists" for annexation of the Danish West Indies, for which Seward had successfully negotiated.[27]

Andrew Johnson had urged annexation of the Dominican Republic and Haiti, with which it shared the island, in 1868, but the House of Representatives rejected making the Dominican Republic and Haiti American protectorates or acquiring the former. Annexationists were undeterred. Their interest in the island focused on its natural resources, its sites for a naval base and a coaling station, and the perceived benefits to the native population of American governance. In addition, Grant pointed to the importance of asserting the Monroe Doctrine. He also reminded Americans that Santo Domingo was a potential "consumer of the products of Northern farms and manufactories" and that it would provide "remunerative wages to tens of thousands of laborers not now upon the island."[28] Grant saw another benefit: because African Americans faced inevitable racial discrimination in the United States, Santo Domingo would provide a refuge for those who wished to emigrate, and thus would provide leverage in convincing white Southerners to treat their black laborers well.

In 1869 Grant's close friend and private secretary, Orville Bab-cock—the same man defended by the president for his involvement in the Whiskey Ring—went to Santo Domingo as a special agent. He returned with a draft protocol of annexation for either the entire coun-try or for Samana Bay; President Buenaventura Baez was to receive $100,000 and munitions worth $50,000. Unfortunately, Babcock's negotiating tactics and partners were questionable, and Baez's govern-ment was near economic collapse. Despite protection from the U.S. navy, Baez was facing threats from internal and Haitian forces. These facts became widely known during public hearings conducted by the Senate.

Such a questionable situation did not deter Grant, but it won no support from Grant's cabinet and undercut the support of such key sen-ators as Charles Sumner. Grant assumed Sumner's support for a treaty that the former believed would help black Americans, and he hoped for a fair hearing of the treaty by Sumner's Senate Foreign Relations Com-mittee. The powerful Senator, however, did not share the president's faith in annexation. He opposed the loss of one of the world's two black republics. Sumner was also concerned about the amount of debt to be inherited by the United States and the difficulty of putting down domestic unrest on the island.

Others who opposed the treaty did so for far different reasons. Southern Democrats saw annexation of a black nation as yet another threat to their society. Others believed that the tropics were not a suit-able breeding ground for democratic institutions; Senator Carl Schurz argued that the country's "indigestible, unassimilable" peoples "could not be trusted with a share in governing our country." Representative James Garfield thought the "strangely degenerated" people had "no place in American life."[29]

After the Senate committee reported against annexation, Grant made support of the treaty a test of party loyalty. Even though he asserted that senators would have to cooperate with his policies if they expected him to honor their patronage selections, the annexation treaty fell far short of achieving the necessary two-thirds vote. The Senate split 28–28 in June 1870, with 19 Republicans voting against the president.

Grant did not accept defeat, however, and the battle over the treaty continued for almost another year. In an effort to win votes, he held out the patronage position of minister to Great Britain—vacant after the recall of Sumner friend John Lathrop Motley, who had frustrated Grant and Secretary of State Fish with his pro-Sumner handling of the *Alabama* claims. In the following months, the rhetoric grew more heated. Indeed, more than one observer wondered about Grant's interests, including Sumner and British minister Edward Thornton, both of whom speculated that the president might have personal reasons for taking such a determined stand on annexation.

Angered by the charges against him and his friends, and frustrated by his cabinet's divided views, Grant suggested annexation by joint resolution (as was done in 1845 to acquire Texas) and, with Congress's approval, sent an investigating committee to the island. The committee, whose membership was largely men associated with the defense of black rights, including Radical Benjamin Wade and black abolitionist Frederick Douglass, returned with a favorable report. While it failed to convince the Senate to ratify the treaty, it did validate Grant's claim that the island offered valuable resources to the United States. On the whole, however, the annexation battle did more harm to the Grant administration than good. Republicans split on yet another issue. The relationship of the president and one of the Senate's and the party's leading figures was beyond repair, with Grant working successfully to depose Sumner as chair of the Foreign Relations Committee in early 1871.

Alabama Claims

At times it seems impossible to find an issue from the Reconstruction years that did not involve Charles Sumner. His efforts to settle the so-called *Alabama* claims once again pitted him against President Grant, though less harmfully than the contemporaneous battle over the Dominican Republic.

In May 1861 Great Britain had issued a proclamation of neutrality that recognized the belligerency of the Confederacy. As a result, Great Britain allowed the building of Confederate ships in British shipyards. The Confederate vessels, including the cruiser *Alabama,* damaged Union ships and shipping. In the two years it sailed, the *Alabama* alone destroyed or captured five dozen Union merchant ships. After the war, Secretary of State Seward argued that Great Britain should pay indemnity for the direct and indirect damages, that is, for the vessels and trade lost, for insurance claims, and for the prolongation of the war caused by the Confederacy's naval successes and Great Britain's moral support of the Southern government. Great Britain refused to admit that it had acted inappropriately and provided, in Sumner's words, not "one soothing word for a friendly power deeply aggrieved."[30]

Negotiations during the Johnson presidency ended with the Johnson-Clarendon Convention of January 1869. The agreement, which stipulated settlement by arbitration of private and individual claims and provided no British apology or expression of regret, was opposed by Sumner, who thought the arbitration process left too much to chance. Sumner spoke against the treaty in a secret session of the Senate, arguing that the British cooperation with the South had added substantially to the costs and length of the conflict. For essentially doubling the length of the war, Great Britain could be held responsible for half of its cost, or $2 billion (although some Americans were willing to accept Canada in lieu of the money).

The treaty was overwhelmingly rejected (54–1) by the Senate just as Grant assumed the presidency. During a period of Anglophobia, both Sumner and the Senate were initially hailed for their stand. British reaction prompted some reevaluation, however. Sumner's arguments and proposal were called "monstrous" by the British *Spectator* and were viewed as signaling a United States ready for war. Sumner countered that his speech was "rather pacific in tone" and that it made "*no DEMAND, whether apology or money.*"[31]

Grant, who had opposed the treaty, and his secretary of state, Hamilton Fish, renewed Seward's efforts. They did so, however, with the interference of Sumner, who believed that his expertise in foreign affairs greatly exceeded theirs and who wished to guide the negotiations through American Minister to Great Britain John Lathrop Motley. Fish, who had no experience in diplomacy before assuming the job, agreed that British actions had extended the length of the war and probably cost the United States at least a billion dollars. Still, he did not expect collection of the money; he hoped that Great Britain would adjust its policy on belligerency and neutrals and that it might pull out of Canada. He also wanted some expression of regret or apology. In mid-1870, Fish, trying to accommodate the powerful Massachusetts senator's view on the various claims, instructed Motley not to bring up the belligerency issue. Motley did not follow his instructions. The negotiations also became entangled with the Santo Domingo annexation efforts. Motley, Sumner's friend, found himself without a job when Grant began his effort to undermine Sumner because of his opposition to the Santo Domingo annexation. But the negotiations with Great Britain continued because of Britain's interest in settling its American problems in order to free itself to handle European problems: it did not want to see its enemies building ships in American shipyards. As a result, in 1871 a Joint High Commission of five Americans and five Britons agreed on the basics of what would become the Treaty of Washington. This agreement, approved by the Senate 50–12 in midsummer, began the settlement of not only the *Alabama* claims but other irritants, such as disagreements over the fishing rights of Americans and Canadians in each other's waters. In addition, the treaty's very first provision expressed Great Britain's regret for the damages caused by the Confederate ships. Sumner spoke in favor of the treaty. Within months the arbitrators agreed that the United States should receive $15,500,000 for damage caused by the *Alabama* and two other ships, the *Florida* and the *Shenandoah*. The United States would receive nothing for damage caused by other Confederate ships.

Reconstruction of the South could not take the public's or their leaders' attention away from such critical concerns as finances and office holding. Even men like Charles Sumner and Thaddeus Stevens, whose commitment to the black Southerner and determination to battle opponents face few challengers today, had to deal with such relatively mundane issues as the type of currency in circulation. The non-Reconstruction issues of the Reconstruction period garnered widespread interest because they affected the day-to-day lives of most Americans in some way. Would a farmer be able to sell his crop for a good price? Would a merchant be able to borrow sufficient funds to expand his business? Would liquor distillers pay a federal tax? Would fishermen be able to fish in traditional waters? Would officeholders provide jobs for their many supporters? Even for many in the South, a predominantly agricultural region with few banks, financial policies could rival those tied to Reconstruction. And for a nation with little understanding of or patience for the freedmen's struggles, non-Reconstruction questions were seldom any easier to answer than questions linked to shaky Republican state governments, but they seemed more in line with questions traditionally faced by the nation.

Notes

1. Quoted in David Donald, *The Civil War and Reconstruction* (New York: W. W. Norton, 2001), 282.

2. Quoted in Robert P. Sharkey, *Money, Class, and Party: An Economic Study of Civil War and Reconstruction* (Baltimore: Johns Hopkins University Press, 1959), 36.

3. Quoted in A. Barton Hepburn, *A History of Currency in the United States* (New York: Macmillan, 1915), 187.

4. Quoted in ibid., 193.

5. Quoted in Irwin Unger, *The Greenback Era: A Social and Political History of American Finance, 1865–1879* (Princeton: Princeton University Press, 1964), 45–46, 47.

6. Quoted in Sharkey, *Money, Class, and Party,* 134, n.

7. Quoted in Thomas Wilson, *The Power "to Coin" Money: The Exercise of Monetary Powers by the Congress* (Armonk, N.Y.: M. E. Sharpe, 1992), 169 (emphasis added).

8. Quoted in Sharkey, *Money, Class, and Party,* 92.

9. Quoted in ibid., 94–96.

10. Quoted in Unger, *The Greenback Era,* 93.

11. *Legal Tender Cases* (*Knox v. Lee*), 12 Wallace 457 (1871).

12. Quoted in Jean Edward Smith, *Grant* (New York: Simon & Schuster, 2001), 579.

13. Summers, *The Era of Good Stealings,* 5; Patrick, *The Reconstruction of the Nation* (New York: Oxford University Press, 1967), 185.

14. Mark Wahlgren Summers, *The Era of Good Stealings* (New York: Oxford, 1993), 99.

15. Quoted in William L. Richter, *The ABC-CLIO Companion to American Reconstruction, 1862–1877* (Santa Barbara, Calif.: ABC-CLIO, 1996), 419.

16. *St. Paul Pioneer,* October 29, 1872, quoted in Summers, *The Era of Good Stealings,* 98.

17. Quoted in Smith, *Grant,* 590.

18. Quoted in ibid., 592; and in Summers, *The Era of Good Stealings,* 181.

19. Summers, *The Era of Good Stealings,* 91, 97.

20. Quoted in Smith, *Grant,* 588.

21. Quoted in ibid.

22. January 23, 1874, quoted in Summers, *The Era of Good Stealings,* 101.

23. Eugene H. Roseboom and Alfred E. Eckes Jr., *A History of Presidential Elections: From George Washington to Jimmy Carter,* 4th ed. (New York: Macmillan, 1979), 91.

24. Quoted in Benedict in Eric Anderson and Alfred A. Moss Jr., eds., *The Facts of Reconstruction: Essays in Honor of John Hope Franklin* (Baton Rouge: Louisiana State University Press, 1991), 73, 74; and in Eric Foner, *Reconstruc-*

tion: America's Unfinished Revolution, 1863–1877 (New York: Harper & Row, 1988), 500.

25. Quoted in William Gillette, *Retreat from Reconstruction, 1869–1879* (Baton Rouge: Louisiana State University Press, 1979), 63.

26. Quoted in James Morton Callahan, *The Alaska Purchase and Americo-Canadian Relations,* West Virginia University Studies in American History, nos. 2–3 (Morgantown: West Virginia University, 1908), 23.

27. Quoted in Smith, *Grant,* 688, n. 25.

28. Quoted in William S. McFeely, *Grant: A Biography* (New York: W. W. Norton, n.d.), 350.

29. Quoted in Geoffrey Perret, *Ulysses S. Grant: Soldier & President* (New York: Random House, 1997), 397.

30. Quoted in David Donald, *Charles Sumner and the Rights of Man* (New York: Knopf, 1970), 375.

31. Quoted in ibid., 379, 391 (emphasis in original).

CHAPTER 6

CONCLUDING
INTERPRETIVE ESSAY

The postwar years were ones of goals, demands, and visions, with no agreement on any of these things. While some Northerners shared the white South's desire for a quick, harmonious, magnanimous return to Union, others believed that only fundamental changes in the South could insure future peace and reflect national ideals of liberty and equality. For the former, little needed to be done; for the latter, the national government's power was essential, just as it had been for winning the war. Unfortunately for the latter—for the Radical Republicans—the nation did not share most of its goals for restructuring of the South, defining freedom, and using federal power to accomplish both. As a result, what was desirable for the Radicals and those who shared their values and visions was not truly possible.

These basic facts explain much of the failure of Reconstruction.

While most Northerners accepted the war-expanded powers of the national government, they (and their representatives and senators) still saw the states as playing the key role in the federal system. And while most believed that black Americans should be protected by the law and should have economic and civil rights, they still saw African Americans as inferiors. Neither of these facts should surprise anyone. The country's first constitution, the Articles of Confederation, sought to prevent the national government from infringing on state powers, and arguments in favor of states' rights had few rivals from the 1790s on. The national government touched few lives directly in the 1860s, and it seemed safer to most Americans that this fact not change. As for issues of race, the general perception was there were few reasons to doubt that races were distinct groups, with their own stages of development and (with the exception of the Caucasian) with their own weaknesses. Science and history seemed to prove this point, and some Americans even expected the quick extinction of black Americans, whose physical and intellectual weaknesses would lead to early deaths without the protection and guidance of their white masters. Federalism and racism blended into a powerful force, especially when economic issues captured voters' attention in the postwar years.

Thus, while race and federalism explain the disappointments of Reconstruction, the problems went far beyond them. Americans were affected by the broad-based desire for a speedy return of national harmony, the reverence for private property rights, the wide-ranging differences within the Republican party, the disagreements between the executive and legislative branches over constitutional responsibilities, the inadequate administrative machinery and the insufficient budget to exert wide-ranging control in the South, and the tensions and conflicts within the Southern states. Still, Reconstruction was able to provide the country with a constitutional base that made possible, albeit a century later, a renewed effort to ensure that black Americans were equal under law.

In the late 1800s, the nation turned from Reconstruction to industrial and urban growth; imperialist expansion completed the removal of the national government as an influence in Southern racial affairs. The Republican party accepted black votes but responded with neither appreciation nor protection. In the South, white Democratic society rescued itself from the errors of congressional Reconstructionists. It had to reform Republican constitutions and statutes and to correct black notions of equality. As a result, the period has been called the nadir of African American history. Segregation, disenfranchisement, debt peonage, and lynching were the Southern solutions to the nagging "Negro problem." The rest of the nation, with its attention on robber barons, protesting farmers, union strikes, immigrants, urban bosses, and child labor, left the South to govern itself.

Segregation was not new, but it spread with impressive vigor to every corner of black Southern life by 1900. In *Plessy v. Ferguson* (1896), the Supreme Court gave its constitutional stamp of approval when it ruled that the Fourteenth Amendment's framers did not intend to counteract nature. The races were different and could not mix without conflict; an equality that involved separation was within the meaning of section one's "equal protection." "Separate but equal" was thus both natural and constitutional. This definition of the Fourteenth Amendment demonstrated how Reconstruction goals and steps could lose their meaning as American society tried to accommodate them to its racial and political views. Backed by this interpretation of the Reconstruction amendments—which allowed two levels of citizenship and equality—segregation spread from residential areas, transportation, and education to virtually every aspect of Southern living, including playgrounds, schools, courtrooms, and government offices. But it was seldom equal; in some cases African Americans were totally denied services. Their schools received as little as a tenth of the appropriations per child as did schools for white children, and black teachers were usually paid half the salaries of white teachers. School buildings were often no more than a single room, and equipment was out of date and worn, if provided at all. Black economic and legal resistance to the Jim Crow (segregation) laws and practices had little support and little success. Even when the Supreme Court prohibited residential segregation achieved through state laws (in the 1917 case of *Buchanan v. Warley*), it did so only because such laws infringed on (white) property rights. Whites turned to private agreements known as restrictive covenants, and blacks reaped no benefits from the ruling. It would not be until 1948, in *Shelley v. Kraemer,* that the Court made racially restrictive contracts impossible to enforce. The private and voluntary agreements did not violate the Constitution, but they could not be enforced by courts. Action by the courts meant action by the states that violated the Fourteenth Amendment.

In terms of disenfranchisement, states followed the lead set by the decision in *United States v. Reese* and found numerous ways to restrict black males from voting without using explicit racial reasons to do so. In addition to continuing the violence that dated back to Reconstruction, states used literacy tests, understanding clauses, poll taxes, grandfather clauses, and, in time, white primaries. In 1915 the Supreme Court in *Guinn v. United States* ruled that the grandfather clause—limiting voting to those who could vote before 1867—was obviously intended to limit black voting (not until in March 1867, with the First Reconstruction

Act, could blacks vote in the South). In general, however, states did what they wished. (For example, not until 1966 did the United States prohibit poll taxes as a requirement for voting in federal elections, and that required a constitutional amendment.) Not surprisingly, black office holding became largely a thing of the past; so too did jury service by African Americans. The government and legal systems were white controlled.

Economically, as W.E.B. Du Bois argued in 1935, "it was the policy of the state to keep the Negro laborer poor, to confine him as far as possible to menial occupations, to make him a surplus labor reservoir and to force him into peonage and unpaid toil."[1] Sharecropping quickly turned from a solution for landless freedmen to a form of economic slavery. Despite the Peonage Act of 1867, which prohibited making a person work in order to pay off debts, there was no federal enforcement until the twentieth century. In the meantime, black (and white) sharecroppers were increasingly in debt and, because of state laws, unable to recover financially by finding more profitable land to farm or nonagricultural work. The statutes prohibited their leaving the land until debts were paid—and landowners, merchants, and bankers did not let that happen. In effect, sharecropping and its system of borrowing from landowners and merchants to start each year's farming had replaced slavery's labor system.

Southern states had a variety of means to control African Americans. They used black convict labor for profit making and race control. It was a profitable arrangement for both state treasuries and private businesses, and it was, according to a Southern white woman, a "hell upon earth" for the black laborer.[2] Southerners also used lynching. Their states had laws against lynching—murder by three or more people to punish someone for a crime or a social violation—but they did not enforce them when the victims were African American, and from the late 1880s to the 1950s, 75 percent of the 5,000 Americans who were victims of lynchers were black. In the 1890s mobs killed 200 victims a year. Often they justified their acts with charges of black rape of white women. Few such allegations were justified. In most cases whites simply sought a way to show dominance. Sometimes the killings involved slow torture before large, approving crowds of men, women, and children; some victims were burned at the stake, their body parts cut off and kept as souvenirs. Newspaper stories alerted whites to upcoming executions, and picture postcards celebrated the charred remains or the bodies dangling from tree limbs. Law enforcement officers frequently led the mob or permitted them access to prisoners. Not surprisingly, few lynchers were even arrested, and white juries refused to convict those who were. In effect, justice for blacks was brutally different than that for whites. Beginning in the late 1890s, there were periodic efforts to pass a federal law against lynching, but they failed. Democrats used arguments of race and federalism to stop all of them.

For some Southern blacks the answer was emigration to Africa. For thousands it was migration to Kansas. Some became early travelers north, although the major movement—the Great Migration—did not begin until the World War I years. Some established black towns, such as Mound Bayou in Mississippi. A few hoped to push the Republicans to respond by threatening to vote Democratic, but even though Republicans ignored their rights, most blacks saw voting for the Democrats as a vote for slavery. Many followed the advice of Booker T. Washington, who urged an emphasis on industrial education and work rather than on voting and other rights.

The twentieth century brought assertions of black citizenship—including black demands to fight for their nation in World Wars I and II—and of black pride. Madame C. J. Walker, who became a millionaire through the sale of hair care products, demonstrated the capability and ambition of African Americans; so too did DuBois, who had earned a Ph.D. from Harvard and wrote a classic history of Reconstruction. Marcus Garvey not only led a "Back to Africa" movement in the 1920s but also a movement to convince African Americans to be proud of their racial heritage and accomplishments. At the same time Carter G. Woodson began the *Journal of Negro History* and Black History Week. The literary accomplishments of such artists as Langston Hughes and Zora Neale Hurston during the Harlem Renaissance won blacks attention and praise, but the assertive "New Negro" of the post–World War I years also prompted a rise in lynching. Even the legal efforts of the National Association for the Advancement of Colored People (NAACP) could not convince the national government to use its Reconstruction-era amendments and laws to end lynching or segregation. Federalism and racism lived on. The "Negro problem" was a Southern problem. Also, as the rest of the nation had contact with the so-called inferior peoples of Latin

America, the Pacific, and Asia—as immigrants and subjects of expansion—they began to better understand Southerners' demands to be left alone to deal with their unique racial situation. The Great Migration of black Southerners to Northern cities was only just beginning to turn African Americans into a national "problem" and political force.

Although it is still not clear exactly how the different pieces of the nation's society came together to form the civil rights movement, its achievements were in many ways the second stage of Reconstruction, enough so that many have argued that Reconstruction ended not in the 1870s but a hundred years later (if it has ever ended). In a striking reversal, the Supreme Court, highlighted by its decision against segregated schools in *Brown v. Board of Education* in 1954, led the way, and a Southern Democratic president—Lyndon Baines Johnson—promised black Americans that "we shall overcome." The Civil Rights Act passed by Congress in 1964 essentially resurrected its 1875 predecessor, but this time Congress relied on its power over interstate commerce. Almost one hundred years after creation of the Fourteenth Amendment, Congress still was not certain that it was possible to base protection of black rights on the Fourteenth Amendment, as the Civil Rights Act of 1875 had done. The Voting Rights Act of 1965 picked up where the Fifteenth Amendment and the Enforcement Acts left off.

One might fairly argue that, while the civil rights movement did not eliminate race as a factor in society, it achieved what the Radical Reconstructionists had in mind: equality under law supported by an activist national government.

Historians and Reconstruction

It was during the "nadir"[3]—the years of the late 1800s and early 1900s—that professional historians replaced participants as analysts of the Reconstruction period. But viewing the period objectively and unemotionally was as impossible for these early students as it was for the participants. The scholarly goal of objectivity is a difficult one to achieve even today as myths, facts, and social values mix in an indecipherable swirl.

The first historical view of Reconstruction focused on 1867 and succeeding years and argued that it was a harsh, vindictive, lengthy period imposed on valiant white Southerners by petty, self-serving Radicals and their white and black stooges. The goal was humiliation and oppression of Southerners; the result was chaos, which white Democrats courageously overcame. Influencing this early (and lingering view) was nationalism, federalism, and racism at the turn of the twentieth century. The Dunning school, named after Columbia University Professor William A. Dunning (whose works and teachings influenced generations of historians), argued in the early 1900s that the Confederates had accepted their defeat and successfully restored their states along the lines required by the lenient policy of Andrew Johnson. Their efforts, led by the correct but often inept and incapable Johnson, were trampled by the vindictive Radicals who sought personal and party benefits; and it was the Radicals who brought corrupt and incompetent governments to the South. For the Radicals, according to Howard K. Beale, the goal was "subjugation," not "conciliation."[4] African Americans were innately inferior and unprepared to carry the responsibilities of citizenship demanded for them by the Radicals, who were guided by "the vain imagination of the political equality of man."[5]

In the 1930s W. E. B. Du Bois stood "virtually alone" in revising this traditional view of Reconstruction. At the heart of his revision was the view of "Negroes as men." As he argued, traditionalists saw "the endless inferiority of the Negro race" and thus "misinterpreted, distorted, even deliberately ignored any fact that challenged or contradicted this assumption."[6] Following Du Bois's lead and that of other African American critics of the Dunning school, the Revisionists transformed perceptions of the period. Researching and writing in the midst of the civil rights movement, they painted a picture of Reconstruction that was barely recognizable when compared to that described by Burgess and Dunning. Beginning in the 1950s, they argued that the Republicans in Congress sought to ensure that the war's accomplishments, which included providing protection for the freedmen, were not lost in the peace. As Kenneth M. Stampp argued, the Radical goal was "to make Southern society more democratic, especially to make the emancipation of the Negroes something more than an empty gesture."[7] When Andrew Johnson blocked Congress's efforts to improve his plan, that body had no choice but to act.

Recent historians—called neorevisionists or postrevisionists—have continued the analysis of the Radicals, often asserting that they attempted too little. They were limited by views on race, constitutional federalism, and the economy. While they were sincere in their calls for reform, they were tied to a social and economic order which they did not want to displace. They were reformers, not revolutionaries. Postrevisionists emphasized continuity between the prewar and the postwar South. They often emphasized the role of Moderate Republicans, thus building on the idea that Reconstruction was hardly radical; according to this view, it was the result of compromise and not a significant shift from national norms. Recent historians, such as Eric Foner, have sought to pull together social, cultural, racial, and local history to give Reconstruction a more comprehensive depiction.

Because most efforts to understand Reconstruction tend to analyze its failures, it becomes fairly easy to conclude that nothing was accomplished. Admittedly, the fate of the African American in the post-Reconstruction decades was a frustrating, limited, and often deadly one. Southern white Democrats' counterreform (if not counterrevolution) eliminated many of the reforms established by the Republican constitutions and governments. In addition, entrenched notions of an inferior Southern black race, raised beyond its capabilities by mistaken notions of racial equality, made it easier for racism to deepen throughout the rest of the country. The African American's failure to reach the level of white accomplishments was explained by his weaknesses, not by an economic, political, social, and constitutional system that was essentially a barrier to all but the rare exception. But because of the Radicals and Reconstruction, the Constitution was changed and became a different document. What those changes would mean for African Americans and for all Americans would become clear only in the next century.

Notes

1. W. E. B. Du Bois, *Black Reconstruction in America, 1860–1880* (1935. Reprint. New York: Atheneum, 1992), 696.

2. Ibid., 698.

3. Rayford W. Logan, *The Betrayal of the Negro from Rutherford B. Hayes to Woodrow Wilson* (New York: Collier [1965]), 11, 88.

4. Howard K. Beale, *The Critical Year: A Study of Andrew Johnson and Reconstruction* (New York: Harcourt, Brace, 1930), 2.

5. John W. Burgess, *Reconstruction and the Constitution, 1866–1876* (New York: Scribner's, 1902), 298.

6. Du Bois, *Black Reconstruction,* 626, 627.

7. Kenneth M. Stampp, *The Era of Reconstruction, 1865–1877* (New York: Knopf, 1965), 214.

BIOGRAPHIES: THE PERSONALITIES OF RECONSTRUCTION

James M. Ashley (1824–1896)

Born near Pittsburgh, Pennsylvania, James Ashley moved to Ohio where his education came from reading the Bible with the guidance of his father, a minister. At a young age he fled his strict father for life on a river steamer. Both in the Ohio Valley (Kentucky and western Virginia) and in the South, Ashley saw slavery and quickly grew to hate it. His outspoken views forced him to leave Virginia for his own safety. His life opposing slavery was only beginning.

After working as a printer, editor, and boat builder, Ashley was admitted to the bar in 1849. He also established a wholesale drug company in Toledo, Ohio. His interest in politics grew during the debate over the territory acquired through the Mexican War of 1846–1848. Until that time he was a member of the Democratic party, whose Southern members generally supported slavery. He became a Free-Soiler in 1848 in order to oppose the expansion of slavery into the new territory. By 1854 he was joining the new Republican party, which also opposed slavery's expansion into the territories.

Ashley was first elected to Congress in 1858 and served through 1868. Known as a Radical Republican, he was involved in many Reconstruction proposals and plans, in part because of his chairmanship of the House Committee on Territories. He introduced a wartime Reconstruction bill in March 1862 that declared Southern states territories and asserted congressional responsibility for their reconstruction. The bill was defeated. Ashley also led the successful fight to abolish slavery in Washington, D.C., and the territories, and he supported the Wade-

Davis Bill, Congress's wartime plan for reconstructing the South, and the Thirteenth Amendment that abolished slavery.

A supporter of black suffrage, Ashley opposed Andrew Johnson's Reconstruction plan. A longtime supporter of Johnson's removal from office, he introduced an impeachment resolution in January 1867. Ashley's antagonism toward the president was caused by their conflicting views on blacks and Reconstruction, but also by Ashley's belief that Johnson played a role in Lincoln's assassination, just as he believed that previous vice-presidents who assumed the presidency upon presidents' deaths had also been complicitous.

Defeated in the 1868 elections, Ashley served briefly as governor of the Montana Territory under Ulysses S. Grant and then built and managed a railroad. He backed the Liberal Republicans in the early 1870s.

Blanche Kelso Bruce (1841–1898)

Bruce, the first African American elected to a full term in the U.S. Senate, began life as a slave in Prince Edward County, Virginia. Light-skinned and likely the son of his white owner, he was tutored along with his white half-brother. After being moved to Missouri and escaping slavery during the Civil War, he established the first black elementary school in Kansas. After the war, he studied for two years (1865–1867) at Oberlin College before becoming a porter on a Mississippi riverboat.

One of many men, white and black, who saw the opportunities offered by the South after the war, Bruce made his way to Mississippi in 1869. Quickly becoming politically active, he held a variety of positions. Starting out as county supervisor of elections, his later positions included sergeant-at-arms of the state senate, tax collector of Bolivar County, sheriff, supervisor of education, and commissioner of elections. In addition, he was a delegate to the Republican national convention from 1868 to 1896. Known as honest, nonvindictive, and capable, he avoided party conflicts.

A wealthy planter who made his fortune through land sales, Bruce was elected to the U.S. Senate in 1874. Four years earlier, Hiram Revels had become the first black elected to that body when he was chosen to fill a short Senate term, filling the seat vacated in 1860 by Jefferson Davis. In the Senate, Bruce introduced few bills but garnered a reputation for efficiency and served on several committees, including education and labor.

He maintained a close alliance with powerful New Yorker Roscoe Conkling. He called for Western land for black migrants and desegregation of army units; he also urged a humane Indian policy. Bruce, who headed a select committee that investigated fraud within the Freedmen's Bureau, called for an investigation of the harassment of a black cadet at West Point.

After a single term in the Senate, Bruce received presidential appointments as registrar of the treasury and recorder of deeds for the District of Columbia. He also wrote articles and toured the country speaking on race issues.

Benjamin Butler (1818–1893)

Benjamin Butler was one of Reconstruction's—and the Civil War's—most controversial figures. Loved by constituents whom he served with devotion, he was hated by those who became victims of his sharp criticisms and even by those within his own party and state who opposed his views on such issues as currency, civil rights for blacks, women's suffrage, and civil service.

After graduating from Waterville (now Colby) College in Maine in 1838 and then teaching school, Butler was admitted to the bar in 1840. A successful criminal attorney, Butler was known for his wit and legal tactics. Soon wealthy, he began his political career as a Democrat in 1853 when he was elected to the House of Representatives; in 1859 he moved to the U.S. Senate, carrying with him the support of laborers, for whom he backed a 10-hour day.

A Unionist, he nevertheless supported Jefferson Davis for the Democratic presidential nomination in 1860. After Stephen Douglas won the nomination, Butler supported the pro-South John Breckinridge. After Fort Sumter was fired on in 1861, Butler, a major general in the state militia, supported the Union and fought for it. Relieving Washington, D.C., and repairing rail lines to the city, he and his men then occupied and secured Baltimore. While at Fortress Monroe he devised the term "contraband" for runaway slaves, defining them as enemy property used to make war and thus liable to seizure.

Sent to New Orleans in May 1862 as military governor, Butler prompted a virtual storm of opposition during his brief stay in Louisiana. He hung one man for insulting the American flag, and he issued Order Number 28, which stipulated that a woman who insulted Union soldiers be treated the same "as a woman of the town plying her avocation." This order earned him the name "Beast" and prompted Jefferson Davis, president of the Confederacy, to order that Butler be hanged if captured.[1]

By the end of the war, Butler was a strong supporter of the freedmen and a Radical Republican. Elected to Congress in 1866, he served until 1875. In the House, Butler stirred the anger of conservative Republicans and Democrats in his state and in Congress as he literally waved the bloody shirt of a Confederate, demanding restrictions on the disloyal South. He inspired opposition by his enthusiastic support for Andrew Johnson's impeachment; he was one of the House impeachment prosecutors. His daughter Blanche married Adelbert Ames, senator and governor of Mississippi during Reconstruction.

Butler, breaking with the Republicans over financial and economic issues, ran for office as a Democrat, Greenbacker, and Anti-Monopolist. He was elected governor of Massachusetts in 1882 as a Democrat and was nominated by the Anti-Monopoly party for president in 1884.

Salmon P. Chase (1808–1873)

Despite his presidential ambitions, Salmon Chase had to settle for "attorney general of fugitive slaves,"[2] secretary of the treasury during the Civil War, and Chief Justice of the Supreme Court from 1864 to his death in May 1873.

Educated in New Hampshire and Ohio, Chase graduated from Dartmouth College in 1826. After teaching in the District of Columbia, he was admitted to the bar in 1829. Practicing law in Cincinnati, Chase became well known but stayed out of politics until the 1840s. Interested in the antislavery cause and free speech issues, he worked for the antislavery Liberty and Free-Soil parties. Chase earned a national reputation defending runaway slaves and the title "attorney general of fugitive slaves."

Elected to the Senate by a Free-Soil–Democratic coalition in 1849, Chase was an opponent of the Compromise of 1850, which temporarily settled sectional arguments over slavery's expansion westward and included a tough federal law for the return of fugitive slaves. He also opposed the Kansas-Nebraska Act of 1854, which essentially opened the middle part of the country to slavery. He was also a founder of the Ohio Republican party. When the Democratic state legislature did not reelect him to the Senate, he served as governor. He was reelected to the Senate in 1860, although his real ambition that year (and every four years from 1856 through 1872) was the presidency, a goal his radicalism put beyond his reach.

Chase's appointment by Abraham Lincoln as secretary of the treasury, despite his inexperience in financial matters, put him in charge of many aspects of the nation's wartime economy. He handled the job capably and helped, sometimes reluctantly, in the creation of greenbacks, the national banking system, and an income tax.

A supporter of the Emancipation Proclamation, the Freedmen's Bureau, black suffrage, the use of black troops, and equal rights, Chase periodically "resigned" during disputes with Lincoln. He found his resignation accepted in 1864 during a disagreement over patronage in his department. Lincoln then appointed him chief justice in December 1864.

Chase's Court decided several important cases. In *ex parte Garland* (1867) and *Cummings v. Missouri* (1867) it ruled against loyalty oaths; in both cases, Chase was on the minority side. Chase concurred in *ex parte Milligan* (1866) with the Court's opinion against military trials when civil courts were functioning. In *Hepburn v. Griswold* (1870), the Chief Justice wrote the majority opinion that ruled against the constitutionality of greenbacks, and in the *Legal Tender Cases* (1871), he was in the minority in opposing the Court's overturning of its *Griswold* ruling. Chase wrote the Court's opinion in both *Texas v. White* (1869), which emphasized the permanence of the Union and the states, and *Mississippi v. Johnson* (1867), in which the Court unanimously refused to halt presidential Reconstruction. In *ex parte McCardle* (1868) Chase explained the Court's unanimous decision to accept a lack of jurisdiction, and in the *Slaughterhouse Cases* (1873) he dissented when the Court argued against the use of the Fourteenth Amendment for nonracial discrimination. As chief justice, Chase was the presiding judge in Andrew Johnson's Senate trial.

Chase sought the presidential nomination of the Liberal Republicans in 1872. He died of a stroke in May 1873.

William Pitt Fessenden (1806–1869)

A graduate of Bowdoin College in 1823 at age 17, William Pitt Fessenden was admitted to the bar in 1827. He moved to Portland, Maine and was elected in 1831 to the legislature as an anti-Jacksonian. His father was not only an abolitionist and Liberty party candidate for governor but also a respected attorney, and soon Fessenden was being compared to him. An active Whig, he served one term in Congress (1841–1843) before losing races for the Senate and the House. He served two terms in the Maine legislature.

Elected to the Senate in 1854 with antislavery support, he opposed the expansion of slavery into the territories and delivered his first speech in the Senate against the Kansas-Nebraska Act, which opened the territory to the expansion of slavery. Appointed to the Senate Finance Committee in 1857, he became its chair in 1861 and thus played a major role during the Civil War helping to devise national policy on taxation, the banking system, and greenbacks. He generally supported the policies of Secretary of Treasury Salmon Chase and, in fact, replaced Chase as secretary in 1864. He accepted the appointment as a short-term commitment because of the country's wartime financial problems. Reelected to the Senate, he resigned his cabinet position.

A Moderate Republican, Fessenden nevertheless believed that Reconstruction was the job of Congress, not the president. He served as chairman of the Joint Committee on Reconstruction and supported the Freedmen's Bureau Bill and the Civil Rights Act of 1866; he believed that the Fourteenth Amendment, which he took a leading role in promoting, was sufficient for concluding Reconstruction. He voted against the Tenure of Office Act on principle and against Andrew Johnson's conviction and removal from office because of the harm such a step would have caused the party and the nation. Fessenden explained that it would have been easy to convict Johnson for "general cussedness" but that was not the charge against the president.[3]

Despite being one of the seven Republican recusants, Fessenden was active in the Republican party after Johnson's trial, campaigning for Grant's election that fall. Up for reelection to the Senate, he died in 1869 before Maine's legislature had the chance to decide whether to reelect him.

Ulysses Simpson Grant (1822–1885)

Born in Ohio near the slave South, Ulysses S. Grant overcame numerous failures to become the commander of the Union army during the last years of the Civil War, commander of the army during the first years of Reconstruction, and eighteenth president of the United States. While his Civil War years were marked by triumph, his two terms as president (1869–1877) were noted for widespread corruption, increasing opposition to the continuation of Reconstruction, and a major economic collapse.

Grant's father wanted him to attend West Point, and he did, receiving above-average grades but not revealing significant ability. After graduating in 1843, Grant served 11 years in the army, including service during the Mexican War of 1846–1848. Bored with Western assignments and drinking heavily, he left the army and moved to St. Louis with his wife. Before becoming a storekeeper in Galena, Illinois at his brothers' leather shop, he had little success as a farmer, rent collector, and clerk. Uninterested in politics, he voted Democratic if he voted at all.

The Civil War changed everything. Grant returned to the army as a colonel of the Twenty-first Illinois Volunteer Infantry. Lincoln soon promoted him to brigadier general. From successes in Missouri, Tennessee, and Mississippi in 1861–1863, Grant moved East to command all Union armies in 1864 and, finally, to accept Robert E. Lee's surrender in 1865.

After the war Grant was one of the most popular men in the country, sought out by both Democrats and Republicans for the presidential race of 1868. Before then, however, he traveled the South in late 1865 to provide President Andrew Johnson with information on Southern behavior and attitudes, joined Johnson on his 1866 "swing around the circle," oversaw much of Reconstruction from his position as commander of the army, briefly served as secretary of war when Johnson sought to remove William Stanton in 1867, and moved steadily into the Radical camp.

Grant's presidency was famous for the corruption associated with it, although Grant himself is usually described as honest and well-meaning but politically naïve and inept with poor political judgment. He was devoted to his friends who often took advantage of his trust. In addition, while he did not abandon Reconstruction efforts—using the Enforcement Acts to help break the Ku Klux Klan and using federal troops periodically to support Southern Republican governments under pressure—his commitment to the freedmen and to the Southern Republican party was less than that of the Radicals. Still, his efforts in the South, along with the corruption, helped prompt the Liberal Republican opposition he faced in the 1872 election.

While unsuccessful in his efforts to acquire Santo Domingo, his administration settled the *Alabama* claims over Great Britain's responsibility for the destruction of Union shipping during the Civil War. In response to the role played by Senator Charles Sumner in the former, Grant helped in Sumner's removal as chair of the Senate's Foreign Affairs Committee.

Despite considering a run for a third term in 1876, Grant left office after eight years, criticized but still popular. Bankrupt in the 1880s because of poor investments, he supported his widow after his death from throat cancer with the 1885 publication of his still highly regarded wartime remembrances, *Personal Memoirs of U. S. Grant*.

Horace Greeley (1811–1872)

Horace Greeley was the foremost editor of his time and one of the major reformers of the nineteenth century.

Greeley, who received little formal education, began his career at age 14 as an apprentice to a newspaper publisher in Vermont. At age 20 he moved to New York with $25; three years later he founded a literary magazine, the *New Yorker*. Earning a reputation for articles and commentaries, he edited a variety of publications before founding New York's only Whig newspaper, the *New York Tribune*, in 1841. In it he took stands against the expansion of slavery, for temperance, for Western expansion ("Go west!"),[4] and for industrial development. His only political office was two years in the House of Representatives (1848–1849).

The newspaperman's life was full of controversial and changing positions. During the secession crisis, he favored letting the Southern states secede if a majority of Southerners wished to do so. Once the war began, however, he supported it; still, by 1864 he was ready for peace at any price, and after the war he paid half of Jefferson Davis's bond, a step that cost the *Tribune* half of its subscribers. He supported Lincoln's 1860 election and emancipation; he opposed the renomination of Abraham Lincoln in 1864 but supported him thereafter. He wanted a mild Reconstruction, but he supported Johnson's impeachment. In 1868 Greeley backed Grant's run for the presidency, but in 1872 he ran against him. He ran for the presidency while supporting a single term for the chief executive.

Greeley's controversial and shifting positions went beyond war, race, and politics. He supported communal living, free Western land, freedom of speech, women's rights (except suffrage), temperance, phrenology, and the protective tariff. He opposed the death penalty, land grants to railroads, the exploitation of workers, the expansion of slavery in the territories, and the *Dred Scott* decision, commenting that the Supreme Court's 1857 ruling on black citizenship and Congress's power in the territories was "entitled to just so much moral weight as would be the judgment of a majority of those congregated in any Washington barroom."[5]

Increasingly disenchanted with Reconstruction and Grant's administration, Greeley joined others in the Liberal Republican party in 1872 and received its (and the Democrats') nomination for the presidency. Although he had long opposed the Democrats and held positions different from the party's platform, he ran a vigorous race. Still, he was handily defeated. An easy figure to lampoon—he wore a wide-brimmed hat, disheveled and baggy pants, and a long linen duster with numerous pockets filled with notes he wrote to himself—he was the target of numerous political attacks and cartoons, including some by Thomas Nast, throughout the campaign. With his wife's death the week before his election defeat and loss of control of the *Tribune* the week after, Greeley broke down physically and mentally and died on November 30, 1872.

Oliver Otis Howard (1830–1909)

Oliver Howard served courageously in the Civil War, but his fame came afterward when he was chosen to head the Bureau of Refugees, Freedmen, and Abandoned Lands.

Like William Pitt Fessenden, Howard graduated from Bowdoin College in Maine (1850); he then attended West Point, graduating in 1854. After serving as an ordnance officer and in the Third Seminole War of 1855–1858, Howard returned to West Point, where he taught math until 1861. During the Civil War, he fought in over 20 major engagements, including Antietam and Gettysburg, and was promoted to general. He lost his right arm at Fair Oaks in 1862 but returned to fighting in less than four months. He commanded a wing of William Tecumseh Sherman's army as it marched to the sea.

The Freedmen's Bureau, created in 1865, was headed by Howard throughout its entire existence. An honest man who cared about blacks, saw the value of education, and was a devout Christian, Howard alienated many with his commitment; he was called the Bible general and Yankee Stepfather. Yet his conscientiousness and his faith in God and the power of education helped him carry out a difficult assignment.

Howard founded several black colleges, including Howard University in the District of Columbia (1869) and, in the 1890s, Lincoln Memorial University in Tennessee. After the demise of the Bureau, he helped negotiate the end of the Apache Wars in the Southwest in 1872 and headed one of the Army's eight departments, the Department of the Columbia, during the Nez Percé War later in the decade. After serving as superintendent of West Point in the early 1880s, he served in the army's Department of the East until his retirement in 1894.

Andrew Johnson (1808–1875)

Born in a two-room shack in frontier North Carolina, Andrew Johnson was the child of landless poor whites who worked as tavern servants. Apprenticed at age 14 to a tailor in Raleigh, he began his education memorizing materials provided by a paid reader to the shop. After deserting the apprenticeship and moving to eastern Tennessee, Johnson set up a tailor shop, learned writing and basic math from his wife, and became increasingly involved in politics. After election as alderman and mayor, he won a seat in the state legislature; he then moved to the state senate in 1841. An independent Democrat, he next served in the House of Representatives for ten years and as governor of Tennessee for two terms. In 1857, he reached the U.S. Senate.

The owner of four house slaves, Johnson accepted the Southern racial order but opposed the slave-owning elite's domination of the state, even the parts of Tennessee where there were few slaves and where Johnson lived. When the South seceded in 1860–1861, however, Johnson was the only Southerner in Congress who did not leave the Union with his state. To him, secession was no more than treason. As a result of his views, he was unpopular in much of Tennessee, yet in 1862 Abraham Lincoln chose him as military governor under his Ten Percent Plan for wartime Reconstruction.

As a Southerner who took a stand for the Union, Johnson made a controversial choice for Lincoln's vice-president in 1864. When Lincoln was assassinated in April 1865, many Republicans hoped that the new president shared their views on Reconstruction of the South. Johnson's lenient plan—based in large part on his view that the Southern states had never left the Union and thus were outside of Congress's authority—led to increasing conflicts with the Radical Republicans and even the party's Moderates. In February 1868, the House of Representatives impeached Johnson; in March the Senate tried him on 11 charges. Johnson avoided conviction by one vote, 35–19.

After leaving the White House in 1869, Johnson returned to Tennessee. In 1875 he was once again elected to the Senate; however, he died only a few weeks into his term. He was buried with his head on a copy of the Constitution; the granite marker over him proclaims that "his faith in the people never wavered."[6]

Pinckney Benton Stewart Pinchback (1837–1921)

Born in Macon, Georgia, P. B. S. Pinchback was one of eight children fathered by a white planter (William Pinchback) and a slave (Eliza Stewart) who was freed about the time of his birth. He described himself as a quadroon (one-quarter black). He moved his mother and siblings north and escaped potential reenslavement after his father's death in 1848. Schooled in Cincinnati, Ohio, the young Pinchback went to work at age 12 as a cabin boy on Ohio river canal boats.

In 1862, Pinchback enlisted in the Union army as part of the First Louisiana Volunteers; a captain, he received permission to raise a company of blacks. Complaining about the unequal treatment of black soldiers, he resigned his commission. His effort to raise a company of black cavalry ended when he was not allowed to captain it.

A supporter of Radical Reconstruction in Alabama, the light-skinned Pinchback continued to speak out for black rights. With the start of congressional Reconstruction in 1867, Pinchback moved to New Orleans where he began his political career by organizing the Fourth Ward Republican Club. He also served as a delegate to the state constitutional convention of 1868. An opponent of race-based (rather than merit-based) appointments and of the disenfranchisement of former Confederates, Pinchback was responsible for the inclusion in the new state constitution of an equal rights provision, as well as a public accommodations provision.

While he was owner of the Mississippi River Packet Company and a cotton broker, Pinchback was elected to the state senate in 1868. He served during the governorship of "carpetbagger" Henry Clay Warmoth, who came to distrust him. He also faced a black rival, Lieutenant Governor James Dunn. All three men were competitors for the governor's office in 1872; however, Dunn died under somewhat mysterious circumstances (probably accidental poisoning), and unrest and conflict grew in both the party and the legislature. With Dunn's death and Pinchback's serving as president pro tem of the Senate in 1871, he was next in line for governor. When Warmoth was impeached and convicted in 1872, Pinchback became governor for a month (December 1871–January 1872).

After the U.S. Senate rejected Pinchback's claim to a Senate seat, he kept busy with a variety of other jobs: he served on the state board of education, and he was an internal revenue agent and surveyor of customs in New Orleans. Approaching 50, he was admitted to the bar. He then served as U.S. marshal in New York in the 1890s and practiced law in the District of Columbia in 1900.

A supporter of Booker T. Washington, he was part of the Washington social elite and grandfather of Jean Toomer, a novelist of the Harlem Renaissance.

William Henry Seward (1801–1872)

A leading opponent of slavery in the 1850s, William Henry Seward became one of the country's most successful secretaries of state, serving from 1861 to 1872.

The son of a New York businessman and county judge, Seward graduated from Union College in 1820 and was admitted to the bar in 1822. His first foray into politics in 1830 was successful: he was elected to the state senate as a member of the Anti-Masonic party. In 1838 and 1840, having become a Whig, he was New York's first Whig governor. A reformer, Seward supported a law that required the state to provide fugitive slaves with jury trials and counsel. After a brief return to law, he was elected to the Senate in 1849 and became an adviser to President Zachary Taylor.

Seward's Senate speeches drew attention to his views on slavery. In 1850 he argued that there was a "higher law" above both statute and Constitution; God's law required opposition to the Compromise of 1850 and to the expansion of slavery into the territories. Eight years later, only months after Abraham Lincoln's little-noted comments on "a house divided against itself," Seward warned of an "irrepressible conflict between opposing and enduring forces [slavery and free labor]."[7]

Seward lost the Republican nomination for president in both 1856 (to John C. Fremont) and 1860 (to Lincoln), but Lincoln appointed him secretary of state. Like Edwin Stanton, he initially thought little of Lincoln's capabilities; however, Seward soon changed his mind. His achievements as secretary were numerous. He extracted the United States from the wartime *Trent* Affair, involving the controversial capture of two Confederate agents, and he prevented foreign recognition of the Confederacy. Seward's major Reconstruction-era accomplishments included France's withdrawal from Mexico, the settlement of the *Alabama* claims against Great Britain for its aid to the Confederacy, the purchase of Alaska from Russia, and the acquisition of Midway Island. He failed in his efforts to acquire the Danish West Indies.

Despite angering Radicals with his cooperation with Lincoln (and later Johnson), Seward supported both the Emancipation Proclamation and the Thirteenth Amendment. He stayed in office after Lincoln's death, surviving an attack at his home by an accomplice of John Wilkes Booth, which severely wounded him. Democrats sought his removal from the Johnson cabinet, which he increasingly influenced; at the same time Radicals worried that he was supporting the Democrats. While attempting to modify some of Johnson's vetoes and messages, he generally backed the president and opposed impeachment. His wartime radicalism had ebbed, and he believed that freedmen should not threaten the nation's reunion.

Seward retired in March 1869 when a new Administration took office. He traveled widely and wrote until his death three years later.

Edwin M. Stanton (1814–1869)

Admitted to the bar in 1835, Edwin Stanton moved from Ohio to Pittsburgh in 1847 and developed a national reputation as a trial and corporation attorney (earning at least $50,000 annually by the 1860s). A staunch Unionist opposed to slavery, he was appointed attorney general in December 1860 and urged President James Buchanan to be firm against Southern secession. While doing so, he passed administration information to Congress in the hope of finding a way to avoid destruction of the Union before Abraham Lincoln assumed the presidency.

After a return to private practice, Stanton succeeded Simon Cameron as secretary of war (for an annual salary of $8,000) in January 1862. His tasks were to make a weak department more efficient, organized, and effective as a central military authority; to end corruption associated with the War Department; to control army commanders whose "policies" conflicted with the Administration's; to maintain internal security; and to make the army a fighting force that could win the war. He handled his job capably and successfully, if not without controversy.

A Democrat at the start of the war who had little confidence in Abraham Lincoln's ability, he was soon a Republican and a close friend of the president. He stayed on as secretary after Andrew Johnson became president; with the war over, his job centered on the army's handling of Western Indians and its occupation of and maintenance of order in the defeated South. Increasingly, however, Stanton came into conflict with the new president, because Stanton worried that Johnson's policy was returning disloyal men to power and undermining the army's role in the South. Stanton, although not a Radical, was providing information to the Republicans. He was a supporter of black rights and even black suffrage, and he was increasingly the supporter of Congress, if not the opponent of Johnson. Although Stanton generally kept his views from the public, Democrats sought his removal from the Cabinet. Johnson finally suspended Stanton in 1867, a step Congress refused to accept under the 1867 Tenure of Office Act. When Johnson removed him again, the House impeached the president. Upon the Senate's failure to convict Johnson in May 1868, Stanton resigned.

Ulysses S. Grant appointed Stanton to the Supreme Court in late 1869, but the former secretary of war died of a heart attack three days after his Senate confirmation that December.

Thaddeus Stevens (1792–1868)

Born with a clubfoot and deserted by his father during adolescence, Thaddeus Stevens rose from poverty and was educated because of the efforts of his mother Sarah. A graduate of Dartmouth College, he moved to Pennsylvania in 1815, where he became an iron manufacturer and a lawyer who defended without pay runaway slaves. An opponent of the Fugitive Slave Act of 1850, he believed that slavery in the United States "was the most disgraceful institution that the world had ever witnessed." He also refused to sign a new state constitution that he helped write because it did not provide for black suffrage. He believed that "this is not 'a white man's Government.'"[8]

Elected to the House of Representatives in 1848 as a Whig and Free-Soiler, he was defeated in 1852 but reelected in 1858. With only three other Congressmen, he opposed the Crittenden Resolution, which stated that the Union's goal in the Civil War was only the salvation of the Union. Chairman of the House Ways and Means Committee, he was a critic of Abraham Lincoln, seeing the president as too cautious despite the opportunity provided by the war to spark a revolution. Stevens supported land confiscation and redistribution—in 40-acre plots—to freedmen. He argued that the Southern states were conquered territories and under congressional authority.[9]

The leading Radical in the House, Thaddeus Stevens was a member of the Joint Committee on Reconstruction that evaluated Southern Reconstruction under Andrew Johnson's plan. Increasingly opposed to Johnson's mild treatment of the South, Stevens helped organize the House's impeachment of Johnson.

During Reconstruction, Stevens's personal life was fuel for opponents. His housekeeper Lydia Smith began working for him in 1848; Stevens never married, and rumors were widespread that Smith, 21 years his junior and a mulatto, was his mistress. Such was the picture presented in Thomas Dixon's *The Clansman* (1905) and the film based on his book, *Birth of a Nation* (1915).

Stevens was unwavering when it came to his principles. He is famous for refusing a burial plot because the cemetery was segregated. When, plagued by heart problems, he died only weeks after the Senate failed to convict Johnson, he was buried in an integrated cemetery under an epitaph which he wrote:

> . . . finding other Cemeteries limited as to Race . . . ,
> I have chosen this [one] that I might illustrate in my death
> The Principles which I advocated
> Through a long life:
> EQUALITY OF MAN BEFORE HIS CREATOR.[10]

His state posthumously elected him to another term in the House.

Charles Sumner (1811–1874)

Few men in American history are known as the moral voice of the nation. Charles Sumner was one such man; he stood against slavery and for equality before the law, equal rights, and suffrage for all Americans.

Born in Massachusetts, Sumner studied at Harvard under Justice Joseph Story and, like his father, became a lawyer. A "Conscience Whig," he opposed the Mexican War and the expansion of slavery into the territories. He argued against segregated schools before the Supreme Court, asserting that such institutions had harmful effects. Elected to the U.S. Senate in 1851, he opposed the Kansas-Nebraska Act of 1854, which made possible the expansion of slavery into territory from which it had been previously barred, and he helped formed the Republican party in Massachusetts. In his "Crime Against Kansas" speech on the floor of the Senate in May 1856, he attacked slavery and Southern support for the institution and its spread. As a result, he was caned by Representative Preston Brooks of South Carolina; reelected in 1857, he did not return to the Senate until December 1859 because of his injuries.

For Sumner, defending the Union meant ending slavery because it was "the single cause" of the rebellion.[11] Fully committed to the idea of equality, he supported black testimony in federal courts, equal pay for black troops, and desegregation of streetcars in Washington, D.C., as well as an end to segregated schools and to public discrimination on the basis of race. During the Civil War Sumner supported emancipation as early as October 1861 and equal rights by 1862. He also supported the Wade-Davis bill, Congress's wartime plan for the Reconstruction of the South.

In the battle over Reconstruction authority, Sumner's belief that the Southern states had committed suicide meant that Congress was responsible for their postwar treatment. Unable to achieve the radical Reconstruction he sought, he accepted the Fourteenth Amendment, although it did not include a provision for black suffrage, and the Reconstruction Acts. As Andrew Johnson attempted to undermine even moderate congressional Reconstruction in 1867 and 1868, Sumner voted to convict and remove the president.

As chairman of the Senate Committee on Foreign Relations, Sumner's expansionist views led him to support William Seward's acquisition of Alaska. On the other hand, he opposed Ulysses Grant's plan to annex Santo Domingo, which led to a break with Grant and the president's successful effort to remove Sumner as chair of the committee. By 1871, Sumner supported the Liberal Republican opposition to Grant's reelection.

Although Sumner died in 1874, the Civil Rights Act of 1875, a much diluted version of the bill he long demanded, was passed in large part in his memory. Upon his death even Southerner L.Q.C. Lamar could remark about the South's frequent opponent, "[for him] . . . freedom [was] the natural and indefeasible right of every intelligent being . . ."; ". . . he would tolerate no halfway measures upon a point so vital" as full citizenship for black Americans.[12]

Lyman Trumbull (1813–1896)

One of the Senate's most moderate, respected, and influential members during the Civil War and Reconstruction, Lyman Trumbull was one of many young men during the mid-1800s who moved from teaching to law. After completing college in Connecticut, he taught school in Georgia for three years before being admitted to the bar in 1836. He began his legal practice in the relatively new state of Illinois near St. Louis. He quickly established himself as a community leader and at age 27 was elected to the state legislature as a Democrat. He then served briefly as Illinois's secretary of state.

Returning to his law practice, he won 60 percent of his cases before the state supreme court, although he lost all three of the cases he argued against another young attorney, Abraham Lincoln. Elected to the state supreme court in 1848, he earned the title "Judge," which many people called him until his death.

Trumbull, who ran for the U.S. House and won in 1854, saw slavery as degrading for both slave and master and opposed its expansion into the territories. He argued cases that helped end the legal life of slavery in Illinois, a free state that allowed virtual slavery in the form of black indentureship. Opposed by the Democrats because of his opposition to the expansion of slavery in the Nebraska Territory, Trumbull turned to the Republicans. He opposed Illinois's other Senator—Democrat Stephen Douglas—over the Kansas-Nebraska Act, believing that Congress had full power in a territory until it became a state. He opposed the 1857 Dred Scott decision that denied black citizenship and Congress's power over slavery in the territories. He was also the topic of debate in most of the Lincoln-Douglas debates in 1858 because of charges of inconsistency he leveled against Douglas for the latter's support of both popular sovereignty (which argued that voters, not Congress, had power over slavery in the territories) and the Dred Scott ruling.

Trumbull played a significant role during the Civil War and Reconstruction because of his chairmanship of the Senate Judiciary Committee. Although he opposed talk of black suffrage, he supported the Wade-Davis Bill, abolition of slavery in the District of Columbia, and the use of black troops, and he introduced a rewritten resolution for the Thirteenth Amendment abolishing slavery. Playing the role of middleman between Congress and President Andrew Johnson, he proposed the Freedmen's Bureau Bill and the Civil Rights Act of 1866, which he saw as moderate measures.

Johnson's vetoes of the two bills prompted Trumbull's cooperation with the Radicals; a conservative on race, he nevertheless believed that lives and property should be protected. He supported the Reconstruction Act of 1867 because Southern behavior seemed to offer "no other way of protecting loyal men."[13] He refused to vote for the president's conviction in 1868 and was one of the famous seven Republican recusants. Despite early criticism of his vote, Trumbull continued his career but switched to the Liberal Republicans, supporting women's suffrage and the end of Reconstruction and opposing high tariffs and internal taxes. He spent considerable time after 1868 arguing cases before the Supreme Court (in 1869 representing the government in *ex parte McCardle*, and also representing the Illinois Central Railroad). Retiring after the 1872 election, he returned to his law practice. (Among those who studied at his firm was William Jennings Bryan, who would unsuccessfully run for the presidency three times in the 1890s and early 1900s.) He served as counsel for Samuel Tilden during the latter's presidential fight after the 1876 election. In 1896 he died while considering a switch to the Populist party.

Trumbull's role in Reconstruction is hard to overestimate but also often forgotten. As one biographer notes, "The history of the United States would have been different had Trumbull never entered politics." He did not believe in blacks' political equality, but was proud of citing his role in the addition of the Thirteenth Amendment to the Constitution.

Benjamin Franklin Wade (1800–1878)

Ben Wade's importance to Reconstruction history involved more than his possible ascendancy to the presidency if Andrew Johnson was convicted by the Senate in 1868.

The ninth of 10 children, Wade was educated by his mother and local schools in Massachusetts. After moving to Ohio he worked as a drover, a farmer, and a laborer on the Erie Canal. After teaching for a brief period, he was admitted to the bar (in 1828). Because of his interest in politics, he soon found himself in a variety of political jobs, including local prosecutor, state senator, and judge of the Third Judicial District, before being elected to the U.S. Senate in 1851. He served there until 1869.

Wade's opposition to slavery led to his opposition to the Fugitive Slave Act of 1850, slavery's expansion into the territories, the Kansas-Nebraska Act, and Southern secession. A supporter of Abraham Lincoln's candidacy in 1860, he nevertheless believed him to be too weak and cautious in his handling of the Southern rebels; he supported both a determined prosecution of the war and abolition of slavery. Logically, then, he joined Maryland Representative Henry Winter Davis in proposing a counterplan to Lincoln's Ten Percent Plan, which Lincoln pocket-vetoed. As chairman of the Joint Committee on the Conduct of the War, he viewed any opposition to the war as disloyalty to the Union. As chairman of the Senate Committee on Territories, he argued that the Southern states had become territories through their rebellion, thus bringing them under the authority of Congress.

After supporting Salmon Chase rather than Lincoln in the 1864 battle for the Republican presidential nomination, Wade was hopeful that Andrew Johnson would take the strong hand Lincoln had not. Soon, however, Johnson's mild Reconstruction plans made Wade one of his staunchest foes. When Wade became president pro tem of the Senate in March 1867, he became next in line for the presidency because Johnson had no vice-president. Wade had many enemies because of his views on Reconstruction and financial issues; thus, some Senators who voted not to convict Johnson after his impeachment undoubtedly did so because they feared a Wade presidency.

After losing the Republican nomination for vice-president on Ulysses Grant's 1868 ticket, Wade retired. Never again running for political office, he returned to the practice of law in Ohio.

Notes

1. H. L. Trefousse, *Ben Butler: The South Called Him Beast!* (New York: Twayne, [1957]), 111.

2. William L. Richter, *The ABC-CLIO Companion to American Reconstruction, 1862–1877* (Santa Barbara, Calif.: ABC-CLIO, 1996), 85.

3. Quoted in Lately Thomas [Robert Steele], *The First President Johnson: The Three Lives of the Seventeenth President of the United States of America* (New York: William Morrow, 1968), 593.

4. William Harlan Hale, *Horace Greeley: Voice of the People* (New York: Harper & Row, [1950]), 41.

5. Glyndon G. Van Deusen, *Horace Greeley: Nineteenth-Century Crusader* (Philadelphia: University of Pennsylvania Press, 1953), 220.

6. Thomas, *The First President Johnson,* 635.

7. John M. Taylor, *William H. Seward: Lincoln's Right Hand* (New York: HarperCollins, 1991), 85, 107.

8. Quoted in H. L. Trefousse, *Thaddeus Stevens: Nineteenth-Century Egalitarian* (Chapel Hill: University of North Carolina Press, 1997), 51, 177.

9. Quoted in Patrick W. Riddleberger, *1866: The Critical Year Revisited* (Carbondale: Southern Illinois University Press, 1979), 42.

10. Fawn M. Brodie, *Thaddeus Stevens: Scourge of the South* (New York: W. W. Norton, 1959), 366.

11. David Donald, *Charles Sumner and the Rights of Man* (New York: Knopf, 1970), 34.

12. William M. Cornell, ed., *Charles Sumner: Memoir and Eulogies* (Boston: James H. Earle, 1874), 311, 313.

13. Mark M. Krug, *Lyman Trumbull: Conservative Radical* (New York: A. S. Barnes, 1965), 250.

PRIMARY DOCUMENTS
OF RECONSTRUCTION

Andrew Johnson's Proclamation of Amnesty (May 29, 1865)

While the nation watched and hoped, Andrew Johnson explained to the former Confederate states the steps they needed to follow to be readmitted to the Union. His plan was similar to Lincoln's Ten Percent Plan; it required an oath of present and future loyalty, and it did not demand suffrage for African Americans in the South. Its terms were mild and thus worried Radicals in Congress. Their response to the plan and to how the Southern states carried it out was to delay admission of new Southern congressmen and to investigate conditions in the South.

. . . I, Andrew Johnson, President of the United States, do proclaim and declare that I hereby grant to all persons who have, directly or indirectly, participated in the existing rebellion, except as hereinafter excepted, amnesty and pardon, with restoration of all rights of property, except as to slaves and except in cases where legal proceedings under the laws of the United States providing for the confiscation of property of persons engaged in rebellion have been instituted; but upon the condition, nevertheless, that every such person shall take and subscribe the following oath (or affirmation) and thenceforward keep and maintain said oath inviolate, and which oath shall be registered for permanent preservation and shall be of the tenor and effect following, to wit: I, _____ _____, do solemnly swear (or affirm), in presence of Almighty God, that I will henceforth faithfully support, protect, and defend the Constitution of the United States and the Union of the States thereunder, and that I will in like manner abide by and faithfully support all laws and proclamations which have been made during the existing rebellion with reference to the emancipation of slaves. So help me God.

The following classes of persons are excepted from the benefits of this proclamation:

First. All who are or shall have been pretended civil or diplomatic officers or otherwise domestic or foreign agents of the pretended Confederate government.

Second. All who left judicial stations under the United States to aid the rebellion.

Third. All who shall have been military or naval officers of said pretended Confederate government above the rank of colonel in the army or lieutenant in the navy.

Fourth. All who left seats in the Congress of the United States to aid the rebellion.

Fifth. All who resigned or tendered resignations of their commissions in the Army or Navy of the United States to evade duty in resisting the rebellion.

. . . Thirteenth. All persons who have voluntarily participated in said rebellion and the estimated value of whose taxable property is over $20,000.00.

. . . *Provided,* That special application may be made to the President for pardon by any person belonging to the excepted classes, and such clemency will be liberally extended as may be consistent with the facts of the case and the peace and dignity of the United States.

SOURCE: James D. Richardson, ed., *A Compilation of the Messages and Papers of the Presidents, 1789–1899,* 20 vols. (New York: Bureau of National Literature, 1897), 8:3508–10.

The Radicals and the South (1865)

In this October 20, 1865 letter to Senator Carl Schurz, Charles Sumner reveals some of the Radicals' concerns about Johnson's Reconstruction of the South. Schurz had traveled through the South that summer; his report would soon be before the Senate. Congress would meet in December to decide the fate of the Johnson governments.

. . . I wish you could give me briefly an outline of your impressions [from your tour of the South]. My own convictions are now stronger than ever with regard to our duty. *The rebel States must not be allowed at once to participate in our Government.* This privilege must be postponed. Meanwhile all parties must be prepared for the great changes in their political relations. *There must be delay.* The President does not see this and every step he takes is toward perdition.

Never was the way so clear or the opportunity so great. The President might have given peace to the country and made it a mighty example of justice to mankind. Instead of this consummation, he revives the old Slave Oligarchy, envenomed by the war, and gives it a new lease of terrible power. This Republic cannot be lost; but the President has done very much to lose it. We must work hard to save it. . . .

SOURCE: Harold M. Hyman, ed., *The Radical Republicans and Reconstruction, 1861–1870* (Indianapolis: Bobbs-Merrill, 1967), 292.

Andrew Johnson's Report on Southern Reconstruction

On December 4 and 18, 1865, President Johnson reported to Congress and the Senate, respectively, on the restoration of the former Confederate states under his plan. His reports indicated his satisfaction with the states' carrying out of his terms. Congressional Republicans, however, were not so satisfied (as indicated in the next document and in the later report by the Joint Committee on Reconstruction). The capable, moderate message of December 4 was written by historian George Bancroft.

[Message of December 4]
    . . . It has been my steadfast object to escape from the sway of momentary passions and to derive a healing policy from the fundamental and unchanging principles of the Constitution.
    . . . [T]he true theory is that all pretended acts of secession were from the beginning null and void. The States can not commit treason nor screen the individual citizens who may have committed treason any more than they can make treaties or engage in lawful commerce with any foreign power. . . .
    . . . I have . . . gradually and quietly, and by almost imperceptible steps, sought to restore the rightful energy of the General Government and of the States. To that end provisional governors have been appointed for the States, conventions called, governors elected, legislatures assembled, and Senators and Representatives chosen to the Congress of the United States. At the same time the courts of the United States, as far as could be done, have been re-opened, so that the laws of the United States

may be enforced through their agency. The blockade has been removed and the customs-houses re-established in ports of entry, so that the revenue of the United States may be collected. The Post-Office Department renews its ceaseless activity, and the General Government is thereby enabled to communicate promptly with its officers and agents. The courts bring security to persons and property; the opening of the ports invites the restoration of industry and commerce; the post office renews the facilities of social intercourse and of business. . . .

I know very well that this policy is attended with some risk; that for its success it requires at least the acquiescence of the States which it concerns. . . . But it is a risk that must be taken. In the choice of difficulties it is the smallest risk. . . .

[Message of December 18]

As the result of the measures instituted by the Executive with the view of inducing a resumption of the functions of the States, . . . the people in North Carolina, South Carolina, Georgia, Alabama, Mississippi, Louisiana, Arkansas, and Tennessee have reorganized their respective State governments, and "are yielding obedience to the laws and Government of the United States" with more willingness and greater promptitude than under the circumstances could reasonably have been anticipated. The proposed [Thirteenth] amendment to the Constitution, providing for the abolition of slavery forever within the limits of the country, has been ratified by each one of those States, with the exception of Mississippi, from which no official information has yet been received, and in nearly all of them measures have been adopted or are now pending, to confer upon freedmen the privileges which are essential to their comfort, protection, and security. In Florida and Texas the people are making commendable progress in restoring their State governments, and no doubt is entertained that they will at an early period be in a condition to resume all of their practical relations to the General Government.

In "that portion of the Union lately in rebellion" the aspect of affairs is more promising than, in view of all circumstances, could well have been expected. The people throughout the entire South evince a laudable desire to renew their allegiance to the Government and to repair the devastations of war by a prompt and cheerful return to peaceful pursuits, and abiding faith is entertained that their actions will conform to their professions, and that in acknowledging the supremacy of the Constitution and the laws of the United States their loyalty will be unreservedly given to the Government whose leniency they can not fail to appreciate. . . . [I]n some of the States the demoralizing effects of the war are to be seen in occasional disorders; but these are local in character, not frequent in occurrence, and are rapidly disappearing as the authority of civil law is extended and sustained. Perplexing questions are naturally to be expected from the great and sudden change in the relations between the two races; but systems are gradually developing themselves under which the freedman will receive the protection to which he is justly entitled, and by means of his labor, make himself a useful and independent member of the community in which he has his home.

. . . I am induced to cherish the belief that sectional animosity is surely and rapidly merging itself into a spirit of nationality, and that representation, connected with a properly adjusted system of taxation, will result in a harmonious restoration of the relations of the States to the National Union.

SOURCE: James D. Richardson, ed., *A Compilation of the Messages and Papers of the Presidents, 1789–1899,* 20 vols. (New York: Bureau of National Literature, 1897), 8:3554–56 and 3570–71.

Thaddeus Stevens and the South (December 18, 1865)

When Congress met in December 1865, the southern governments had been restored under Andrew Johnson's plan. Radical leader Thaddeus Stevens explained to the House his view of the "conquered provinces" and how they should be treated.

. . . [I]t is very plain that it requires the action of Congress to enable them to form a State government and send representatives to Congress. Nobody, I believe, pretends that with their old constitution and frames of government they can be permitted to claim their old rights under the Constitution. They have torn their constitutional States into atoms, and built on their foundations fabrics of a totally different character. . . .

. . . The late war between two acknowledged belligerents served their original compacts, and broke all the ties that bound them together. The future condition of the conquered power depends on the will of the conqueror. They must come in as new States or remain as conquered provinces. Congress . . . is the only power that can act in the matter. . . .

Congress alone can do it . . . . Hence a law of Congress must be passed before any new State can be admitted; or any dead ones revived. Until then no member can be lawfully admitted into either House. . . . Congress must create States and declare when they are entitled to be represented. Then each House must judge whether the members presenting themselves from a recognized State possess the requisite qualifications of age, residence, and citizenship; and whether the election and returns are according to law. . . .

It is obvious from all this that the first duty of Congress is to pass a law declaring the condition of these outside or defunct States, and providing proper civil government for them. . . . I know of no arrangement so proper for them as territorial governments. There they can learn the principles of freedom and eat the fruit of foul rebellion. . . . In Territories Congress fixes the qualifications of electors; and I know of no better place nor better occasion for the conquered rebels and the conqueror to practice justice to all men, and accustom themselves to make and to obey equal laws. . . .

But this is not all that we ought to do before inveterate rebels are invited to participate in our legislation. We have turned, or are about to turn, loose four million slaves without a hut to shelter them or a cent in their pockets. The infernal laws of slavery have prevented them from acquiring education, understanding the commonest laws of contract, or of managing the ordinary business of life. This Congress is bound to provide for them until they can take care of themselves. If we do not furnish them with homesteads, and hedge them around with protective laws; if we leave them to the legislation of their late masters, we had better have left them in bondage. . . . If we fail in this great duty now, when we have power, we shall deserve and receive the execration of history and of all future ages.

SOURCE: *Congressional Globe*, 39th Cong., 1st sess., 1865, 72–75.

The Civil Rights Act of 1866

To clarify the status of the freedmen, Congress passed the Civil Rights Act in early 1866. Andrew Johnson's veto of it, after his veto of the bill extending the life of the Freedmen's Bureau, helped create the conflict between him and congressional Republicans that ended in his impeachment two years later. The statute, which was put into permanent form in the first section of the Fourteenth Amendment, provides a definition of American citizenship and of the rights of American citizens.

Be it enacted, . . That all persons born in the United States and not subject to any foreign power, excluding Indians not taxed, are hereby declared to be citizens of the United States; and such citizens, of every race and color, without regard to any previous condition of slavery or involuntary servitude, except as a punishment for crime whereof the party shall have been duly convicted, shall have the same right, in every State and Territory of the United States, to make and enforce contracts, to sue, be parties, and give evidence, to inherit, purchase, lease, sell, hold, and convey real and personal property, and to full and equal benefit of all laws and proceedings for the security of person and property, as is enjoyed by white citizens, and shall be subject to like punishment, pains and penalties, and to none other, any law, statute, ordinance, regulation, or custom, to the contrary notwithstanding.

Sec. 2 . . . Any person who, under color of any law, statute, ordinance, regulation, or custom, shall subject, or cause to be subjected, any inhabitant of any State or Territory to the deprivation of any right secured or protected by this act, or to different punishment, pains, or penalties on account of such person having at any time been held in a condition of slavery or involuntary servitude, except as a punishment for crime whereof the party shall have been duly convicted, or by reason of his color or race, than is prescribed for the punishment of white persons, shall be deemed guilty of a misdemeanor, and, on conviction, shall be punished by fine not exceeding one thousand dollars, or imprisonment not exceeding one year, or both, in the discretion of the court.

Sec. 3 . . . The district courts of the United States . . . shall have, exclusively of the courts of the several States, cognizance of all crimes and offenses committed against the provisions of this act. . . .

SOURCE: Walter L. Fleming, ed., *Documentary History of Reconstruction: Political, Military, Social, Religious, Educational and Industrial, 1965 to the Present Time,* 2 vols. (Cleveland: Arthur H. Clark, 1906–1907), 1:197–200.

The Joint Committee on Reconstruction Reports on the Condition of the Southern States (July 1866)

In December 1865 Congress decided to investigate conditions in the South before it determined whether the men elected by the Southern states should be seated in the House and the Senate. After months of testimony, the Committee concluded that the eleven Southern states were not reconstructed.

. . . A claim for the immediate admission of senators and representatives from the so-called Confederate States has been urged, which seems to your committee not to be founded either in reason or in law, and which cannot be passed without comment. Stated in a few words, it amounts to this: That inasmuch as the lately insurgent States had no right to separate themselves from the Union, they still retain their positions as States, and consequently the people thereof have a right to immediate representation in Congress without the imposition of any conditions whatever; and further, that until such admission Congress has no right to tax them for the support of the government. It has even been contended that until such admission all legislation affecting their interests is, if not unconstitutional, at least unjustifiable and oppressive.

It is believed by your committee that all these propositions are not only wholly untenable, but, if admitted, would tend to the destruction of the government.

It must not be forgotten that the people of these United States, without justification or excuse, rose in insurrection against the United States. . . .

. . . That a government thus outraged had a most perfect right to exact indemnity for the injuries done, and security against the recurrence of such outrage in the future, would seem too clear for dispute. . . .

It is moreover contended . . . that, from the peculiar nature and character of our government, no such right on the part of the conqueror can exist; that from the moment when rebellion lays down its arms and actual hostilities cease, all political rights of rebellious communities are at once restored. . . . If this is indeed true, then is the government of the United States powerless for its own protection, and flagrant rebellion, carried to the extreme of civil war, is a pastime which any State may play at, not only certain that it can lose nothing in any event, but may even be the gainer by defeat. . . .

. . . It is more than idle, it is a mockery, to contend that a people who have thrown off their allegiance, destroyed the local government which bond their States to the Union as members thereof, defied its authority, refused to execute its laws, and abrogated every provision which gave them political rights within the Union, still retain, through all, the perfect and entire right to resume, at their own will and pleasure, all their privileges with the Union, and especially to participate in its government, and to control the conduct of its affairs. . . .

. . . It is the opinion of your comments—

I. That the States lately in rebellion were, at the close of the war, disorganized communities, without civil government, and without constitutions or other forms. . . .

II. That Congress cannot be expected to recognize as valid the election of representatives from disorganized communities. . . .

III. That Congress would not be justified in admitting such communities to a participation in the government of the country without first providing such constitutional or other guarantees as will tend to secure the civil rights of all citizens of the republic; a just equality of representation; protection against crime founded in rebellion and crime; a temporary restoration of the right of suffrage to those who have not actively participated in the efforts to destroy the Union. . . .

We now propose to re-state, as briefly as possible, the general facts and principles applicable to all the States recently in rebellion:

First, the seats of the senators and representatives from the so-called Confederate States became vacant in the year 1861 . . . by the voluntary withdrawal of their incumbents. . . . This was done as a hostile act against the Constitution and government of the United States, with a declared intent to overthrow the same. . . .

Second. The States thus confederated prosecuted their war against the United States to final arbitrament. . . .

Third. Having voluntarily deprived themselves of representation in Congress for the criminal purpose of destroying the federal Union, and having reduced themselves, by the act of levying war, to the condition of public enemies, they have no right to complain of temporary exclusion from Congress; but, on the contrary . . . the burden now rests upon them, before claiming to be reinstated in their former condition, to show that they are qualified to resume federal relations. In order to do this, they must prove that they have established, with the consent of the people, republican forms of government in harmony with the Constitution and laws of the United States, that all hostile purposes have ceased, and should give adequate guarantees against future treason and rebellion. . . .

. . . Fifth. . . . The authority to restore rebels to political power in the federal government can be exercised only with the concurrence of all the departments in which political power is vested. . . .

SOURCE: Joint Committee on Reconstruction, 39th Cong., 1st sess., 1866, S. Rept. 112, x–xxi.

The New Orleans Riot (1866)

The white massacres of blacks in summer 1866 in Memphis and New Orleans raised many concerns in the North about the effectiveness of Andrew Johnson's Reconstruction plan and about white Southerners' willingness to respect black lives and rights. Over 80 people died, all but a half-dozen black. Undoubtedly, the violence in allegedly reconstructed states influenced some Northern voters who went to the polls that fall. Philip H. Sheridan was the military commander, appointed by Andrew Johnson, in Texas and Louisiana. The president later replaced him with the more politically conservative Winfield S. Hancock.

New Orleans, Aug. 1, 1866.

U. S. Grant, General:

You are doubtless aware of the serious riot which occurred in this city on the 30th. A political body styling itself the Convention of 1864, met on the 30th, for, as it is alleged, the purpose of remodelling the present constitution of the State. The leaders were political agitators and revolutionary men, and the action of the convention was liable to produce breaches of the public peace. I had made up my mind to arrest the head men if the proceedings of the convention were calculated to disturb the tranquility of the Department, but I had no cause for action until they committed the overt act. In the mean time official duty called me to Texas, and the Mayor of the city, during my absence, suppressed the convention by the use of the police force, and, in so doing, attacked the members of the convention and a party of two hundred negroes with fire-arms, clubs and knives, in a manner so unnecessary and atrocious as to compel me to say that it was murder. About forty whites and blacks were thus killed, and about one hundred and sixty wounded. Every thing is now quiet, but I deem it best to maintain a military supremacy in the city for a few days, until the affair is fully investigated. I believe the sentiment of the general community is great regret at this unnecessary cruelty, and that the police could have made any arrest they saw fit without sacrificing lives.

P. H. SHERIDAN
Major–General Commanding.

New Orleans, La., August 2, 1866

U. S. Grant, General, Washington, D.C.

The more information I obtain of the affair of the 30th, in this city, the more revolting it becomes. It was no riot; it was an absolute massacre by the police, which was not excelled in murderous cruelty by that of [black Union soldiers at] Fort Pillow [during the war]. It was a murder which the Mayor and police of the city perpetrated without the shadow of a necessity; furthermore, I believe it was premeditated, and every indication points to this. . . . There has been a feeling of insecurity on the part of the people . . . that the safety of life and property does not rest with the civil authorities, but with the military.

P. H. SHERIDAN,
Major–General Commanding.

SOURCE: Harvey Wish, ed., *Reconstruction in the South, 1865–1877: First-Hand Accounts of the American Southland after the Civil War, by Northerners and Southerners* (New York: Farrar, Straus and Giroux, 1965), 52–53.

Thaddeus Stevens Explains the Conflict Between Andrew Johnson and Congress (January 1867)

In early 1867 Radical congressman Thaddeus Stevens proposed a bill to disenfranchise most former Confederates for five years. It failed, but in arguing for it Stevens discussed many of the issues of Reconstruction: disagreements between president and Congress, the power of the traditional Southern white elite, suffrage for the freedmen, and legal and social equality.

. . . . What are the great questions which now divide the nation?. . . .

. . . . To reconstruct the nation, to admit new States, to guaranty republican governments to old States are all legislative acts. The President claims the right to exercise them. Congress denies it and asserts the right to belong to the legislative branch. They have determined that while in their keeping the Constitution shall not be violated with impunity. This I take to be the great question between the President and Congress. He claims the right to reconstruct by his own power. Congress denied him all power in the matter, except those of advice, and has determined to maintain such denial. . . .

Beyond this I do not agree that the "policy" of the parties are defined. To be sure many subordinate items of the policy of each may be easily sketched. The President is for exonerating the conquered rebels from all the expense and damages of the war. . . . He desires that the traitors . . . shall be exempt from further fine, imprisonment, forfeiture, exile, or capital punishment, and be declared entitled to all the rights of loyal citizens. . . .

In opposition . . . , a portion of Congress seems to desire that the conquered belligerent shall, according to the law of nations, pay at least a part of the expenses and damages of the war. . . . A majority of Congress desires that treason shall be made odious. . . .

Congress refuses to treat the States created by him as of any validity, and denied that the old rebel States have any existence which gives them any rights under the Constitution. . . .

. . . . Unless the rebel States, before readmission, should be made republican in spirit, and placed under the guardianship of loyal men, all our blood and treasure will have been spent in vain. . . . Having these States . . . entirely within the power of Congress, it is our duty to take care that no injustice shall remain in their organic laws. Holding them "like clay in the hands of the potter," we must see that no vessel is made for destruction. . . . Possibly with [black Southerners'] aid loyal governments may be established in most of these States. Without it all are sure to be ruled by traitors; and loyal men, black and white, will be oppressed, exiled, or murdered. . . . Have not loyal blacks quite as good a right to choose rulers and make laws as rebel whites? In the second place, it is a necessity in order to protect the loyal white men in the seceded States. The white Union men are in a great minority in each of those States. With them the blacks would act in a body; and it is believed that in each of said States, except one, the two united would form a majority, control the States, and protect themselves. Now they are the victims of daily murder. . . .

Another good reason is, it would insure the ascendancy of the Union [Republican] party. Do you avow the party purpose? Exclaims some horror-stricken demagogue. I do. For I believe, on my conscience, that on the continued ascendancy of that party depends the safety of this great nation. . . . For these, among other reasons, I am for negro suffrage in every rebel State. If it be just, it should not be denied; if it be necessary, it should be adopted; if it be punishment to traitors, they deserve it.

But it will be said, as it has been said, "This is negro equality!" What is negro equality, about which so much is said by knaves, and some of which is believed by men who are not fools? It means, as understood by honest Republicans, just this much, and no more: every man, no matter what his race or color; every earthly being who has an immortal soul, has an equal right to justice, honesty, and fair play with every other man; and the law should secure him those rights. The same law which condemns or acquits an African should condemn or acquit a white man. . . . Such is the law of God and such ought to be the law of man. This doctrine does not mean that a negro shall sit on the same seat or eat at the same table with a white man. That is a matter of taste which every man must decide for himself. The law has nothing to do with it. . . . I know there is between those who are influenced by this cry of "negro equality" and the opinion that there is still danger that the negro will be the smartest, for I never saw even a contraband slave that had not more sense than such men. . . .

SOURCE: *Congressional Globe*, 39th Cong., 2d sess., 1867, 251–53.

First Reconstruction Act (March 2, 1867)

Dissatisfied with Johnson's lenient plan, Republicans in Congress replaced it in early 1867 with a new procedure that put the South under military districts and increased the requirements to include black suffrage and ratification of the Fourteenth Amendment. Thanks to the election of 1866, they had enough votes to override Johnson's veto of the measure, as well as the three succeeding ones which provided clarification and fine tuning.

An Act To Provide the More Efficient Government of the Rebel States.

Whereas no legal State governments or adequate protection for life or property now exists in the rebel States of Virginia, North Carolina, South Carolina, Georgia, Mississippi, Alabama, Louisiana, Florida, Texas, and Arkansas; and whereas it is necessary that peace and good order should be enforced in said State until loyal and republican State governments can be legally established: Therefore,

Be it enacted by the Senate and House of Representatives of the United States of America in Congress assembled, That said rebel States shall be divided into military districts and made subject to military authority of the United States as hereinafter prescribed, and for that purpose Virginia shall constitute the first district; North Carolina and South Carolina the second district; Georgia, Alabama, and Florida, the third district; Mississippi, and Arkansas fourth district; and Louisiana and Texas the fifth district.

Section 2. And be it further enacted, That it shall be the duty of the President to assign to the command of each of said districts an officer of the army, not below the rank of brigadier-general. . . .

Section 3. And be it be further enacted, That it shall be the duty of each officer assigned as aforesaid, to protect all persons in their rights of person and property, to suppress insurrection, disorder, and violence, and to punish, or cause to be punished, all disturbers of the public peace and criminals; and to this end he may allow local civil tribunals to take jurisdiction of and to try offenders, or, when in his judgment it may be necessary for the trial of offenders, he shall have power to organize military commissions or tribunals for that purpose, and all interference under color of the State authority with the exercise of military authority under this act, shall be null and void. . . .

Section 5. And be it further enacted, That when the people of any one of said rebel States shall have formed a constitution of government in conformity with the Constitution of the United States in all respects, framed by a convention of delegates elected by the male citizens of said State, twenty-one years old and upward, of whatever race, color, or previous condition, who have been resident in said State for one year previous to the day of such election, except such as may be disfranchised for participation in the rebellion or for felony at common law, and when such constitution shall provide that the elective franchise shall be enjoyed by all such persons as have the qualifications herein stated for electors of delegates, and when such constitution shall be ratified by a majority of the persons voting on the question of ratification who are qualified as electors for delegates, and when such constitution shall have been submitted to Congress for examination and approval, the Congress shall have approved the same, and when said State, by a vote of its legislature elected under said constitution, shall have adopted the amendment to the Constitution of the United States, proposed by the Thirty-ninth Congress, and known as article fourteen, and when said article shall have become a part of the Constitution of the United States, and said State shall have declared entitled to representation in Congress. . . . *Provided,* That no person excluded from the privilege of holding office by said proposed amendment to the Constitution of the United States, shall be eligible to election as a member of the convention to frame a constitution for any said rebel States, nor shall any such person vote for members of such convention. . . .

SOURCE: Walter L. Fleming, ed., *Documentary History of Reconstruction: Political, Military, Social, Religious, Educational and Industrial, 1965 to the Present Time,* 2 vols. (Cleveland: Arthur H. Clark, 1906–1907), 1:401–3.

Southern Whites and Black Troops (1865)

After the war, the presence in the South of African Americans in uniforms of the Union army was particularly upsetting for whites who were used to unarmed and controlled black slaves. For many Southerners, these troops were representative of the upheaval brought by the war, as this selection from a New Orleans newspaper demonstrates.

Our citizens, who had been accustomed to meet and treat the negroes only as respectful servants, were mortified, pained, and shocked to encounter them in towns and villages, and on the public roads, by scores and hundreds and thousands, wearing Federal uniforms, and bearing bright muskets and gleaming bayonets. They often recognized among them those who had once been their own servants. They were jostled from the sidewalks by dusky guards marching four abreast. They were halted, in rude and sullen tones by negro sentinels, in strong contrast with the kind and fraternal hail of the old sentinels in threadbare gray or dilapidated homespun. The ladies of villages so

guarded, ceased to appear on the streets, and it was with much reluctance that the citizens of the surrounding country went to town on
imperative errands. All felt the quartering of negro guards among them
to be a deliberate, wanton, cruel act of insult and oppression. Their
hearts sickened under what they deemed an outrageous exercise of
tyranny. They would have received white troops, not indeed with
rejoicing, but with kindness, satisfaction and respect; but when they
saw their own slaves, freed, armed, and put on guard over them, they
treated all hope of Federal magnanimity or justice as an idle dream.

SOURCE: Whitelaw Reid, *After the War: A Southern Tour: May 1, 1865, to May 1, 1866*
(Cincinnati: Moore, Wilstach & Baldwin, 1866), 422.

Southern Whites React to Congressional Reconstruction
(1867–1868)

George Browder, a Methodist minister from Kentucky, was one of
millions of Southern whites who found Congress's replacement of
Andrew Johnson's Reconstruction plan to be a horrifying step. His
diary presents his views.

May 1 [1866]—. . . President Johnson is gaining favor rapidly
with conservative men, while the radicals & disorganizers are deserting
him. He has vetoed two egregiously unconstitutional bills, the Freedmen[']s bureau & the Civil Rights. . . . Rebels who hated Andy Johnson
with a perfect hatred now endorse & support him.

March 4 [1867]—This day the new Congress goes into effect. Our
state is not represented at present. The Southern States are not, & the
most extreme, unjust, illiberal, & radical measures prevail in Congress.
The president vetoes, but the [Republican] party is powerful & carry
measures over the veto. The future is dark. . . .

July 4 [1867]—Day once sacred in the annals of freedom. What
strange sights do you behold this day in the Land of Washington &
Patrick Henry? Military law superior to civil authority! News papers
suppressed, courts overthrown, judges removed, citizens imprisoned, property confiscated, elections controlled by military authority. Negroes admitted to suffrage & their masters disfranchised. The
Southern states held as conquered provinces & the public confidence
destroyed! The good people ground down with oppressive taxation,
& nine states not allowed representation in the national council!

Verily the shouts of jubilation that once ring in these states, will be few or feigned to day.

. . . April 14, 1868—Three years ago this day, President Lincoln was assassinated. The excitement of that day is almost repeated now in the trial & impeachment of Andrew Johnson. He will almost surely be expelled for trying to preserve the constitution against radical schemers. The country is in a deplorable state and growing worse. Clouds are darker & denser. . . .

SOURCE: Richard L. Troutman, ed., *The Heavens Are Weeping: The Diaries of George Richard Browder* (Grand Rapids, Mich.: Zondervan Publishing House, 1987), 208, 210–11, 213, 214.

White South Carolinians and Reconstruction

Just a few months after Thaddeus Stevens presented his views of Andrew Johnson, Southern rebels, and black suffrage, a convention of white South Carolinians protested the very things the Radical congressman supported. When compared to Stevens's views, their positions suggest why Reconstruction was such a complex and intense period.

We desire peace for its own sake, for its holy Christian influence, and for the civilization and refinement which spring up in its path. Do the Reconstruction acts of Congress propose to give us this peace? No—they give us war and anarchy, rather. They sow the seeds of discord in our midst and place the best interests of society in the hands of an ignorant mob. They disfranchise the white citizen and enfranchise the newly emancipated slave. The slave of yesterday, who knew no law but the will of the master, is today about to be invested with the control of the government. . . . By the Reconstruction acts of Congress these powers [of suffrage and jury service] are conferred upon the negro—he can make and unmake the Constitution and the laws which he will administer according to the dictates of another or his own caprice.

We are not unfriendly to the negro. . . . In his property, in his life and in his person we are willing that the black man and the white man shall stand together upon the same platform and be shielded by the same equal laws. . . . But upon a question involving such great and momentous issues we should be untrue to ourselves and unfair to our opponents were we to withhold the frank and full expression of our opinions. We, therefore, feeling the responsibility of the subject and the occasion, enter our most solemn protest against the policy of investing the negro with political rights. The black man is what God and nature and circumstances have made him. That he is not fit to be invested with these important rights may be no fault of his. But the fact is patent to all that the negro is utterly unfitted to exercise the highest functions of the citizens. The government of the country should not be permitted to pass from the hands of the white man into the hands of the negro. The enforcement of the Reconstruction acts by military power under the guise of negro voters and negro conventions cannot lawfully reestablish civil government in South Carolina. It may for a time hold us in subjection to a quasi-civil government backed by military force, but it can do no more. As citizens of the United States we should not consent to live under negro supremacy, nor should we acquiesce in negro equality. Not for ourselves only, but on behalf of the Anglo-Saxon race and blood in this country, do we protest against this subversion of the great social law, whereby an ignorant and depraved race is placed in power and influence above the virtuous, the educated and the refined. By these acts of Congress intelligence and virtue are put under foot, while ignorance and vice are lifted into power.

SOURCE: Walter L. Fleming, ed., *Documentary History of Reconstruction: Political, Military, Social, Religious, Educational and Industrial, 1965 to the Present Time*, 2 vols. (Cleveland: Arthur H. Clark, 1906–1907), 1:424–26.

Southern White Frustrations Were Wide-Ranging (1870)

Southern whites were plagued not just by the loss of slave labor but by hard economic times. Even poor whites, many of whom had opposed slavery as a tool that helped keep the large planters in power, were struggling against the realities of postwar economic and political conditions. Alabaman William F. Samford explained their situation.

We are to-day . . . poorer than we were on the day of the surrender of the Southern armies. Our carpetbaggers and nigger scalawags have imposed intolerable taxation upon a people already crushed to the earth. A deep and sullen gloom is settling upon the Southern heart. Twelve cents for cotton and twenty-five cents for bacon and one hundred and fifty dollars and rations for a negro idler;—for laborer he will not be—winds up the plantation business. Why don't we raise hogs and make our own bacon? Why a hog has no more chance to live among these thieving negro farmers than a juney bug in a gang of puddle ducks. . . . All this great staple producing region is essentially upon the sheriff's block.

SOURCE: Walter L. Fleming, ed., *Documentary History of Reconstruction: Political, Military, Social, Religious, Educational and Industrial, 1965 to the Present Time*, 2 vols. (Cleveland: Arthur H. Clark, 1906–1907), 2:310.

The Reconstruction Amendments to the Constitution

Probably the most important achievements of Reconstruction were the three constitutional amendments ending slavery, defining citizenship, limiting the power of states in dealing with rights, and eliminating race as a criterion for voting. Each amendment stipulates the national government's power to enforce its provisions.

Amendment 13 (1865)

Section 1. Neither slavery nor involuntary servitude, except as a punishment for crime whereof the party shall have been duly convicted, shall exist within the United States, or any place subject to their jurisdiction.

Section 2. Congress shall have power to enforce this article by appropriate legislation.

Amendment 14 (1868)

Section 1. All persons born or naturalized in the United States, and subject to the jurisdiction thereof, are citizens of the United States and of the State wherein they reside. No State shall make or enforce any law which shall abridge the privileges and immunities of citizens of the United States; nor shall any State deprive any person of life, liberty, or property, without due process of law; nor deny to any person within its jurisdiction the equal protection of the laws.

Section 2. . . . [W]hen the right to vote at any election for the choice of Electors for President and Vice President of the United States, Representatives in Congress, the executive and judicial officers of a State, or the members of the legislature thereof, is denied to any of the male inhabitants of such State, being twenty-one years of age and citizens of the United States, or in any way abridged, except for participation in rebellion, or other crime, the basis of representation therein shall be reduced in the proportion which the number of such male citizens shall bear to the whole number of male citizens twenty-one years of age in such State.

Section 3. No person shall be a Senator or Representative in Congress or Elector of President and Vice President, or hold any office, civil or military, under the United States, or under any State, who, having previously taken an oath, as a member of Congress, or as an officer of the United States, or as a member of any State legislature, or as an executive or judicial officer of any State, to support the Constitution of the United States, shall have engaged in insurrection or rebellion against the same, or given aid and comfort to the enemies thereof. Congress may, by a vote of two-thirds of each house, remove such a disability.

Section 4. The validity of the public debt of the United States . . . shall not be questioned. But neither the United States nor any State shall assume or pay any debt or obligation incurred in aid of insurrection or rebellion against the United States, or any claim for the loss or emancipation of any slave; but all such debts, obligations, and claims shall be held illegal and void.

Section 5. The Congress shall have the power to enforce, by appropriate legislation, the provisions of this article.

Amendment 15 (1870)

Section 1. The right of citizens of the United States to vote shall not be denied or abridged by the United States or by any State on account of race, color, or previous condition of servitude.

Section 2. The Congress shall have power to enforce this article by appropriate legislation.

Articles of Impeachment against Andrew Johnson
(March 3, 1868)

The House of Representatives voted on February 24, 1868, to impeach Andrew Johnson. On March 3 it determined the charges on which the Senate would try him. The first nine focused on Johnson's alleged violations of the Tenure of Office Act and of the rider to the Army Appropriations Act and involved his firing of Edwin Stanton and his appointment of Lorenzo Thomas as secretary of war. According to the Tenure of Office Act, both the firing and the appointment required Senate approval, which Johnson did not have. The final articles emphasized Johnson's deportment as president and his political battles with Congress.

Article I

That said Andrew Johnson, President of the United States, on the twenty-first day of February, in the year of our Lord one thousand eight hundred and sixty-eight, at Washington, in the District of Columbia, unmindful of the high duties of his office, of his oath of office, and of the requirement of the Constitution that he should take care that the laws be faithfully executed, did lawfully, and in the violation of the Constitution and laws of the United States issue and order in writing for the removal of Edwin M. Stanton from the office of Secretary for the Department of War, said Edwin M. Stanton having been theretofore duly appointed and commissioned, by and with the advice and consent of the Senate of the United States, as such Secretary . . . and said Senate . . . having refused to concur in said suspension, whereby and by force of the provisions of act entitled "An act regulating the tenure of certain civil officers," . . . said Edwin M. Stanton did forthwith resume the functions of his office. . . . [Johnson then] contrary to the said Senate then and there being in session . . . remove[d] said Edwin M. Stanton from the office of Secretary for the Department of War . . . [Thus] Andrew Johnson, President of the United States, did then and there commit and was guilty of a high misdemeanor in office.

Article II

[C]ontrary to the provisions of an act entitled "An act regulating the tenure of certain civil offices," passed March 2, 1867, without the advice and consent of the Senate of the United States, and said Senate then and there being in session, and without authority of law, did, with intent to violate the Constitution of the United States and the act aforesaid, issue and deliver to one Lorenzo Thomas a letter of authority. . . .

Article X

That said Andrew Johnson, President of the United States, unmindful of the high duties of his office and the dignity and proprieties thereof, and of the harmony and courtesies which ought to exist and be maintained between the legislative branches of the Government of the United States, designing and intending to set aside the rightful authority and powers of Congress, did attempt to bring into disgrace, ridicule, hatred, contempt, and reproach the Congress of the United States and the several branches thereof, to impair and destroy the regard and respect of all the good people of the United States for the Congress and legislative power thereof, (which all officers of the Government ought inviolably to preserve and maintain,) and to excite the odium and resentment of all the good people of the United States against Congress and the laws by it duly and constitutionally enacted. . . . [He did] make and deliver with a loud voice certain intemperate, inflammatory, and scandalous harangues, and did therein utter loud threats and bitter menaces as well against Congress as the laws of the United States duly enacted thereby, amid the cries, jeers, and laughter of the multitudes then assembled and within hearing. . . . [He said,] "We have witnessed in one department of the Government every endeavor to prevent the restoration of peace, harmony, and Union. . . . We have seen this Congress pretend to be for the Union, when its every step and act tended to perpetuate disunion and make a disruption of the States inevitable." . . .

[Johnson's comments] . . . are peculiarly indecent and unbecoming in the Chief Magistrate of the United States, by means whereof said Andrew Johnson has brought the high office of the President of the United States into contempt, ridicule, and disgrace, to the great scandal of all good citizens. . . .

Article XI

That said Andrew Johnson, President of the United States, unmindful of the high duties of his office and of his oath of office, and in disregard of the Constitution and laws of the United States, did heretofore, to wit: on the 18th day of August, 1866, at the city of Washington, in the District of Columbia, by public speech, declare and affirm in substance that the Thirty-Ninth Congress of the United States was not a Congress of the United States authorized by the Constitution to exercise legislative power under the same; but, on the contrary, was a Congress of only part of the States, thereby denying and intending to deny that the legislation of said Congress was valid or obligatory upon him . . . except in so far as he saw fit to approve the same, and also thereby denying and intending to deny the power of the said Thirty-Ninth Congress to propose amendments to the Constitution. . . .

SOURCE: Walter L. Fleming, ed., *Documentary History of Reconstruction: Political, Military, Social, Religious, Educational and Industrial, 1965 to the Present Time,* 2 vols. (Cleveland: Arthur H. Clark, 1906–1907), 1:458–70.

Amnesty Act of 1872

One of the major complaints from Southern whites during Reconstruction—and by many historians thereafter—involved the restricted political rights of former Confederates. The Fourteenth Amendment barred them from office holding until Congress removed the "disability." Only four years after the amendment became part of the Constitution, Congress removed the restriction from all but a few men. This step helped the Democratic Redeemers regain power in their states.

Be it enacted . . . ,That all political disabilities imposed by the third section of the fourteenth article of amendments to the Constitution of the United States are hereby removed from all persons whomsoever, except Senators and Representatives of the thirty-sixth and thirty-seventh Congresses, officers in the judicial, military, and naval service of the United States, heads of departments, and foreign ministers of the United States.

SOURCE: Walter L. Fleming, ed., *Documentary History of Reconstruction: Political, Military, Social, Religious, Educational and Industrial, 1965 to the Present Time,* 2 vols. (Cleveland: Arthur H. Clark, 1906–1907), 2:431.

Charles Sumner and Black Rights

In an 1871 letter encouraging members of an African American convention in South Carolina, Charles Sumner reviewed many of the discriminations faced by Southern blacks only a few years after the Civil War. He also revealed his deeply held commitment to equal rights and much of the reasoning behind his proposed civil rights act.

In the first place, you must at all times insist upon your rights, and here I mean not only those already accepted, but others still denied, all of which are contained in equality before the law. Wherever the law supplies a rule, there you must insist upon equal rights. How much remains to be obtained you know too well in the experiences of life. Can a respectable colored citizen travel on steamboats or railways, or public conveyances generally, without insult on account of race? Let Lieutenant-Governor [James] Dunn, of Louisiana, describe his journey from New Orleans to Washington. Shut out from proper accommodations in the cars, the doors of the Senate Chamber opened to him, and there he found the equality a railroad conductor had denied. Let our excellent friend, Frederick Douglass, relate his melancholy experience, when, within sight of the executive mansion, he was thrust back from the dinner-table where his brother commissioners were already seated. . . . I might ask the same question with regard to hotels, and even common schools. An hotel is a legal institution, and so is a common school. As such each must be for the equal benefit of all. Now, can there be any exclusion from either on account of color? It is not enough to provide separate accommodations for colored citizens even if in all respects as good as those of other persons. . . . The discrimination is an insult and a hindrance, and a bar, which not only destroys comfort and prevents equality, but weakens all other rights. The right to vote will have new security when your equal rights in public conveyances, hotels, and common schools, is at last established; but here you must insist for yourselves by speech, by petition, and by vote. . . .

Among the cardinal objects in education which must be insisted on must be equality, side by side with the alphabet. It is in vain to teach equality if you do not practise [*sic*] it. It is in vain to recite the great words of the Declaration of Independence if you do not make them a living reality. What is lesson without example? As all are equal at the ballot-box, so must all be equal at the common school. Equality in the common school is the preparation for equality at the ballot-box; therefore do I put this among the essentials of education.

SOURCE: Walter L. Fleming, ed., *Documentary History of Reconstruction: Political, Military, Social, Religious, Educational and Industrial, 1965 to the Present Time*, 2 vols. (Cleveland: Arthur H. Clark, 1906–1907), 2:292–93.

The Civil Rights Act of 1875 (March 1, 1875)

Proposed by Charles Sumner, the Civil Rights Act, passed after his death in 1874, was the last major legislative achievement of Reconstruction. Its coverage of private acts of discrimination faced significant opposition throughout the country in 1875 and was attacked by the Supreme Court in 1883 as not being based on the Fourteenth Amendment, which, the Court said, restricted official state action only.

An Act To Protect All Citizens in their Civil and Legal Rights

Whereas, it is essential to just government we recognize the equality of all men before the law, and hold that it is the duty of government in dealings with the people to mete out equal and exact justice to all, of whatever nativity, race, color, or persuasion, religious or political; and it being the appropriate object of legislation to enact great fundamental principles into law: Therefore,

Be it enacted that the Senate and the House of Representatives of the United States of America in Congress assembled, That all persons within the jurisdiction of the United States shall be entitled to the full and equal enjoyment of the accommodations, advantages, facilities, and privileges of inns, public conveyances on land or water, theaters, and other places of public amusement; subject only to the conditions and limitations established by law, and applicable alike to citizens of every race and color, regardless of any previous condition of servitude.

Section 2: That any person who shall violate the foregoing section by denying to any citizen, except for reasons by law applicable to citizens of every race and color, and regardless any previous condition of servitude, the full enjoyment of any of the accommodations, advantages, facilities, or privileges in said section enumerated, or by aiding or inciting such denial, shall for every such offence, forfeit and pay the sum of five hundred dollars to the person aggrieved thereby. . . .

SOURCE: Walter L. Fleming, ed., *Documentary History of Reconstruction: Political, Military, Social, Religious, Educational and Industrial, 1965 to the Present Time,* 2 vols. (Cleveland: Arthur H. Clark, 1906–1907), 295–97.

The South and the Civil Rights Act of 1875

As Congress considered Sumner's proposed bill guaranteeing blacks' access to privately owned public accommodations, the *Atlanta News* called Southern whites to arms.

Let there be White Leagues formed in every town, village and hamlet of the South, and let us organize for the greater struggle which seems inevitable. If the October elections which are to be held at the North are favorable to the radicals, the time will have arrived for us to prepare for the very worse. The radicalism of the republican party must be met by the radicalism of white men. We have no war to make against the United States Government, but against the republican party our hate must be unquenchable, our war interminable and merciless. Fast fleeting away is the day of wordy protest and ideal appeals to the magnanimity of the republican party. By brute force they are endeavoring to force us into acquiescence to their hideous programme. We have submitted long enough to indignities, and it is time to meet brute-force with brute-force. Every Southern state shall swarm with White Leagues, and we should stand ready to act the moment Grant signs the civil-rights bill. It will not do to wait till radicalism has fettered us to the car of social equality before we make an effort to resist it. The signing of the bill will be a declaration of war against the southern whites. It is our duty to ourselves, it is the duty of our children, it is our duty to the white race whose prowess subdued the wilderness of this continent, whose civilization filled it with cities and towns and villages, whose mind gave it power and grandeur, and whose labor imparted to it prosperity, and whose love made peace and happiness dwell within its homes, to take the gage of battle the moment it is thrown down. If the white democrats of the North are men, they will not stand idly by and see us borne down by northern radicals and half-barbarous negroes. But no matter what they may do, it is time for us to organize. We have been temporizing long enough. Let northern radicals understand that military supervision of southern elections and the civil-rights bill mean war, that war means bloodshed, and that we are terribly in earnest, and even they, fanatical as they are, may retrace their steps before it is too late.

SOURCE: *Atlanta News*, September 10, 1874.

More Southerners React to the Civil Rights Act of 1875

When Congress was considering Charles Sumner's public accommodations bill, many in the South were willing to stand up and do battle against the Radicals over the prospect of "negro equality." Among those upset were some of the Southern white "scalawags" who had no interest in black rights. In *The Cotton States in the Spring and Summer of 1875*, Charles Nordhoff explained their views.

The agitation of the Congressional Civil Rights Bill did more, even, than Republican misrule, to give the State [Alabama] to the Democrats last fall [1874]. Alabama has a large population of whites—small farmers, collected in the northern counties, where there are but few negroes. These people, who had pretty generally voted the Republican ticket in previous years, became alarmed at the prospect of "negro equality," . . . and last fall, under the representations of adroit and earnest Democratic speakers, they went over in a body to the Democratic party. The passage of the absurd Civil Rights Bill by Congress has probably allayed their fears, because it is now found to be substantially a dead letter. The blacks do not attempt to have it enforced, and it is probable that its only use will be to annoy the Republicans in Northern States, and in regions South where there are but few negroes, and where the Democrats propose to arouse the race prejudice by hiring negroes to board at hotels, and to otherwise insist on the enforcement of the law during the next year's canvass.

SOURCE: Charles Nordhoff, *The Cotton States in the Spring and Summer of 1875* (New York: B. Franklin, 1876), 91.

Black Southerners View Freedom

During the 1930s, men and women long freed from slavery shared their memories with interviewers. In the following excerpts, African Americans in their late eighties look back 60 years to explain what freedom was like in the South of the 1860s.

After freedom a heap of people say they was going to name theirselves over. They named theirselves big names, then went roaming round like wild, hunting cities. They changed up so it was hard to tell who or where anybody was. Heap of 'em died, and you didn't know when you hear about it if he was your folks hardly. Some of the names was Abraham, and some called theirselves Lincum. Any big name 'cepting the master's name. It was the fashion. . . .

*　　*　　*

. . . We knowed freedom was on us, but we didn't know what was to come with it. We thought we was going to get rich like the white folks. We thought we was going to be richer than the white folk, 'cause we was stronger and knowed how to work, and the whites didn't, and they didn't have us to work for them any more. But it didn't turn out that way. We soon found out that freedom could make folks proud, but it didn't make 'em rich. . . .

        *   *   *

Seemed like they thought if they be free they never have no work to do and just have plenty to eat and wear. They found it different, and when it was cold they had no wood like they been used to. I don't believe in the colored race being slaves 'cause of the color, but the war didn't make times much better for a long time. Some of them had a worse time. So many soon got sick and died. They died of consumption and fevers and nearly froze. Some ner 'bout starved. The colored folks just scattered 'bout hunting work after the war.

        *   *   *

I went down to Augusta to the Freedmen's Bureau to see if 'twas true we was free. I reckon there was over a hundred people there. The man got up and stated to the people: "You all is just as free as I am. You ain't got no mistress and no master. Work when you want." On Sunday morning Old Master sent the house gal and tell us to all come to the house.

He said: "What I want to send for you all is to tell you that you are free. You have the privilege to go anywhere you want, but I don't want none of you to leave me now. I wants you-all to stay right with me. If you stay, you must sign to it."

I asked him: "What you want me to sign for? I is free."

"That will hold me to my word and hold you to your word," he say.

All my folks sign it, but I wouldn't sign. Master call me up and say, " Willis, why wouldn't you sign? I say: "If I is already free, I don't need to sign no paper. If I was working for you and doing for you before I got free, I can do it still, if you wants me to stay with you."

        *   *   *

I worked for Massa 'bout four years after freedom, 'cause he forced me to, said he couldn't 'ford to let me go. His place was near ruint, the fences burnt, and the house would have been, but it was rock. . . . When the war was over, Massa come home and says, "You son of a gun, you's supposed to be free, but you ain't, 'cause I ain't gwine give you freedom." So I goes on working for him till I gits the chance to steal a hoss from him. . . . I don't know as I 'spected nothing from freedom, but they turned us out like a bunch of stray dogs, no homes, no clothing, no nothing, not 'nough food to last us one meal.

        *   *   *

The owners went to work and notified the slaves that they were free. After the proclamation was issued, the government had agents who went all through the country to see if the slaves had been freed. They would see how the proclamation was being carried out. They would ask them, "How are you working?" "You are free." "What are you getting?" Some of them would say, "I ain't getting nothing now." Well, the agent would take that up, and they would have that owner up before the government. Maybe he would be working people for a year and giving them nothing before they found him out.

SOURCE: B. A. Botkin, ed., *Lay My Burden Down: A Folk History of Slavery* (Chicago: University of Chicago Press, 1945), 66, 223–24, 240–41, 243, 246–47, 249.

A Freedman Views Slavery and Freedom

Soon after the Civil War ended, a freedman from Tennessee who had moved to Ohio wrote his former owner. He explained the benefits of freedom, the horrors of slavery, and the debt the South owed its former slaves.

Dayton, Ohio, August 7, 1865.

To My Old Master, Col. P. H. Anderson
Big Spring, Tennessee
Sir:

I got your letter and was glad to find that you had not forgotten Jourdon, and that you wanted me to come back and live with you again, promising to do better for me than anyone else can. I have often felt uneasy about you. I thought the Yankees would have hung you long before this for harboring Rebs they found at your house. . . . Although you shot at me twice before I left you, I did not want to hear of your being hurt, and am glad you are still living. It would do me good to go back to the dear old home again and see Miss May and Miss Martha and Allen, Esther, Green, and Lee. Give my love to them all, and tell them I hope we will meet in the better world, if not in this. . . .

I want to know particularly what the good chance is you proposed to give me. I am doing tolerably well here; I get $25 a month, with victuals and clothing; have a comfortable home for Mandy (the folks here call her Mrs. Anderson), and the children Milly, Jane and Grundy, go to school and are learning well; the teacher says Grundy has a head for a preacher. They go to Sunday-School, and Mandy and me attend church regularly. We are kindly treated; sometimes we overhear others saying, "Them colored people were slaves" down in Tennessee. The children feel hurt when they hear such remarks, but I tell them it was no disgrace in Tennessee to belong to Col. Anderson. Many darkies would have been proud, as I used to was, to call you master. Now, if you will write and say what wages you will give me, I will be better able to decide whether it would be to my advantage to move back again.

. . . Mandy says she would be afraid to go back without some proof that you are sincerely disposed to treat us justly and kindly—and we have concluded to trust your sincerity by asking you to send us our wages for the time we served you. This will make us forget and forgive old s[c]ores, and rely on your justice and friendship in the future. I served you faithfully for thirty-two years, and Mandy twenty years. At $25 a month for me, and $2 a week for Mandy, our earnings would amount to $11,680. Add to this the interest for the time our wages has been kept back and deduct what you paid for our clothing and three doctor's visits to me, and pulling a tooth for Mandy, and the balance will show what we are in justice entitled to. Please send the money by Adams Express, in care of V. Winters, esq., Dayton, Ohio. . . . Here I draw my wages every Saturday night, but in Tennessee there was never any pay day for the negroes any more than for the horses and cows. Surely there will be a day of reckoning for those who defraud the laborer of his hire.

In answering this letter please state if there would be any safety for my Milly and Jane, who are now grown up and both good looking girls. You know how it was with poor Matilda and Catherine. I would rather stay here and starve and die if it comes to that than have my girls brought to shame by the violence and wickedness of their young masters. You will also please state if there has been any schools opened for the colored children in your neighborhood, the great desire of my life now is to give my children an education, and have them form virtuous habits.

From you old servant,
Jourdon Anderson.

P.S.—Say howdy to George Cater, and thank him for taking the pistol from you when you were shooting at me.

SOURCE: *New York Tribune*, August 22, 1865.

A Southern White Views the Freedmen

Caleb G. Forshey, a Southern white who had supported secession, shared his views on the Freedmen's Bureau and the freedmen with the Joint Committee on Reconstruction on March 28, 1866.

. . . *Question:* What is your opinion as to the necessity and advantages of the Freedmen's Bureau, or an agency of that kind, in Texas?

Answer: My opinion is that it is not needed; my opinion is stronger than that—that the effect of it is to irritate, if nothing else. . . . [E]xcept where the Freedmen's Bureau had interfered, or rather encouraged troubles, such as little complaints, especially between negro and negro, the negro's disposition was very good, and they had generally gone to work, a vast majority of them with their former masters . . . The impression in Texas at present is that negroes under the influence of the Freedmen's Bureau do worse than without it.

I want to state that I believe all former owners of negroes are the friends of negroes; and that the antagonism paraded in the papers of the north does not exist at all. . . .

. . . I think freedom is very unfortunate for the negro; I think it is sad; his present helpless condition touches my heart more than anything else I ever contemplated, and I think that is the common sentiment of our slaveholders. . . .

. . . [M]y judgment is that the highest condition the black race has ever reached or can reach, is one where he is provided for by a master race. That is the result of a great deal of scientific investigation and observation of the negro character by me ever since I was a man . . . The negro will not take care of his offspring unless required to do it, as compared with the whites. The little children will die; they do die, and hence the necessity of very rigorous regulations on our plantations which we have adopted in our nursery system.

Another cause is that there is no continence among the negroes. . . .

. . . [P]erhaps nine-tenths of our people, believe that the distinctions between the races should not be broken down by any such community of interests in the management of the affairs of the State. I think there is a very common sentiment that the negro, even with education, has not a mind capable of appreciating the political institutions of the country to such an extent as would make him a good associate for the white man in the administration of the government. . . .

SOURCE: The Report of the Committees of the House of Representatives Made during the First Session, Thirty-Ninth Congress, 1865–1866, vol. 2 (Washington, D.C.: Government Printing Office, 1866), 129–32.

The South and Abolition (1866)

J.D.B. DeBow, editor of *DeBow's Review,* reveals some of the impact of abolition on both Southern whites and Southern blacks. He also reveals white concerns about the recovery of the Southern agricultural economy and the changing work patterns of blacks. His comments suggest some of the reasons for the development of sharecropping.

If we can get the same amount of labor from the same persons [negroes], there is no doubt of the result in respect to *economy.* Whether the same amount of labor can be obtained, it is too soon yet to decide. We must allow one summer to pass first. They are working now very well on the plantations . . . The negro women are not disposed to field work as they formerly were, and I think there will be less work from them in the future than there has been in the past. The men are rather inclined to get their wives in[to] other employment, and I think that will be the constant tendency, just as it is with the whites. Therefore, the real number of agricultural laborers will be reduced. I have no idea the efficiency of those who work will be increased. If we can only keep up their efficiency to the standard before the war, it will be better for the south, without doubt, upon the mere money question, because it is cheaper to hire the negro than to own him. Now a plantation can be worked without any outlay of capital by hiring the negro and hiring the plantation.

SOURCE: Walter L. Fleming, *Documentary History of Reconstruction: Political, Military, Social, Religious, Educational and Industrial, 1965 to the Present Time,* 2 vols. (Cleveland: Arthur H. Clark, 1906–1907), 300.

A Southerner Struggles after the War

On February 12, 1867, W. Gilmore Simms wrote a friend in Charleston, South Carolina. In it he reveals that life in the South during the 1860s involved more than decisions made in Washington about suffrage and office holding.

I trust you & yours are well. I am not. My head aches while I write, and my heart is not free from its aches also. Everything is dark here before us. We are all dreadfully anxious about our future—not about the political but the physical condition of the country. Nobody but our politicians cares a straw about reconstruction. The terror before our people is physical misery, privation, want, hunger, starvation. . . .

SOURCE: James P. Shenton, ed., *The Reconstruction: A Documentary History of the South after the War, 1865–1877* (New York: G. P. Putnam's Sons, 1963), 114.

Southern Feelings about the Radicals

Like many Southerners, the *Planters' Banner* of Louisiana celebrated the death of Radical Thaddeus Stevens. Its August 15, 1868 edition demonstrated the anger which many felt toward the leading congressional Reconstructionists:

THAD. STEVENS IS DEAD.—The prayers of the righteous have at last removed the congressional curse! May old Brownlow, Butler, and all such political monsters, soon follow the example of their illustrious predecessor! May his new iron-works wean him from earth, and the fires of his new furnaces never go out! The devil will get on a big "bender" now. With Thad. Stevens in his cabinet and Butler in Washington, he can manage things in both kingdoms to his liking. Lucky Devil!

SOURCE: House Misc. Doc. no. 154, 41st Cong., 2d sess., 1870, 544.

A Southern Scalawag Discusses Race and Civil Rights

Not all Southern whites opposed steps for the benefit of freedmen's rights, but they were in the small minority. Among them was an Alabama scalawag, Charles Hays, who served as a Republican in Congress from 1869 to 1877.

I am very well aware sir, that in taking the step I do I shall receive the censure of those who sit and worship in the temples of a dead past, forgetful of the great events which have been indelibly recorded upon the pages of our country's history within the last decade. I am aware, sir, that the hate of the ignorant and the scorn of the untutored will be invoked against me. All these things are sources of profound regret; but they shall not deter me from the faithful discharge and sacred observance of a duty which God, reason, and conscience tell me is right.

Coming from the far South, being once the owner of a large number of slaves, thoroughly conversant with their history in the past and present, I feel that I have some idea of what should be accorded them now. Set free by the strong arm of Federal power, cut adrift upon the cold charities of an inhuman world in ignorance and penury that they did not bring upon themselves, struggling against adverse winds and storms of hate . . . the colored race have set an example that fairly entitles them to the plaudit of "Well done, ye good and faithful servants."

The discussion of this question of "civil rights" has brought about a state of feeling in the South which is to be deplored. . . . Newspapers, politicians, demagogues, and inciters of sectional hate have preached to the white masses of the South that Congress was upon the verge of enacting a law enforcing "social equality" and blotting out the lines between knowledge and ignorance. . . .

The appeal is made that such an underlying antipathy exists between the races as will render this law dangerous to be passed. I believe no such twaddle. Thousands of the most intelligent men of the South were born and raised upon the old plantations. Childhood's earlier days were passed listening to the lullaby song of the negro nurse, and budding manhood found them surrounded by slave association. Was there prejudice then? Was cry against "social equality" raised then? Never, sir; but now that they are free and receiving the enlightenments of education, for the first time the fact is discovered that the negro, who molded our fortunes, built our railroads, erected our palatial mansions, and toiled for our bred, is a curse upon the face of the earth, and not entitled to the protection of society.

Sir, for one, as a southern man, I feel a debt of gratitude to them. . . . [During the war they] protected our defenseless homes, and fed our destitute widows and starving children. In that hour of bondage and slavery they proved to me and mine, and now it lies in my power to pay the debt, the instincts of honor tell me to do it willingly and cheerfully, "as best becomes a man."

No possible harm can come to the white man by the passage of this law. . . . Has not southern men associated with them for ages? Has any great conflict arisen heretofore? . . . .

. . . [Social equality] is the cry of the old-time office-holder and cod-fish aristocrat, who uses the negro now as he once did the poor white man—to make capital of. . . . If . . . any one is responsible for the present state of affairs it is the southern democracy themselves, who would not listen to reason [about the Thirteenth, Fourteenth, and Fifteenth Amendments], but rushed blindly on in the wonted paths of prejudice and hate.

SOURCE: *Congressional Record*, 43d Cong., 1st sess., 1874, 1096–97.

Sharecropping: A Solution Gone Awry

Sharecropping began during Reconstruction. It satisfied the freedmen's desire for land and independence and the landowners' desire for laborers at a time when capital was scarce. The system became increasingly exploitative, making it hard for many sharecroppers to get out of the debt that their contracts committed them to pay. As explained by D. Augustus Straker in *The New South Investigated* (1888), there were many angles in sharecropping that undermined the system.

At the close of the war, added to the renting of small farms to the colored man by whites, to be paid in certain proportions of the crop, was the system of making advances to this class of farmers of such necessary farming utensils and necessities for food and clothing, as would enable them to produce said crop. This system in its incipiency had nothing in its intent discommendable, but it afterwards grew into the strongest engine of power, political and civil, as turned against the colored laborer and the poor white. The profit to be delivered from such an occupation, in which total ignorance had to compete with panoplied intelligence, soon caused numerous small merchants . . . to set up small stores on every plantation cultivated. In most instances the merchant was also landlord, and in this combination commenced a system of usury, unrivalled by the Jews of Lombardy in ancient times. The poor, ignorant colored and white man, renting small farms and relying on the merchant for advances to make his crop, were and still are compelled to pay the exorbitant interest, frequently of fifty per cent and not unusually of seventy or ninety per cent. A coat which cost the merchant one dollar, was frequently sold for two; a pound of meat that cost six cents, was sold for twelve; a hat which cost fifty cents, was sold for $1.50; so likewise shoes and other things. . . . I have seen colored men who, having a large family, rent a small farm and take advances for a year to make a crop, and at the end of said year, after paying such debts to the merchant as were incurred in making said crop, [do] not have money enough to buy a suit of clothing for any one of the family. I have also seen the taking of all the crop by the merchant, and also, the horse or mule and other chattels which were given as collateral security for the debt in making a crop in one year. And, added to this, was the practice of either refusing to sell lands to the colored farmer, or, when contracting to do so, cheating him in the end by some artifice or design.

SOURCE: D. Augustus Straker, *The New South Investigated* (Detroit: Ferguson Printing, 1888), 87–89.

Frederick Douglass and Black Rights (April 1865)

Speaking to the Massachusetts Anti-Slavery Society, black abolitionist Frederick Douglass presented arguments in favor of black suffrage. In doing so, he also argued for letting the freedman prove his ability without restrictions or aids.

I have had but one idea for the last three years to present to the American people, and the phraseology in which I clothe it is the old abolition phraseology. I am for the "immediate, unconditional, and universal" enfranchisement of the black man, in every State in the Union. [Loud applause.] Without this, his liberty is a mockery; without this, you might as well almost retain the old name of slavery for his condition; for in fact, if he is not the slave of the individual master, he is the slave of society, and holds his liberty as a privilege, not as a right. He is at the mercy of the mob, and has no means of protecting himself.

It may be objected, however, that this pressing of the Negro's right to suffrage is premature. Let us have slavery abolished, it may be said, let us have labor organized, and then, in the natural course of events, the right of suffrage will be extended to the Negro. I do not agree with this. . . . This is the hour. Our streets are in mourning, tears are falling at every fireside, and under the chastisement of this Rebellion we have almost come up to the point of conceding this great, this all-important right of suffrage. I fear that if we fail to do it now, if abolitionists fail to press it now, we may not see, for centuries to come, the same disposition that exists at this moment. [Applause.] Hence, I say, now is the time to press this right.

It may be asked, "Why do you want it? Some men have got along very well without it. Women have not this right." Shall we justify one wrong by another? This is a sufficient answer. Shall we at this moment justify the deprivation of the Negro of the right to vote, because some one else is deprived of that privilege? I hold that women, as well as men, have the right to vote [applause], and my heart and my voice go with the movement to extend suffrage to woman; but that question rests upon another basis than that on which our right rests. We may be asked . . . why we want it. I will tell you why we want it. We want it because it is our *right,* first of all. No class of men can, without insulting their own nature, be content with any deprivation of their rights. We want it again, as a means for educating our race. . . . If nothing is expected of a people, that people will find it difficult to contradict that expectation. By depriving us of suffrage, you affirm our incapacity to form an intelligent judgment respecting public men and public measures; you declare before the world that we are unfit to exercise the elective franchise, and by this means lead us to undervalue ourselves. . . . Again, I want the elective franchise, for one, as a colored man, because ours is a peculiar government, based upon a peculiar idea, and that idea is universal suffrage. If I were in a monarchical government, or an autocratic or aristocratic government . . . , there would be no special stigma resting upon me, because I did not exercise the elective franchise. . . . [B]ut here where universal suffrage is the rule, where that is the fundamental idea of the Government, to rule it out is to make us an exception, to brand us with the stigma of inferiority, and to invite to our heads the missiles of those about us; therefore, I want the franchise for the black man. . . .

. . . What I ask for the Negro is not benevolence, not pity, not sympathy, but simple *justice.* [Applause.] The American people have always been anxious to know what they shall do with us. . . . Everybody has asked the question, and they learned to ask it early of the abolitionists, "what shall we do with the Negro?" I have had but one answer from the beginning. Do nothing with us! Your doing with us has already played the mischief with us. Do nothing with us! If the apples will not remain on the tree of their own strength, if they are wormeaten at the core, if they are early ripe and disposed to fall, let them fall! . . . And if the Negro cannot stand on his own legs, let him fall also. All I ask is, give him a chance to stand on his own legs! Let him alone! If you see him on his way to school, let him alone, don't disturb him! If you see him going to the dinner-table at a hotel, let him go! If you see him going to the ballot-box, let him alone, don't disturb him! [Applause.] If you see him going into a workshop, just let him alone,—your interference is doing him a positive injury.... Let him fall if he cannot stand alone! ...If you will only untie his hands, and give him a chance, I think he will live. He will work as readily for himself as the white man....

SOURCE: Philip S. Foner, *The Life and Writings of Frederick Douglass* (New York: International Publishers, 1950), 158–65.

White Southerners Seek Immigrants (1866)

Frustrated by the adjustments required by free black labor and certain that freedmen would not work as efficiently and cooperatively as they did as slaves, Southern states sought alternative sources of population and production. Although their efforts generally proved ineffective—few immigrants were willing to work in the conditions they found in the South—they tried various methods of recruitment, as this South Carolina law from late 1866 indicates.

I.   Be it enacted by the Senate and House of Representatives ..., That for the purpose of encouraging, promoting and protecting European immigration to and in this State, the sum of ten thousand dollars be appropriated. . . .

II.   That the Governor ... shall appoint a Commissioner of Immigration, who shall open an office ... in Charleston, to perform such duties as may appertain to his office. . . .

III.   That it shall be the duty of said Commissioner of Immigration to advertise in all the gazettes of the State for lands for sale ... [and made available to immigrants].

IV.   That the said Commissioner shall periodically publish, advertise and cause to be distributed in the Northern and European ports and states, descriptive lists of such lands as have been registered and offered for sale, together with this Act, and a statement of such advantages as this State offers in soil, climate, productions, social improvements, etc., to the industrious, orderly and frugal European immigrant.

SOURCE: Walter L. Fleming, ed., *Documentary History of Reconstruction: Political, Military, Social, Religious, Educational and Industrial, 1965 to the Present Time,* 2 vols. (Cleveland: Arthur H. Clark, 1906–1907), 299–300.

Mississippi's Black Codes (1865)

Mississippi's Black Codes were not only the first in the South but also among the most restrictive. While they provided for a variety of rights and protections, they also limited freedmen's civil and criminal rights and restrained them economically.

Sec. 1. [of Mississippi's 1865 laws] Be it enacted, . . . that all freedmen, free negroes, and mulattoes may sue and be sued, implead and be impleaded, in all the courts of law and equality of this State, and may acquire personal property . . . by descent or purchase, and may dispose of the same in the same manner and to the same extent that white people may. . . .

Sect. 3. . . . All freedmen, free negroes, or mulattoes who do now and have here before lived and cohabited together as husband and wife shall be taken and held in law as legally married, and the issue shall be taken and held as legitimate for all purposes: that it shall not be lawful for any freedman, free negro, or mulatto to intermarry with any white person. . . .

Sect. 4. . . . In addition to cases in which freedmen, free negroes, and mulattoes are now by law competent witnesses, freedmen, free negroes, or mulattoes shall be competent in civil cases, when a party or parties to the suit, either plaintiff or plaintiffs, defendant or defendants, and a white person or white persons, is or are the opposing party or parties, plaintiff or plaintiffs, defendant or defendants. . . .

Sect. 7. . . . Every civil officer shall, and every person may, arrest and carry back to his or her legal employer any freedman, free negro, or mulatto who shall have quit the service of his or her employer before the expiration of his or her term of service without good cause. . . .

Sect. 9. . . . If any person shall persuade or attempt to persuade, entice, or cause any freedman, free negro, or mulatto to desert from the legal employment of any person before the expiration of his or her term of service, or shall knowingly employ any such deserting freedman, free negro, or mulatto, or shall knowingly give or sell to any deserting freedman, free negro, or mulatto, any food, raiment, or other thing, he or she shall be guilty of a misdemeanor. . . .

Sec. 2. [of Mississippi's 1865 vagrancy law] . . . All freedmen, free negroes and mulattoes in this State, over the age of eighteen years, found on the second Monday in January, 1866, or thereafter, with no lawful employment or business, or found unlawfully assembling themselves together, either in the day or night time, and all white persons so assembled themselves with freedmen, free negroes or mulattoes, or usually associating with freedmen, free negroes or mulattoes, on terms of equality, or living in adultery or fornication with a freed woman, free negro or mulatto, shall be deemed vagrants. . . .

Sec. 7. . . . If any freedman, free negro, or mulatto shall fail or refused to pay any tax levied according to the provisions of the sixth section of this act, it shall be prima facie evidence of vagrancy, and it shall be the duty of the sheriff to arrest such freedman, negro, or mulatto or such person refusing or neglecting to pay such tax, and proceed at once to hire for the shortest time such delinquent tax-payer to any who will paid the said tax, with accruing costs, giving preference to the employer, if there be one.

Sec. 1. [of Mississippi's 1865 penal laws] Be it enacted, . . . That no freedman, free negro or mulatto, not in the military service of the United States government, and not licensed so to do by the board of police of his or her county, shall keep or carry firearms of any kind, or any ammunition, dirk or bowie knife. . . .

Sec. 2. . . . Any freedman, free negro, or mulatto committing riots, affrays, trespasses, malicious mischief, cruel treatment to animals, seditious speeches, insulting gestures, language, or acts, or assaults on any person, disturbance of the peace, exercising the function of a minister of the Gospel without a license from some regularly organized church, vending spirituous or intoxicating liquors, or committing any other misdemeanor, the punishment of which is not specifically provided by the law, shall, upon conviction thereof in the county court, be fined not less than ten dollars, and not more than one hundred dollars, and may be imprisoned at the discretion of the court, not exceeding thirty days. . . .

SOURCE: Walter L. Fleming, ed., *Documentary Collection of Reconstruction: Political, Military, Social, Religious, Educational and Industrial, 1965 to the Present Time*, 2 vols. (Cleveland: Arthur H. Clark, 1906–1907), 286–90.

Violence Against "Union Men" and Freedmen

By the late 1860s violence was widespread throughout the South. A state such as Texas, which was on the frontier and suffered from insufficient law enforcement in general, paid a heavy price. This

June 30, 1868 report details some of the dangers of the Reconstruction period for Republicans, white and black.

We have been challenged to produce cases of Union men and
freedmen being persecuted for their loyalty. We now do so: Judge Black
was a Republican; he was murdered in 1867, in Uvaldi county, by a
rebel. Milton Biggs was a Union man, and had been appointed County
Judge of Blanco county; he was murdered, 1867, while plowing in this
field, before he could qualify. Judge Christian, a loyal man, of Bell
county, was pursued into Missouri, and murdered by a party of rebels.
Mr. Wade and seven other gentlemen were killed in Lamar county, last
year, for their Unionism. Four men were recently murdered in the
county of Hunt, and six in Bell county, for their loyalty. Within the present month, the County Judge and the District Clerk of Hunt county
have been driven from their homes, and compelled to fly their lives,
because of their unyielding attachment to the Government. Hundreds
of loyal men, to our knowledge, are, at this time, forsaking their homes
in Texas, fleeing from the assassin—forced away by rebel intolerance.
And we here put it to record, that Honorable members of this Convention are to-day exiles from their friends, and dare not return to their
families, for the only reason that they will not forswear their principles.

Now, whilst it remains true that the Union men of Texas constitute
a very small proportion of the white population, and whilst it is true
that they are being killed by the rebels, it is impossible to escape the
conclusion that they are killed for their Unionism. In other words, if
they were rebels they would be killed.

And when we come to examine the persecutions suffered by the
freed people, the mass of testimony is so overwhelming that no man of
candor can for a moment question the statement that they are, in very
many parts of the State, wantonly maltreated and slain, simply because
they are free, and claim to exercise the rights of freedmen. Some months
ago, in Panola county, a party of whites rode up on a cabin wherein
some freed people were dancing, and deliberately fired upon them,
killing four, one woman and seriously wounding several others. In
1867, in DeWitt county, a white man met a freedman riding, and asked
him what he was going to do with the whip he had in his hand, and on
being answered, "Nothing," shot the freedman, killing him instantly. In
the county of Fort Bend, last year, a white man was riding through

town, and seeing a negro man standing on the steps of the office of the Freedman's Bureau, he drew his revolver and shot him dead. The criminal had never seen or spoken to the freedman before. In Newton county, 1867, a white man met a colored man driving a team; the former made the freedman get out of his wagon, and then shot him seven times in cold blood. In Fort Bend county, same year, the freed people were holding a fair to procure funds to finish their church, and while they were singing a hymn two white men rode by and fired their pistols into the church. In October, 1867, a white man was traveling in Grayson county and met a freedman; after passing him a few yards, he turned and fired upon him, hitting him in the back. The freedman died in a few hours; he had not spoken a word to the murderer; he had never seen him before. But a few days ago a party of white men assaulted the family of an unoffending freedman in Falls county, killing one and dangerously wounding another freedman. In the same county, a few weeks ago, two armed white men, in open day, went to he house of a colored man, and without any provocation murdered him. Soon after this a white man, in the same neighborhood, rode up to two freedmen, and, without any known cause, shot one of them dead and fired at the other. Last week the colored Registrar in Burleson county was found murdered; and in January last the colored Registrar of Milam county was called to his door at night and shot. And so the bloody story runs.

We mention some minor outrages. In April last, a party of white men visited the cabins of two quiet industrious freedmen in Freestone county, captured one of them and took him to the woods to murder him; he, however, escaped, being fired at several times and received one wound. In that and adjoining countries the whites are driving the freedmen from their homes and from their crops, some of whom are in this city to-day, fugitives, from rebel violence. In the county of Marion bands of armed whites are traversing the county, forcibly robbing the freedmen of their arms, and committing other outrages upon them. Last week a colored woman was whipped in Parker county by a white man; and some time ago, in another county, a white man cut off the ears of a freedwoman. It is openly proclaimed by many of the perpetrators of these wrongs that their object is to compel the negroes to give up loyal leagues, and to get satisfaction out of them for supporting Yankees . . .

SOURCE: James P. Shenton, ed., *The Reconstruction: A Documentary History of the South after the War: 1865–1877* (New York: G. P. Putnam's Sons, 1963), 130–31.

The Ku Klux Klan's Principles

The Ku Klux Klan was one of many organizations in the South in the 1860s and 1870s that used violence and intimidation to remove African Americans and white Republicans from political, economic, and social influence. According to KKK members, their organization sought to protect the South and its long traditions of white rule. The Klan was formed in Pulaski, Tennessee, in 1866 by six young Confederate veterans seeking amusement. Their organization adopted a mysterious name and rituals and relied on secrecy, including identification of members to achieve the latter, and to be in tune with the popularity of masquerading. Not until 1867–1868, when the following precepts were written, did the organization expand throughout the South and resort to increasing violence. The "Interrogations" indicate the group's political stance against Republican Reconstruction, national involvement in the Southern states, and black rights.

Creed

We, the Order of the * * * , reverentially acknowledge the majesty and supremacy of the Divine Being, and recognize the goodness and providence of the same. And we recognize our relation to the United States Government, the supremacy of the Constitution, the Constitutional Laws thereof, and the Union of States thereunder.

Characters and Objects of the Order

This is an institution of Chivalry, Humanity, Mercy, and Patriotism; embodying in its genius and its principles all that is chivalric in conduct, noble in sentiment, generous in manhood, and patriotic in purpose; its peculiar objects being

First: To protect the weak, the innocent, and the defenseless, from the indignities, wrongs, and outrages of the lawless, the violent, and the brutal; to relieve the injured and oppressed; to succor the suffering and unfortunate, and especially the widows or orphans of Confederate soldiers.

Second: To protect and defend the Constitution of the United States, and all laws passed in conformity thereto, and to protect the States and the people thereof from all invasion from any source whatever.

Third: To aid and assist in the execution of all constitutional laws, and to protect the people from unlawful seizure, and from trial except by their peers in conformity to the laws of the land.

Interrogations to be asked

. . . 2d. Are you now, or have you ever been, a member of the Radical Republican party, or either of the organizations known as the "Loyal League" and the "Grand Army of the Republic?"

3d. Are you opposed to the principles and policy of the Radical party, and to the Loyal League, and the Grand Army of the Republic, so far as you are informed of the character and purposes of those organizations?

4th. Did you belong to the Federal army during the late war, and fight against the South during the existence of the same?

5th. Are you opposed to negro equality, both social and political?

6th. Are you in favor of a white man's government in this country?

7th. Are you in favor of Constitutional liberty, and a Government of equitable laws instead of a Government of violence and oppression?

8th. Are you in favor of maintaining the Constitutional rights of the South?

9th. Are you in favor of the re-enfranchisement and emancipation of the white men of the South, and the restitution of the Southern people to all their rights, alike proprietary, civil, and political?

10th. Do you believe in the inalienable right of self-preservation of the people against the exercise of arbitrary and unlicensed power?

SOURCE: Walter L. Fleming, *Documentary History of Reconstruction: Political, Military, Social, Religious, Educational and Industrial, 1965 to the Present Time,* 2 vols. (Cleveland: Arthur H. Clark, 1906–1907), 347–49.

Carpetbaggers in Louisiana

Northerners in the South quickly became suspect; they were tied to the era's corruption, often deservedly so. The view of them as exploitative outsiders—an interpretation supported by many early historians—helped Democrats win sufficient votes to redeem their states. Two Republicans—B. F. Joubert, a quadroon, and S. W. Scott, a former Army officer—explain the Southern perception of the carpetbagger.

Joubert:

. . . What we call a carpet-bagger is a man who comes here . . . to occupy public position, and make the best of it, and then leave the State where he has made his money . . . There is Mr. Conway, superintendent of education. His wife is very often away, and they do not keep house. That is the reason they call them carpet-baggers; they do not bring their families here . . . The Southern people have been deceived a great deal and taken in by strangers . . . The northern people who come here prejudice the blacks even against me and my class of people. They call me an aristocrat, and put into the heads of the black people that I am an aristocrat. They will associate with the negro, because they want to use him and get his vote; but as soon as they get his vote they don't care about him. They want to make money out of him and get a position . . .

Scott:

. . . I understand the use of the term carpet-bagger, as it is used by the respectable citizens of the State of Louisiana, to mean northern men who come here expressly for political purposes, and excite the animosity of the colored class against their old masters for the purpose of receiving their votes and obtaining office. These men locate themselves in different portions of the State, and fill any place they can get, without any reference to the location where they are supposed to reside, and, and it is generally believed, obtain these offices for the purpose of robbing the people, having no intention of remaining here after the time when they shall stop making money through their official positions . . . I have traveled extensively through the South—through nearly every parish of the State of Louisiana. I am what is termed by many a carpet-bagger; but I have never yet seen the place where I have been better treated or received than in the South, by the old families and residents here.

SOURCE: House Misc. Doc. No. 211, 42d Cong., 2d sess., 1872, 454, 478.

Republican Governments in the South (April 1874)

Southern Republican governments faced charges of corruption and wastefulness. Some of the charges were legitimate; others were the result of Southern Democrats' opposing new services and their costs. Black newspapers printed this explanation of South Carolina's financial record in the early 1870s. It was written by F. L. Cardozo. The son of a Jewish father and free black woman, Cardozo began his education in Charleston, South Carolina and completed it at the University of Glasgow. A wartime minister, he became secretary of state in South Carolina.

. . . The State having been organized on a free basis necessarily created a large number of officers, and, therefore, a large amount of salaries. We are not ashamed of the fact that our appropriation for schools in 1872–73 is four times greater than in 1859–60. Ignorance was the corner-stone of slavery, and essential to its perpetuity. . . .

Now in every hamlet and village in our state, "the schoolmaster is abroad."

In 1857 the number of scholars attending the free schools was only 19,356, while in 1873 the number of scholars attending the schools was 85, 753 (of which 37, 218 were white, 46, 535 colored).

It will be observed that there were no appropriations for the State Lunatic Asylum and Penitentiary in 1859–60. The Lunatic Asylum was then supported by the friends of its wealthy inmates and the counties, but in 1872–73 . . . the State assumed its support and made liberal appropriations for its unfortunate patients.

The erection of the Penitentiary was not begun until after the war, and there was, therefore, no appropriation for it in 1859–60.

. . . There was no appropriation in 1859–60 for a colored State Orphan Home. The colored orphans that were then uncared for were free, but their parents, when living, were heavily taxed to support white orphans, while their own children, after their death, were neglected. . . .

It is . . . a fact that the present system of taxation, like that of almost all civilized countries, is based chiefly upon real estate. In the days of slavery before the war it was not so. Taxes were levied by the large planters, who absolutely controlled the State, upon trade, professions, free colored persons, a mere nominal *per capita* tax upon slaves, and upon the lands assessed at one-third their true value.

The method of taxing land enabled the planters to acquire and retain large and uncultivated tracts of land, and thus form that most dangerous of all oligarchies—a landed aristocracy.

. . . It is stated that "the committees have received large sums as compensation for reporting favorably on private bills." Whatever corruption may exist in the Legislature is to be attributed to the Democrats as well as the Republicans. They never hesitate to offer bribes when they have a private bill to pass. Bur corruption existed long before the advent of the Republican party of this State into power, only it was carried on then with the artistic skill of more experienced operators, and not easily seen.

. . . The Republicans admit the existence of evils among them. They acknowledge they have committed mistakes and errors in the past which they deeply regret. But those mistakes and errors are being daily corrected, and they see no necessity whatever to resort to the desperate remedies asked for by the convention of the so-called tax-payers. . . .

In this work the difficulties under which they have labored have been naturally great, and have been increased ten-fold by the determined hostility and opposition of the Democratic party ever since reconstruction. . . .

SOURCE: *New National Era*, April 16, 1874.

Rutherford Hayes and the South (1876)

Rutherford B. Hayes's election to the presidency came after a special commission of congressmen, senators, and Supreme Court justices decided that the disputed electoral votes of Florida, Louisiana, and South Carolina (as well as one vote from Oregon) should go to him rather than Democrat Samuel Tilden. Whether Southern Democrats had been promised the abandonment of support for Republican governments in the South has been the cause of much historical debate. Hayes's inaugural address, delivered on March 5, 1877, indicates that, regardless of any "deal" to assure his election, he was committed to Southern home rule rather than further reconstruction.

. . . The people of those [Southern] States are still impoverished, and the inestimable blessing of wise, honest, and peaceful local self-government is not fully enjoyed. . . . [I]t must not be forgotten that only a local government which recognizes and maintains inviolate the rights of all is a true self-government.

. . . [I]t must be a government which guards the interests of both races carefully and equally. . . .

. . . The question we have to consider for the immediate welfare of those States of the Union is the question of government or no government; of social order and all the peaceful industries and the happiness that belong to it, or a return to barbarism. . . .

. . . [W]hile in duty bound and fully determined to protect the rights of all by every constitutional means at the disposal of my Administration, I am sincerely anxious to use every legitimate influence in favor of honest and efficient local *self*-government as the true resource of those States for the promotion of the contentment and prosperity of their citizens. . . .

Let me assure my countrymen of the Southern States that it is my earnest desire to regard and promote their truest interests—the interests of the white and of the colored people both and equally—and to put forth my best efforts in behalf of a civil policy which will forever wipe out in our political affairs the color line and the distinction between North and South, to the end that we may have not merely a united North or a united South, but a united country. . . .

[The nation's goal should be] . . . a union depending not upon the constraint of force, but upon the loving devotion of a free people. . . .

SOURCE: James D. Richardson, *A Compilation of the Messages and Papers of the Presidents,* vol. 10 (New York: Bureau of National Literature, 1897), 10:4395–96, 4399.

ANNOTATED BIBLIOGRAPHY

Abbott, Richard H. *Cobbler in Congress: The Life of Henry Wilson, 1812–1875.* Lexington: University of Kentucky Press, 1972.

Argues that Wilson, called a Radical in his day, had a "penchant for seeking the middle way" (262).

Anderson, Eric, and Alfred A. Moss Jr., eds. *The Facts of Reconstruction: Essays in Honor of John Hope Franklin.* Baton Rouge: Louisiana State University Press, 1991.

Essays cover a wide range of topics and emphasize historical debates.

Ayers, Edward L. *Vengeance and Justice: Crime and Punishment in the 19th-Century American South.* New York: Oxford University Press, 1984.

Part two provides an analysis of Southern whites' thinking about law and race during Reconstruction and the late 1800s.

Bardaglio, Peter W. *Reconstructing the Household: Families, Sex, and the Law in the Nineteenth-Century South.* Chapel Hill: University of North Carolina Press, 1995.

Looks at how the Civil War changed Southern families by ending the "linchpin" (xiv) of slavery; traditional structures of household authority, as well as the larger Southern society, saw "an unprecedented intrusion of the state" (xvi).

Barney, William L. *The Civil War and Reconstruction: A Student's Companion.* New York: Oxford, 2001.

The most recent encyclopedia; easy to read, with many illustrations and photographs.

Beale, Howard K. *The Critical Year: A Study of Andrew Johnson and Reconstruction.* New York: Harcourt, Brace, 1930.

Presents congressional Reconstruction as "harsh and unwise" (vii).

Belz, Herman. *Reconstructing the Union: Theory and Policy during the Civil War.* Ithaca, N.Y.: Cornell University Press, 1969.

An excellent study of Congress's wartime Reconstruction views and steps.

Benedict, Michael Les. *A Compromise of Principle: Congressional Republicans and Reconstruction, 1863–1869.* New York: Norton, 1974.

Republicans compromised rather than united in opposition to the policies of Abraham Lincoln. Benedict provides almost 60 pages of lists related to party, policy, and voting among Congressmen.

———. *The Impeachment and Trial of Andrew Johnson.* New York: W. W. Norton, 1973.

Argues that the Republicans, divided over impeachment, were guided by views on such economic issues as the currency and tariffs, as well as by views on race, the South, and Johnson.

Boles, John B. *Black Southerners, 1619–1869.* Lexington: University Press of Kentucky, 1983.

Readable, well-paced look at African American history to readmission of the Southern states as a result of their completing congressional Reconstruction.

Botkin, B. A., ed. *Lay My Burden Down: A Folk History of Slavery.* Chicago: University of Chicago Press, 1945.

Slaves' often-emotional perspectives on their experiences and treatment; includes insightful descriptions of emancipation and the early struggles of freedmen.

Bowen, David Warren. *Andrew Johnson and the Negro.* Knoxville: University of Tennessee Press, 1989.

Analyzes Johnson's racial attitudes in the context of his times and argues that these attitudes were partially responsible for the Tennesseean's actions and decisions.

Bowers, Claude. *The Tragic Era: The Revolution after Lincoln.* 1929. Reprint. Safety Harbor, Fla.: Simon, 2001.

Helped establish the myth of Reconstruction as "tragedy" (v).

Brabson, Fay Warrington. *Andrew Johnson: A Life in Pursuit of the Right Course, 1808–1875: The Seventeenth President of the United States.* Durham, N.C.: Seeman Printery, 1972.

One of the more recent pro-Johnson studies that sees Johnson as a "man of stature" (vii) with organizational and leadership abilities and a determination "to bring a truer democratic form of government to the Republic" (269).

Brock, William R. *An American Crisis: Congress and Reconstruction, 1865–1867.* New York: Harper & Row, 1966.

Sees the Radicals as a positive force. Although they failed to reform the South, they were responsible for three new constitutional amendments.

Brodie, Fawn M. *Thaddeus Stevens: Scourge of the South*. New York: Norton, 1959.
   Presents Stevens as flawed. but a seeker of justice.

Burgess, John W. *Reconstruction and the Constitution, 1866–1876*. New York:
   Scribner's, 1902.
   Burgess helped begin the "Dunning school" interpretation with this
   study of the constitutional conflict dividing Johnson and Congress.

Butchart, Ronald E. *Northern Schools, Southern Blacks, and Reconstruction*.
   Westport, Conn.: Greenwood, 1980.
   Contends that Northern white leaders supported the education of freed-
   men as a step to economic and social advancement.

Callahan, James Morton.*The Alaska Purchase and Americo-Canadian Relations*.
   West Virginia University Studies in American History, nos. 2–3. Morgantown: West Virginia University, 1908.
   A forty-four page study that traces Alaska's history from the late 1700s to
   the region's acquisition by the United States in 1867, with emphasis on
   the twenty years before the purchase.

Carter, Dan. *When the War Was Over: The Failure of Self-Reconstruction in the
   South, 1865–1867*. Baton Rouge: Louisiana State University Press, 1985.
   One of the few studies of why Southerners did what they did. Argues that
   Southern leaders, while politically moderate as a whole, refused to
   acknowledge Northern concerns for the freedmen and interest in a
   reformed South.

Castle, Albert. *The Presidency of Andrew Johnson*. Lawrence: Regents Press of
   Kansas, 1979.
   Sees Johnson as guided by Jacksonian principles and failing to recognize
   and respond to "the postwar mood of the North" (227).

Cimbala, Paul A., and Randall M. Miller, eds. *The Freedmen's Bureau and Reconstruction: Reconsiderations*. New York: Fordham University Press, 1999.
   Essays on the Bureau's overall work and its efforts in specific areas.

Cornell, William M., ed. *Charles Sumner: Memoir and Eulogies*. Boston: James
   H. Earle, 1874.
   A celebratory essay and 14 eulogies emphasizing character and accom-
   plishments.

Coulter, E. Merton. *The South during Reconstruction, 1865–1877*. Baton Rouge:
   Louisiana State University Press, 1947.
   Covers everything from education and fashion to race and economics.

Cox, LaWanda, and John Cox. *Politics, Principle, and Prejudice, 1865–1866: The
   Dilemma of Reconstruction America*. New York: Free Press of Glencoe,
   1963.
   Focuses on the Democrats and the role of Johnson's inflexible principles
   in pushing Moderate Republicans to work with Radicals.

Craven, Avery. *Reconstruction: The Ending of the Civil War.* New York: Holt, Rinehart, 1969.

Argues that Reconstruction, the final phase of the Civil War, sought equal rights but was defeated by "good old-fashioned democratic doctrine" (307).

Current, Richard Nelson. *Old Thad Stevens: A Story of Ambition.* Madison: University of Wisconsin Press, 1942.

Sees Stevens as being guided by frustrated ambitions and by economic and party interests.

Curry, Richard O., ed. *Radicalism, Racism, and Party Alignment: The Border States during Reconstruction.* Baltimore: Johns Hopkins Press, 1969.

Nine essays, plus a bibliographic essay, on Reconstruction in Missouri, Tennessee, West Virginia, Kentucky, Maryland, and Delaware, noting the sharp stands and divisions within each.

———. *Those Terrible Carpetbaggers: A Reinterpretation.* New York: Oxford University Press, 1988.

A revisionist look at carpetbaggers through 10 interwoven character sketches. Concludes that they did not match the stereotype of corrupt, greedy, ill-educated, and self-serving exploiters.

———, ed. *Reconstruction in Retrospect: Views from the Turn of the Century.* Baton Rouge: Louisiana State University Press, 1969.

Excerpts from writings by eight historians, including W.E.B. DuBois, William Dunning, and Woodrow Wilson.

Degler, Carl N. *The Other South: Southern Dissenters in the Nineteenth Century.* New York: Harper & Row, 1974.

Proves that the South "is not and never has been a monolith" (2) by looking at Southern "losers" (1) who opposed slavery and secession and who supported Reconstruction and the Populist party of the 1890s.

Dewitt, David Miller. *The Impeachment and Trial of Andrew Johnson.* 1903; Madison: State Historical Society of Wisconsin, 1967.

A lengthy and sympathetic account of the president's ordeal that supports Johnson's reconstruction efforts and finds fault with the Republicans' methods and policies.

Donald, David. *Charles Sumner and the Rights of Man.* New York: Knopf, 1970.

A study of Sumner's life from 1850 to his death in 1874 that emphasizes Sumner's status as a man of ideas and sincerity.

———. *The Politics of Reconstruction, 1863–1867.* Baton Rouge: Louisiana State University Press, 1965.

A short look (82 pages) at the early years of Reconstruction with appendices on voting and congressmen.

————, Jean Harvey Baker, and Michael F. Holt. *The Civil War and Reconstruction*. New York: W. W. Norton, 2001.

Thorough, readable text with valuable notes and suggested readings.

DuBois, W.E.B. *Black Reconstruction in America, 1860–1880*. 1935. Reprint. New York: Atheneum, 1992.

A pathbreaking economic reinterpretation of Reconstruction that argues that black Southerners played a major role in the fate of the postwar South.

Dunning, William A. *Reconstruction, Political and Economic, 1865–1877*. 1907. Reprint. New York: HarperTorchbook, 1982.

Thoughtful topics and quotable lines from the traditional school; little on the freedmen.

Edwards, Laura F. *Gendered Strife and Confusion: The Political Culture of Reconstruction*. Urbana: University of Illinois Press, 1997.

Focuses on Granville County, North Carolina, but looks at all of the South, rich and poor, black and white. Gender and economic status, as well as race, defined the postwar South.

Ely, James W., Jr. *The Guardian of Every Other Right: A Constitutional History of Property Rights*. New York: Oxford University Press, 1998.

A short overview with a chapter on the Civil War and Reconstruction periods.

Fleming, Walter L., ed. *Documentary History of Reconstruction: Political, Military, Social, Religious, Educational and Industrial, 1865 to the Present Time*. 2 vols. Cleveland: Arthur H. Clark, 1906–1907.

Provides a large selection of original sources, including government documents.

Foner, Eric. *Freedom's Lawmakers: A Directory of Black Officeholders during Reconstruction*. Revised ed. Baton Rouge: Louisiana State University Press, 1996.

Biographical sketches of over 1,500 African American officeholders, plus bibliographies and indexes.

————. *Politics and Ideology in the Age of the Civil War*. New York: Oxford University Press, 1980.

A brief collection of essays that blend political, social, and intellectual history.

————. *Reconstruction: America's Unfinished Revolution, 1863–1877*. New York: Harper & Row, 1988.

A lengthy work that emphasizes the central role played by Southern African Americans.

————, and Olivia Mahoney. *America's Reconstruction: People and Politics after the Civil War*. New York: HarperPerennial, 1995.

A short account with numerous pictures and illustrations.

Foster, Gaines. *Ghosts of the Confederacy: Defeat, the Lost Cause, and the Emergence of the New South, 1865–1913.* Oxford: Oxford University Press, 1987.

Argues that celebrations in the late 1800s of the Confederate effort helped reunite the nation. Part one deals with the Reconstruction years.

Frankel, Noralee. "Breaking the Chains: 1860–1880." In *To Make Our World Anew: A History of African Americans,* edited by Robin D. G. Kelley and Earl Lewis, 227–80. Oxford: Oxford University Press, 2000.

Emphasizes the struggles and accomplishments of the freedmen.

Franklin, John Hope. *Reconstruction: After the Civil War.* Chicago: University of Chicago Press, 1961.

A brief, pioneering, revisionist study that sees hope turned to failure as a result of the efforts of the traditional Southern ruling class and the ebbing interest in Reconstruction by Republicans.

————, and Alfred A. Moss Jr. *From Slavery to Freedom: A History of African Americans.* 7th ed. New York: McGraw-Hill, 1994.

A standard text for 50 years.

Gambill, Edward L. *Conservative Ordeal: Northern Democrats and Reconstruction, 1865–1868.* Ames: Iowa State University Press, 1981.

Looks at the interplay among Democrats, Andrew Johnson, and Republicans during Johnson's years as president.

Gerteis, Louis. *From Contraband to Freedman: Federal Policy Toward Southern Blacks, 1861–1865.* Westport, Conn.: Greenwood, 1973.

A study of policy and the people carrying it out. Concludes that federal policy was not based on reform and equality, thus ensuring the ultimate failure of those who sought full freedom for the Southern black.

Gienapp, William E., ed. *The Civil War and Reconstruction: A Documentary Collection.* New York: Norton, 2001.

Over 50 selections on Reconstruction, including Abraham Lincoln's veto of the Wade-Davis Bill, descriptions of life in the South for whites and blacks, an account of the work of the Freedmen's Bureau, and Rutherford B. Hayes's description of his Southern policy.

Gillette, William. *Retreat from Reconstruction, 1869–1879.* Baton Rouge: Louisiana State University Press, 1979.

One of the few works that concentrates on the later years of Reconstruction. Focuses on national policy making.

Hale, William Harlan. *Horace Greeley: Voice of the People.* New York: Harper & Row, 1950.

A sympathetic look at the journalist whom Hale describes as "experimental, self-contradictory, explosive, irascible, and often downright wrongheaded" (x).

Harris, William C. *With Charity for All: Lincoln and the Restoration of the Union.* Lexington: University Press of Kentucky, 1997.

The most recent and the most complete account of Lincoln's Reconstruction ideas and steps; argues that Lincoln saw wartime Reconstruction as a critical first step in the restoration of the nation after the war, not just as a tactic for winning the conflict.

Hart, Albert Bushnell. *The Reconstruction Era: Eyewitness Accounts.* Westwood, Mass.: PaperBook, 1992.

Fifteen pages of documents for high school students.

Hearn, Chester G. *The Impeachment of Andrew Johnson.* Jefferson, N.C.: McFarland, 2000.

The most recent study to view Johnson as a hero and the Radicals as threats to the nation and the Constitution.

Hepburn, A. Barton. *A History of Currency in the United States.* New York: Macmillan, 1915.

Discussion of greenbacks is intended to provide facts rather than interpretation; includes insightful comments by various Reconstruction figures.

Hesseltine, William B. *Lincoln's Plan of Reconstruction.* Tuscaloosa, Ala.: Confederate, 1960.

A short analysis that sees Lincoln failing to restructure the South but succeeding in reshaping the nation.

———. *Ulysses S. Grant: Politician.* New York: Dodd, Mead, 1935.

Over half of this book, which presents Grant as a weak and generally ineffective political leader, focuses on his involvement in Reconstruction.

Hine, Darlene Clark, William C. Hine, and Stanley Harrold. *The African-American Odyssey.* 2 vols. 2d ed. Upper Saddle River, N.J.: Prentice Hall, 2003.

Chapters 12 and 13 focus on the Southern black and Reconstruction; useful timelines and bibliographies.

Hollandsworth, James G. *An Absolute Massacre: The New Orleans Race Riot of July 30, 1866.* Baton Rouge: Louisiana State University Press, 2001.

Uses eyewitness testimony to explain the riot's origins in racial and political tensions and to describe its impact.

Holzman, Robert S. *Stormy Ben Butler.* New York: Macmillan, 1954.

A generally positive biography despite acknowledgment of Butler's many flaws.

Horowitz, Robert F. *The Great Impeacher: A Political Biography of James M. Ashley.* New York: Brooklyn College Press, 1979.

An analysis of the motives of a dedicated abolitionist who supported black rights as a Radical but whose personal weaknesses undermined both his career and his historical reputation.

Howard, Victor B. *Religion and the Radical Republican Movement, 1860–1870.* Lexington: University Press of Kentucky, 1990.

Looks at evangelical and liberal churches and their contributions to the "moral tone" of the 1860s.

Hyman, Harold M. *A More Perfect Union: The Impact of the Civil War and Reconstruction on the Constitution.* Sentry ed. Boston: Houghton Mifflin, 1975.

A lengthy and in-depth argument against the theory that the use of national power during Reconstruction disturbed the national-state relationship; Republican accomplishments were moderate and tended to bring only temporary adjustments to the federal system and to black rights.

———. *The Reconstruction Justice of Salmon P. Chase: In Re Turner and Texas v. White.* Lawrence: University Press of Kansas, 1997.

Argues that, as chief justice, Chase helped end slavery's lingering existence but without threatening the federal system; his personal history and beliefs led him to support equal rights and a revised state-national relationship.

———, ed. *The Radical Republicans and Reconstruction, 1861–1870.* Indianapolis: Bobbs-Merrill, 1967.

Over five dozen documents on the history of the Radicals, with useful commentaries and a review of Reconstruction historiography.

———, and William M. Wiecek. *Equal Justice under Law: Constitutional Development, 1835–1875.* New York: Harper & Row, 1982.

Explains how social and economic changes during the Civil War and Reconstruction helped define the modern Constitution by shifting "the gravity of liberty and of authority, from states to nation" (xiii).

Jensen, Ronald J. *The Alaska Purchase and Russian-American Relations.* Seattle: University of Washington Press, 1975.

A brief look at one of the Reconstruction era's successes in foreign policy.

Jones, Robert H. *Fields of Conflict: The Civil War and Reconstruction in America.* Malabar, Fla.: Krieger, 1998.

The last three chapters explain the war's "aftermath" (249).

Kendrick, Benjamin B. *The Journal of the Joint Committee of Fifteen on Reconstruction, Thirty-Ninth Congress, 1865–1867.* New York: Columbia University and Longmans, Green, 1914.

A history of the committee with biographies of members edited by a historian from Columbia University (Dunning school).

Kennedy, Stetson. *After Appomattox: How the South Won the War.* Gainesville: University Press of Florida, 1995.

Argues that the South used the racism it shared with the North to resist Reconstruction.

Korngold, Ralph. *Thaddeus Stevens: A Being Darkly Wise and Rudely Great.* New York: Harcourt, Brace, 1955.

A positive study of Stevens that depicts him battling an unbending South and an obstructionist president.

Krug, Mark M. *Lyman Trumbull: Conservative Radical.* New York: A. S. Barnes, 1965.

A biography based on the Trumbull Family Papers; depicts the Senator as "the father of the Thirteenth Amendment, of the first civil rights bill, and of the first civil service bill" (353).

Kutler, Stanley L. *Judicial Power and Reconstruction Politics.* Chicago: University of Chicago Press, 1968.

Nine essays on the Supreme Court during Reconstruction; finds the Court playing a decisive and activist role.

Linden, Glenn M., ed. *Voices from the Reconstruction Years, 1865–1877.* Fort Worth, Tex.: Harcourt Brace, 1999.

Selections provide participants' opinions during Moderate, Radical, and Counter Reconstruction.

Logan, Rayford W. *The Betrayal of the Negro from Rutherford B. Hayes to Woodrow Wilson.* New York: Collier, 1965.

Sees the half-century after Reconstruction as "the lowest point in the American Negro's struggle for civil rights" (11).

Lunde, Erik S. *Horace Greeley.* Twayne's United States Authors Series, edited by Lewis Leary. Boston: Twayne, 1981.

A short, analytical look at a complex man, with discussions of his various aspects (chapters titled "The Editor," "The Reformer," "The Campaigner," etc.).

McAfee, Ward. *Religion, Race and Reconstruction.* Albany: State University of New York Press, 1998.

Looks at efforts in the 1870s to educate the freedmen.

McCaslin, Richard B. *Andrew Johnson: A Bibliography.* Bibliographies of the Presidents of the United States, no. 17. Westport, Conn.: Greenwood, 1992.

Lists and annotates 2,025 sources, including unpublished personal papers, biographies, newspapers, and films.

McFeely, William S. *Grant: A Biography.* New York: W. W. Norton, 1981.

Looks at the general's personal and professional life in detail. Argues that Grant was not guided by principles and failed to take necessary steps to assure the success of Reconstruction.

———. *Yankee Stepfather: General O. O. Howard and the Freedmen.* New Haven, Conn.: Yale University Press, 1968.

Concludes that Howard's contributions to the Freedmen's Bureau's task in the South were limited by his decisions not to push for black rights.

McKay, Ernest. *Henry Wilson: Practical Radical–A Portrait of a Politician.* Port Washington, N.Y.: Kennikat Press, 1971.

Emphasizes Wilson's interest in party politics, support for freedmen's civil rights and suffrage, desire to forgive the South, and opposition to Andrew Johnson.

McKitrick, Eric L. *Andrew Johnson and Reconstruction.* Chicago: University of Chicago Press, 1960.

Shows Johnson's flaws as the reasons for his failure as president.

Maltz, Earl M. *Civil Rights, the Constitution, and Congress, 1863–1869.* Lawrence: University Press of Kansas, 1990.

A brief study; focuses on debates in Congress on the three Reconstruction amendments.

Mantell, Martin E. *Johnson, Grant, and the Politics of Reconstruction.* New York: Columbia University Press, 1973.

Looks at political struggles between Johnson and Congress and between the president and General Ulysses Grant, with a focus on the Republicans and on the 1868 elections as "the culminating major event of Johnson's administration" (4).

Meier, August, and Elliott Rudwick. *From Plantation to Ghetto.* 3d ed. New York: Hill and Wang, 1976.

Chapter four looks at Reconstruction

Meyer, Howard N. *The Amendment that Refused to Die: Equality and Justice Deferred: A History of the Fourteenth Amendment.* Updated ed. Lanham, Md.: Madison Books, 2000.

Looks at the intent of the amendment's framers, how the Supreme Court distorted that intent, how interpreters defined the amendment after Reconstruction, and how the amendment was used in favor of black rights by the 1960s.

Morris, Robert C. *Reading, 'Riting,' and Reconstruction: The Education of Freedmen in the South, 1861–1870.* Chicago: University of Chicago Press, 1981.

Looks at Northern teachers of the freedmen, as well as Southern whites; sees the former as moderate in their attitudes and goals.

Nash, Howard P., Jr. *Andrew Johnson: Congress and Reconstruction.* Rutherford, N.J.: Fairleigh Dickinson University Press, 1972.

A brief work relying heavily on first-person accounts rather than narrative.

Nelson, Scott Reynolds. *Iron Confederacies: Southern Railways, Klan Violence, and Reconstruction.* Chapel Hill: University of North Carolina Press, 1999.

Analyzes the importance of the railroad to white Southerners and Northerners during Reconstruction and Redemption.

Nelson, William E. *The Fourteenth Amendment: From Political Principle to Judicial Doctrine.* Cambridge: Harvard University Press, 1988.

The story of the amendment from its drafting through its interpretation by the Supreme Court in the late 1800s and early 1900s.

Nieman, Donald G. *Promises to Keep: African-Americans and the Constitutional Order, 1776 to the Present.* New York: Oxford University Press, 1991.

A broad but brief look at African Americans and the Constitution.

———. *To Set the Law in Motion: The Freedmen's Bureau and the Legal Rights of Blacks, 1865–1868.* Millwood, N.Y.: KTO Press, 1979.

Looks at one angle of the Bureau's complex job; finds its work undermined by lack of personnel, local white resistance, President Johnson's policies, and the lack of clear legal authority.

Niven, John. *Salmon P. Chase: A Biography.* New York: Oxford University Press, 1995.

Looks at Chase as "a representative nineteenth-century man" (vii) who was a moralist and a realist.

Olsen, Otto H., ed. *Reconstruction and Redemption in the South.* Baton Rouge: Louisiana State University Press, 1980.

Essays on six states that focus on the failure of Republicanism; each is followed by a bibliographical essay.

Osthaus, Carl R. *Freedmen, Philanthropy, and Fraud: A History of the Freedmen's Savings Bank.* Urbana: University of Illinois Press, 1976.

Praises black bank officials as freedmen who saved their money.

Oubre, Charles F. *Forty Acres and a Mule: The Freedmen's Bureau and Black Landownership.* Baton Rouge: Louisiana State University Press, 1978.

Focuses on Alabama, Arkansas, Florida, Louisiana, and Mississippi as it studies such barriers to black landowning as the return of confiscated lands to their white owners, the country's reverence for private property, and blacks' lack of knowledge about steps to acquire land.

Painter, Nell. *Exodusters: The Black Migration to Kansas after Reconstruction.* New York: Knopf, 1976.

Fascinating look at the movement of thousands of blacks from Louisiana, Mississippi, Tennessee, and Texas to Kansas in 1879; presents the exodus to "a Promised Land of freedom and equality" (261) as an alternative to Southern ills for a few thousand black Southerners.

Patrick, Rembert W. *The Reconstruction of the Nation.* New York: Oxford University Press, 1967.

A general history that includes foreign affairs and "the people" (210), including homesteaders, migrants, and immigrants, as well as religion, education, and economics; sees Northern Republicans giving up on their demands for a reformed South.

Perman, Michael. *Reunion without Compromise: The South and Reconstruction: 1865–1868.* London: Cambridge University Press, 1973.

Focuses on "the defeated Southern leadership" (v) who were ultimately successful in their refusal to accept changes to the South.

———. *The Road to Redemption: Southern Politics, 1869–1879.* Chapel Hill: University of North Carolina Press, 1984.

Sees Reconstruction politics as a stage in Southern politics and political battles as contributors to the ultimate failure of Reconstruction. Includes a useful look at Southern Democrats' Redemption governments.

———, ed. *Major Problems in the Civil War and Reconstruction: Documents and Essays.* 2d ed. Boston: Houghton Mifflin, 1998.

Scholarly essays and documents with brief bibliographies.

Perret, Geoffrey. *Ulysses S. Grant: Soldier & President.* New York: Random House, 1997.

Lengthy, readable biography with a brief section on Reconstruction; sees Grant in 1865–1868 as careful and capable, and during his presidency as having little interest in continuing Reconstruction.

Polakoff, Keith Ian. *The Politics of Inertia: The Election of 1876 and the End of Reconstruction.* Baton Rouge: Louisiana State University Press, 1973.

Focuses on Democrats' and Republicans' power structures; argues that party fragmentation, not coordination and action, elected Rutherford B. Hayes president.

Pomerantz, Sidney I. "Election of 1876: Disputed Election." In *The Coming to Power: Critical Presidential Elections in American History,* edited by Arthur M. Schlesinger Jr. New York: Chelsea House, McGraw-Hill, 1972.

A 50-page explanation and analysis of the election and the "Compromise of 1877."

Powell, Lawrence N. *New Masters: Northern Planters during the Civil War and Reconstruction.* New Haven: Yale University Press, 1980.

Focuses on Northerners who farmed cotton in the South from 1862 to 1868; finds that most of them left the South after problems with Southern whites and black laborers.

Quill, J. Michael. *Prelude to the Radicals: The North and Reconstruction during 1865.* Washington, D.C.: University Press of America, 1980.

A brief look at the initial magnanimous Northern public opinion regarding the South; relies heavily on newspapers.

Rabinowitz, Howard N. *Race Relations in the Urban South, 1865–1890.* New York: Oxford University Press, 1978.

Focuses on Atlanta, Montgomery, Nashville, Raleigh, and Richmond in order to explain how racism and black expectations affected Reconstruction and Southern life.

————, ed. *Southern Black Leaders of the Reconstruction Era.* Urbana: University of Illinois Press, 1982.

Covers both the famous, such as Blanche K. Bruce, as well as the more obscure officeholders.

Rable, George C. *But There Was No Peace: The Role of Violence in the Politics of Reconstruction.* Athens: University of Georgia Press, 1984.

A broad look at the violence, including riots and the Ku Klux Klan, that followed the Civil War and defeated Reconstruction.

Ragsdale, Bruce A., and Joel D. Treese. *Black Americans in Congress, 1870–1989.* Washington, D.C.: U.S. Government Printing Office, 1990.

One- to two-page biographies, with pictures, of 66 African Americans who served in the House and Senate from Reconstruction to the nation's bicentennial.

Ransom, Roger L., and Richard Sutch. *One Kind of Freedom: The Economic Consequences of Emancipation.* Cambridge: Cambridge University Press, 1977.

Covers sharecropping and debt peonage in arguing that economic factors, not race, played the key role in defining black freedom.

Reid, Whitelaw. *After the War: A Southern Tour—May 1, 1865, to May 1, 1866.* Cincinatti: Moore, Wilstach & Baldwin, 1866.

Presents Reid's views of white and black Southerners and their reaction to the events related to Reconstruction under Johnson.

Richardson, Heather Cox. *The Death of Reconstruction: Race, Labor, and Politics in the Post–Civil War North, 1865–1901.* Cambridge, Mass.: Harvard University Press, 2001.

Sees the postwar relationship between whites and blacks as being defined by race and by competing concepts of political economy; half of the book looks at 1865–1883.

Richardson, James D., ed. *A Compilation of the Messages and Papers of the Presidents.* 20 vols. 1897. Reprint. New York: Bureau of National Literature, 1917.

Reconstruction presidents are covered in volumes 7–10.

Richter, William L. *The ABC-CLIO Companion to American Reconstruction, 1862–1877.* Santa Barbara, Calif.: ABC-CLIO, 1996.

Includes encyclopedia articles, chronology, and bibliography.

Riddleberger, Patrick W. *1866: The Critical Year Revisited.* Carbondale: Southern Illinois University Press, 1979.

A review and analysis of national politics with a focus on the controversies over civil rights and presidential-congressional powers that defined future years.

Roark, James L. *Masters without Slaves: Southern Planters in the Civil War and Reconstruction.* New York: Norton, 1977.

A study of the South from the perspective of the planter class; emphasizes the changes in Southern culture and economic life brought by the end of slavery.

Rose, Willie Lee. *Rehearsal for Reconstruction: The Port Royal Experiment*. Indianapolis: Bobbs-Merrill, 1964.

Presents the South Carolina sea islands during the war and Reconstruction as "a proving ground" for freemen and "a training and recruiting ground" (xiv) for soldiers, politicians, teachers, and philanthropists.

Roseboom, Eugene H., and Alfred E. Eckes Jr. *A History of Presidential Elections: From George Washington to Jimmy Carter.* 4th ed. New York: Macmillan, 1979.

Chapters five and six explain the elections of 1864, 1868, 1872, and 1876.

Roske, Ralph J. *His Own Counsel: The Life and Times of Lyman Trumbull*. Reno: University of Nevada Press, 1979.

An easy-to-read biography of the Moderate leader that credits his role in the formation of the Republican party and in the framing of the Thirteenth Amendment and the Civil Rights Act of 1866.

Rozwenc, Edwin C., ed. *Reconstruction in the South*. Boston: D. C. Heath, 1952.

Provides excerpts that demonstrate early interpretations of Reconstruction.

Sawrey, Robert D. *Dubious Victory: The Reconstruction Debate in Ohio*. Lexington: University Press of Kentucky, 1992.

Uses Ohio to help understand public interest in non-Reconstruction topics and how that interest affected the fortunes of the Democrats and Republicans in the North.

Schroeder-Lein, Glenna R., and Richard Zuczek. *Andrew Johnson: A Biographical Companion*. Santa Barbara, Calif.: ABC-CLIO, 2001.

An encyclopedia that covers Johnson's life and the people, events, and issues in it; with documents, bibliographies, and a chronology.

Sefton, James E. *Andrew Johnson and the Uses of Constitutional Power*, edited by Oscar Handlin. Boston: Little, Brown, 1980.

A political biography that looks at the Johnson-Congress battle and "the theme of constitutional power" (ix); concludes that Johnson's inability to compromise accounted for his failure in Reconstruction.

———. *The United States Army and Reconstruction, 1865–1877*. Baton Rouge: Louisiana State University Press, 1967.

A rare focus on the military side of Reconstruction that finds the army successful in adjusting to shifting policies from Washington but unsuccessful in protecting the freedmen.

Seip, Terry L. *The South Returns to Congress: Men, Economic Measures, and Intersectional Relationships, 1868–1879*. Baton Rouge: Louisiana State University Press, 1983.

A study of Southern congressmen and Southern economic issues that finds unity among the officeholders and lack of respect for them by Northerners.

Sharkey, Robert P. *Money, Class, and Party: An Economic Study of Civil War and Reconstruction*. Baltimore: Johns Hopkins University Press, 1959.

Covers greenbacks, tariffs, labor, and banking in arguing that the Republican party was not united on economic policies during Reconstruction.

Shenton, James P., ed. *The Reconstruction: A Documentary History of the South after the War: 1865–1877*. New York: G. P. Putnam's Sons, 1963.

Requires much page-turning to find desired selections but includes a wide range of excerpts.

Silber, Nina. *The Romance of Reunion: Northerners and the South, 1865–1900*. Chapel Hill: University of North Carolina Press, 1993.

A rare look at how Northerners in the late 1800s responded to their victory in the Civil War through a "conciliatory culture" (2) and "sentimental rubric" (3); three chapters focus specifically on the Reconstruction years.

Simpson, Brooks D. *Let Us Have Peace: Ulysses S. Grant and the Politics of War and Reconstruction, 1861–1868*. Chapel Hill: University of North Carolina Press, 1991.

Covers Grant's views during the war and during Johnson's presidency and his decision to play a political role in order to aid Congress in achieving "peace."

———. *The Reconstruction Presidents*. Lawrence: University of Kansas Press, 1998.

Thoughtful, insightful look at Lincoln, Johnson, Grant, and Hayes, each in his own chapter; concludes that the issue of black rights affected each man's presidency.

Singletary, Otis A. *Negro Militia and Reconstruction*. Austin: University of Texas Press, 1957.

A brief study of the militias, white resentment of them, and the hesitancy of state governors to use them due to fear of promoting race war.

Smith, Jean Edward. *Grant*. New York: Simon & Schuster, 2001.

A lengthy analysis that presents Grant as a determined, generally capable president whose interest in Reconstruction continued throughout his eight years in the White House.

Stalcup, Brenda, ed. *Reconstruction: Opposing Viewpoints*. San Diego: Greenhaven, 1995.

Includes primary sources on such topics as the Ku Klux Klan and the Fourteenth Amendment, as well as a bibliography and chronology.

Stampp, Kenneth M. *The Era of Reconstruction, 1865–1877*. 1965. Reprint. New York: Vintage Books, 1967.

A brief, readable early synthesis of the revisionist interpretation of Reconstruction.

———, and Leon F. Litwack. *Reconstruction: An Anthology of Revisionist Writings*. Baton Rouge: Louisiana State University Press, 1969.

Twenty-two selections on the presidents, the Radicals, the freedmen, and Southern conditions.

Stanwood, Edward. *American Tariff Controversies in the Nineteenth Century*. 2 vols. Boston: Houghton Mifflin, 1903.

Presents the tariff as "the most persistent issue in American politics" (1) that not even the Civil War and Reconstruction could displace for long; finds the tariff policy during Reconstruction to be based on no clear plan.

Stiles, T. J., ed. *Robber Barons and Radicals: Reconstruction and the Origins of Civil Rights*. New York: Perigee, 1997.

Uses the words of Northerners and Southerners, including O. O. Howard, Andrew Carnegie, and Senator John Sherman, to show how the 12 years after the Civil War make up "a story of struggle, apparent triumph, fatal flaws, and catastrophic loss" (xiii).

Summers, Mark W. *Railroads, Reconstruction, and the Gospel of Prosperity: Aid under the Radical Republicans, 1865–1877*. Princeton: Princeton University Press, 1984.

Emphasizes the key role played by railroads in the Reconstruction South; finds local interests responsible for both railroad building and the resulting corruption.

———. *The Era of Good Stealings*. New York: Oxford, 1993.

An enjoyable, even witty, look at corruption and its political uses.

Swinney, Everette. *Suppressing the Ku Klux Klan: Enforcement of the Reconstruction Amendments, 1870–1877*. New York: Garland, 1986.

Looks at the problems and success of using the Enforcement Acts, whose enforcement declined by 1874 and which faced local resistance.

Taylor, John M. *William H. Seward: Lincoln's Right Hand*. New York: Harper-Collins, 1991.

Focuses on foreign affairs but touches on William Seward's views of and role in Reconstruction; sees him as "a complicated and occasionally devious person" but also "one of the political giants of his generation" (x).

Thomas, Benjamin P., and Harold M. Hyman. *Stanton: The Life and Times of Lincoln's Secretary of War*. New York: Knopf, 1962.

A detailed, lengthy, but readable biography that depicts the secretary of war as sincerely opposed to Johnson's Reconstruction policies.

Thomas, Lately [Robert Steele]. *The First President Johnson: The Three Lives of the Seventeenth President of the United States of America*. New York: William Morrow, 1968.

A sympathetic biography of Johnson that notes his missteps, sees him as the embodiment of the "people" (507) and as "a fighter" (567), and labels impeachment a "farce" (527).

Thornbrough, Emma Lou, ed. *Black Reconstructionists*. Great Lives Observed. Englewood Cliffs, N.J.: Prentice-Hall, 1972.

Useful introduction, chronology, and excerpts from newspapers, government, and histories.

Tourgee, Albion. *A Fool's Errand: By One of the Fools*. New York: Fords, Howard, and Hulbert, 1880.

A classic novel based on Tourgee's experiences in North Carolina as a carpetbagger and judge; finds Reconstruction's problems among the Radicals and among white Southerners.

Trefousse, H. L. *Andrew Johnson: A Biography*. New York: Norton, 1989.

A well-written and balanced study.

———. *Ben Butler: The South Called Him Beast!* New York: Twayne, [1957].

A sympathetic look.

———. *Benjamin Franklin Wade: Radical Republican from Ohio*. New York: Twayne, 1963.

Explains that Wade was motivated by a desire to protect the nation and provide rights for black Americans.

———. *Historical Dictionary of Reconstruction*. New York: Greenwood, 1991.

Includes encyclopedia articles, chronology, and bibliographic references.

———. *The Radical Republicans: Lincoln's Vanguard for Radical Justice*. New York: Knopf, 1969.

Covers from abolitionist roots in 1840s to decline in 1870s; notes the diversity among Radicals and their responsibility for the future expansion of black rights.

———. *Reconstruction: America's First Effort at Racial Democracy*. Updated ed. Anvil Series. Malabar, Fla.: Krieger, 1999.

The first half of this book is a brief history of Reconstruction; the second half is primarily composed of political documents.

———. *Thaddeus Stevens: Nineteenth-Century Egalitarian*. Chapel Hill: University of North Carolina Press, 1997.

The newest biography of the Radical Congressman; argues that, while Stevens was not as powerful as has generally been depicted, he guided the nation toward racial equality.

Trelease, Allen. *White Terror: The Ku Klux Klan Conspiracy and Southern Reconstruction*. 1971; Baton Rouge: Louisiana State University Press, 1995.

A lengthy analysis of the Klan's origins, use, and decline from 1866 to 1872 that emphasizes the organization's base in white supremacy and its willingness to use violence.

Troutman, Richard L., ed. *The Heavens Are Weeping: The Diaries of George Richard Browder.* Grand Rapids, Mich.: Zondervan Publishing, 1987.

Views of the South and Reconstruction by a Kentucky minister who disagreed with much of congressional policy.

Unger, Irwin. *The Greenback Era: A Social and Political History of American Finance, 1865–1879.* Princeton: Princeton University Press, 1964.

Argues that there was much support and opposition for greenbacks and that the wartime paper money split the political parties during Reconstruction.

Van Deusen, Glyndon G. *Horace Greeley: Nineteenth-Century Crusader.* Philadelphia: University of Pennsylvania Press, 1953.

A biography that focuses on Greeley's public life, sees the newspaperman as a symbol of America, and finds him taking a conservative position on Reconstruction.

Werlich, Robert. *"Beast" Butler: The Incredible Career of Major General Benjamin Franklin Butler.* Washington, D.C.: Quaker Press, 1962.

Focuses on the Civil War; finds Butler "in league with Aaron Burr and Benedict Arnold in his services to the country" (x).

Williams, Lou Falkner. *The Great South Carolina Ku Klux Klan Trials, 1871–1872.* Athens: University of Georgia Press, 1996.

A brief look at the federal trials and the Southern whites' often successful resistance to the federal efforts to convict local Klan members for attempting to restrict black power.

Williams, T. Harry. *Lincoln and the Radicals.* 1941. Reprint. Madison: University of Wisconsin Press, 1965.

Sees Lincoln as a moderate battling the Radical "Jacobins" during "savage years" (384).

Williamson, Joel. *The Crucible of Race: Black-White Relations in the American South since Emancipation.* New York: Oxford University Press, 1984.

Sees racism as an outgrowth of the Civil War and abolitionism. Chapters one and two look at Southern blacks; chapter three studies the attitudes of Southern whites.

Wilson, Theodore Brantner. *The Black Codes of the South.* Southern Historical Publications, no. 6. University: University of Alabama Press, 1965.

A brief look at the Codes and their influence on Northern opinion in 1865–1866; finds that Northerners saw them as evidence that the South was not ready to be left on its own.

Wilson, Thomas. *The Power "to Coin" Money: The Exercise of Monetary Powers by the Congress.* Armonk, N.Y.: M. E. Sharpe, 1992.

Looks at the changing constitutional interpretations of Congress's monetary powers.

Winston, Robert W. *Andrew Johnson: Plebeian and Patriot.* New York: Barnes & Noble, 1928.

> One of the first studies to see Johnson as a Reconstruction hero for his support of the Constitution, his faith in the states, and his lack of vindictiveness towards the South.

Wish, Harvey, ed. *Reconstruction in the South, 1865–1877: First-Hand Accounts of the American Southland after the Civil War, by Northerners and Southerners.* New York: Farrar, Straus and Giroux, 1965.

> Documents are preceded by a dated but useful historical and historiographical overview.

Woodward, C. Vann. *Reunion and Reaction: The Compromise of 1877 and the End of Reconstruction.* Boston: Little Brown, 1951.

> Challenges the traditional view of the handling of the 1876 election dispute and argues that Radical goals were betrayed by Rutherford B. Hayes's deal with Southern Democrats.

Web Sources

American Presidents: Life Portraits. Http://www.americanpresidents.org/.

> Provides brief biographies and guides to research; useful for finding other web sites.

Civil War Resources on the Internet: Abolitionism to Reconstruction (1830s–1890s). Http://www.libraries.rutgers.edu.

> Provides links to other sites and to documents from Reconstruction.

Documenting the American South: Beginnings to 1920. Http://docsouth.unc.edu.

> Provides full text of primary sources, including first-person narratives.

Harper's Weekly. Http://harpweek.com.

> Articles, cartoons, editorials, and illustrations from *Harper's Weekly.*

Library of Congress. American Memory. Http://lcweb2.loc.gov/ammem/.

> Library of Congress collection of primary sources in American history.

The Presidents of the United States. Http://www.whitehouse.gov.history/presidents.

> Provides biographical information on the presidents.

Teachers First. Http://www.teachersfirst.com/us/history/.

> Provides aids for teachers and students K–12.

INDEX

About the Author

CLAUDINE L. FERRELL is Associate Professor, History and American Studies, at Mary Washington College.